# MARKET KILLING

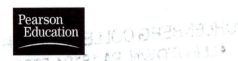

**Pearson Education**

We work with leading authors to develop the strongest educational materials, bringing cutting edge
thinking and best learning practice to a global market.

Under a range of well-known imprints, including Longman, we craft high quality print and electronic publications which help readers to understand and apply their content, whether studying or at work.

To find out about the complete range of our publishing please visit us on the World Wide Web at:

www.pearsoneduc.com

# MARKET KILLING

## What the free market does and what social scientists can do about it

Edited by
GREG PHILO
and
DAVID MILLER

*An imprint of* **Pearson Education**
Harlow, England · London · New York · Reading, Massachusetts · San Francisco
Toronto · Don Mills, Ontario · Sydney · Tokyo · Singapore · Hong Kong · Seoul
Taipei · Cape Town · Madrid · Mexico City · Amsterdam · Munich · Paris · Milan

**Pearson Education Limited**

Edinburgh Gate
Harlow
Essex CM20 2JE
England

and Associated Companies around the world

*Visit us on the World Wide Web at*
*www.pearsoneduc.com*

---

First published in Great Britain in 2001

© Pearson Education Limited 2001

The right of Greg Philo and David Miller to be identified
as authors of this work has been asserted by them in accordance
with the Copyright, Designs and Patents Act 1988.

ISBN 0 582 38236 X

*British Library Cataloguing in Publication Data*
A CIP catalogue record for this book can be obtained from the British Library

*Library of Congress Cataloging-in-Publication Data*
A catalog record for this book can be obtained from the Library of Congress

10  9  8  7  6  5  4  3  2  1
08  07  06  05  04  03  02  01

Typeset by 35
Printed and bound in Malaysia ,LSP

# Contents

Contents

# CONTRIBUTIONS AND COMMENTARIES

# Acknowledgements

Many people have helped us in producing this book and we would like to thank them all. Our colleagues in the Glasgow Media Group have helped by reading the text and making suggestions – thanks to John Eldridge, Jenny Kitzinger, Jacquie Reilly, Lesley Henderson, Alison Hill, Liza Beattie, Emma Miller, Kevin Williams and Howard Davis. Thanks to colleagues in the Stirling Media Research Institute, Raymond Boyle, William Dinan, Amir Saeed and Philip Schlesinger for discussions on some of the issues raised below. Thanks also to Paul Littlewood and Jason Ditton and to Mary, John and Sarah Philo for help with source material. Thanks to Bob Franklin, Hugh Mackay, Sheila Rowbotham and Raymond Tallis for their useful comments on early drafts. For her work in preparing the manuscripts, thanks especially to Lynn Campbell. Thanks very much to Caitlin and Lewis Miller especially for providing empirical analysis of children's television and advertising. A personal note of thanks is also due to Rene and Dick Philo for providing help and accommodation and to Emma Miller for encouragement and tolerance. Thanks also to Jane Powell at our publishers. This is also just about 25 years since we published the first of the Glasgow Media Group Books so on this anniversary we should say thanks to the very large number of people who have helped us over this period and who made all of the subsequent work possible and sometimes even enjoyable.

# Contributors

**Derek Bousé** studied at the Annenberg School for Communication, and was a media studies professor in the USA for several years. He is now an independent scholar and filmmaker, living in Salzburg, Austria. His articles on film, television and other visual media have appeared in *Film Quarterly, Critical Studies in Mass Communication, The Journal of Visual Literacy, The Public Historian,* and most recently in the edited volume *Image Ethics in the Digital Age* (University of Minnesota Press, 2001). His recent book *Wildlife Films* is published by the University of Pennsylvania Press (2000).

**Noam Chomsky**, long-time political activist, writer and professor of linguistics at Massachusetts Institute of Technology, is the author of numerous books and articles on US foreign policy, international affairs and human rights. Among the most recent books are *Year 501, World Orders Old and New, Powers and Prospects, Profit over People* and *The New Military Humanism: Lessons from Kosovo.*

**John Corner** is Professor in the School of Politics and Communication Studies at the University of Liverpool. He has written widely on media topics in books and journals and his most recent publications include a collection of articles (*Studying Media,* Edinburgh University Press, 1998) and a review of television studies (*Critical Ideas in Television Studies,* Oxford, 1999). He is an editor of the journal *Media, Culture, and Society.*

**James Curran** is Professor of Communications, Goldsmiths College, University of London. He has published 14 books about the mass media, including *Power Without Responsibility* (with Jean Seaton) (5th edition, Routledge, 1997); *De-Westernizing Media Studies* (ed., with Myung-Lin Park) (Routledge, 2000); *Media Organisations in Society* (ed.) (Arnold, 2000); and *Mass Media and Society* (ed. with Michael Gurevitch) (3rd edition, Arnold, 2000).

**Barbara Epstein** teaches in the History of Consciousness Department at the University of California, Santa Cruz. She is the author of *Political Protest and Cultural Revolution: Nonviolent Direct Action in the 1970s and 1980s* (University of California Press, 1991).

**Andrew Gamble** is Professor of Politics and Director of the Political Economy Research Centre at the University of Sheffield. He is the author of *The Free Economy and the Strong State* (Macmillan, 1988) and *Hayek: the Iron Cage of Liberty* (Polity, 1996).

**Chris Hamnett** is Professor of Human Geography at King's College London. He was previously Professor of Urban Geography at the Open University. He has held a number of visiting appointments including the George Washington University, Washington, DC, Nuffield College, Oxford, and the Netherlands Institute of Advanced Studies, Wassenaar. He is author of *Winners and Losers: the Home Ownership Market in Modern Britain* (UCL Press, 1999) and he is joint author of *Cities, Housing and Profits* (Hutchinson, 1989), *As Safe as Houses* (Paul Chapman, 1991) and *Shrinking the State* (Oxford University Press, 1998). He has edited and co-edited several books. His current research interest is social change and inequality in London.

**Angela McRobbie** is Professor of Communications at Goldsmiths College London and author of *British Fashion Design: Rag Trade or Image Industry* (Routledge, 1998) and *In the Culture Society: Art, Fashion and Popular Music* (Routledge, 1999). Her current research is on young women and employment in the new cultural economy.

**David Miller** is a member of the Stirling Media Research Institute. He is the author of *Don't Mention the War: Northern Ireland, Propaganda and the Media* (Pluto, 1994), co-author of *The Circuit of Mass Communication: Media Strategies, Representation and Audience Reception in the AIDS Crisis* (Sage, 1998), co-editor of *War and Words: the Northern Ireland Media Reader* (Beyond the Pale, 1996, with Bill Rolston) and editor of *Rethinking Northern Ireland: Culture, Ideology and Colonialism* (Longman, 1998).

**Greg Philo** is Research Director of the Glasgow University Media Unit. He was co-author of the Glasgow University Media Group books *Bad News* (RKP, 1976), *More Bad News* (RKP, 1980), *Really Bad News* (Writers and Readers, 1982) and *War and Peace News* (Open University Press, 1985). He is editor of *Message Received* (Longman, 1999), *Media and Mental Distress* (Longman, 1996) and *The Glasgow Media Group Reader*, volume II (Routledge, 1995) and author of *Seeing and Believing: the Influence of Television* (Routledge, 1990).

**Hilary Rose** is Professor Emerita of Social Policy, University of Bradford, Visiting Research Professor in Sociology City University, Joint Professor of Physic, Gresham College. Her most recent book is *Love, Power and Knowledge: Towards a Feminist Transformation of the Sciences* (Polity, UK and Indiana, USA). She has published some eight other authored and edited books which include *Science and Society* (with Steven Rose, 1969), and the edited collections *The Radicalisation of Science* (1976) and *The Political Economy of Science* (1976). A further edited collection, with Helga Nowotny, *Countermovements in the Sciences*, was published in 1979. More recently she was a founding member and co-chair of the Science, Engineering and Technology (SET) Policy Forum, an independent group whose project was to stimulate fresh thinking in the Labour Party, and co-authored the pamphlet *Shaping the Future* (Open University, 1966). Currently she is writing a book on a feminist sociology of human genetics for Polity and co-editing with Steven Rose a book on evolutionary psychology for Crown Harmony, US, and Cape, UK.

**Danny Schechter** is the Executive Producer of Globalvision Inc. and the author of *The More You Watch, the Less You Know* (Seven Stories Press) and *News Dissector: Passions, Pieces and Polemics* (Electron Press).

**Philip Schlesinger** is Professor of Film and Media Studies at the University of Stirling, Scotland, Director of the Stirling Media Research Institute and Visiting Professor of Media and Communication at the University of Oslo. He is a member of the board of the Scottish Screen agency and co-editor of *Media, Culture and Society*. He is author of *Putting 'Reality' Together* (Routledge, 2nd edition, 1987) and *Media, State and Nation* (Sage, 1991) and has co-authored *Televising 'Terrorism'* (Comedia, 1983), *Women Viewing Violence* (BFI, 1992), *Reporting Crime* (1994) and *Men Viewing Violence* (BSC, 1998). He is at present conducting research on political communication and national identity in the European Union, UK and Scotland.

**Jean Shaoul** is a lecturer in the School of Accounting and Finance at Manchester University where she concentrates on public and business policy. She uses financial information derived from company accounts and other grey literature to evaluate public policy decisions from a public interest perspective. She has written widely in both academic and more popular forums on privatization, the corporatization of the public services, the NHS, the Private Finance Initiative in the NHS and education, public expenditure, the financial context of the BSE crisis and food safety regulation. She is a regular contributor to the *World socialist website* (wsws.org).

**Hilary Wainwright** is editor of *Red Pepper*, a popular British new left magazine, Senior Research Associate at the International Centre for Labour Studies of the University of Manchester and a fellow of the Transnational Institute in Amsterdam. She was a founding member of Charter 88, the movement to democratize Britain's feudal state, and convenor of the economic democracy workshop of the Helsinki Citizens Assembly. She also serves on the editorial board of The Catalyst Trust, a left policy think-tank in the UK. She is currently working on a book, *Whatever Happened to People Power?*, on popular resistance in the face of corporate-driven globalization. A socialist feminist and strong believer in popular democracy – in combination with parliamentary democracy, Wainwright founded the Popular Planning Unit of the Greater London Council during the Thatcher years. Her books include *Beyond the Fragments; Feminism and the Making of Socialism* (with Sheila Rowbotham and Lynne Segal) and her most recent book is *Arguments for a New Left: Answering the Free Market Right* (Blackwell, 1993).

The 'discursive turn' in the social and cultural sciences is one of the most significant shifts of direction in our knowledge of society which has occurred in recent years.

**Stuart Hall, Introduction to Open University course book *Representation: Cultural Representations and Signifying Practices*, 1997**

When the emperor is restocking his wardrobe, he usually shops in Paris.

**Raymond Tallis, *Not Saussure*, 1988**

It's been a busy weekend at the University where I run the Serious Comment section of the media studies course. But it is all grist to my mill: as I say in the brochure, it's my ambition to turn out the next generation of award-winning newspaper commentators like myself, able to express opinions on wide-ranging matters of general importance to the community as a whole. We had a quiet start to the term, with not much happening in the outside world besides the Party Conferences, a couple of natural disasters, a few bombings, some foreign uprisings, a civil war, the Northern Ireland talks and a famine or two. Not much for the serious commentator to get her teeth into there. So for the first few weeks, I taught an important retrospective course on 'Towards a new republicanism: Diana – the semiotics of grief in the zeitgeist of a post-industrial nation'.

**Bel Littlejohn, *Guardian*, 17 October 1997**

# Introduction

This book began as a critique of media and cultural studies. It seemed to us that this area of academic life had lost its critical edge and was no longer able to comment on the central issues and problems of its own society. This was at a time when very powerful changes were occurring to social and cultural relationships. These changes came mostly from the release of the 'free market' and the re-emergence of right wing politics at the end of the twentieth century. The effects were not hard to see on for example the division of social wealth, on the health of citizens, in damage to the public sector and in the rise of individualism and the culture of fame and glamour. In Britain, this was the age of ideology and spin-doctoring as the new relationships were legitimized and promoted as necessary and inevitable features of social life. What the left-wing theorists of the nineteenth century had originally described as the 'internationalization of capital' was now rechristened 'globalization'. This was then celebrated as if the free market had only just been discovered. These social and cultural changes seemed to us a very rich area for analysis by theorists of media and culture. Yet in Britain and the USA many had turned away from empirical and critical research. They were lost instead in the dreams and speculations of what was now termed post-modern theory. One of our responses to this was to write an extended essay which we showed to friends and colleagues asking for comments (it appears here as the first Part of the book). The essay had two main purposes. We wished to analyze the changes in social and cultural life which had resulted from the new release of the free market. We then wanted to ask what had happened to intellectual debate such that it was unable to engage in any serious critique or explanation of these changes. As we worked and discussed these issues with colleagues it was apparent that the intellectual malaise about which we were writing had spread through much of social science and was affecting debates in areas as diverse as geography, history, politics and philosophy as well as the natural sciences. Many people sent us comments and suggestions and we eventually decided that it would be best to invite them and others to contribute short essays to this volume. In practice, these contributions either take up and develop issues which were raised in the first essay or they discuss the impact of post-modernism and the new academic quiescence on specific subject areas.

The first of these essays is contributed by Noam Chomsky. He originally offered us comments on the first draft of Part 1. In this we had argued that social scientists have substantially lost the ability to be critical about their own society. But as he noted:

> I think one might look at it differently. What you are describing seems to me a reversion to the norm. There are moments when a critical stance towards one's own society is (barely) tolerated; periods of popular ferment and struggle, the immediate aftermath of scandals and atrocities too extreme to suppress quickly . . . But these moments are the exceptions in the history of intellectuals and academic social scientists. The usual stance is triumphalism about domestic power and providing the ideological support for it, meanwhile feathering one's own nest.

He also pointed to the impact of recent media and cultural studies in diverting from activism:

> They are highly relevant in diverting young people from activism and critical intelligence, and undermining the linkage of intellectuals to activism which, however limited, has typically been a factor in social change. That seems to me the conclusion implicit in your analysis, and the right one.

In this he had reached the conclusion that the radical post-modernists had nothing to do with left politics: '. . . on the contrary, they seem to me deeply reactionary, and the rise during the Thatcher/Reagan era is quite natural' (correspondence, January·1998). He also drew our attention to a debate in Z *Papers* magazine (now replaced by Z net) to which he had contributed. This debate consisted of a number of essays on post-modernist theory. His own contribution pointed to a series of critical problems about the intellectual basis of post-modernism and which are generic to its theoretical approach. We therefore included his essay here with a new introduction which he has written for this volume. The issue which he raises is what eventually is the nature of rational enquiry. Are conclusions to be consistent with premises or, can we string together thought as we like, calling it an 'argument', taking one story to be as good as another? He asks, are we to abandon the ground rules of rational enquiry and if so what it to replace them other than primal screams? He also notes the political impact of post-modernist thought. The message that we must now abandon the 'illusions' of science and rationality will, he says, gladden the hearts of the powerful, delighted to monopolize these instruments for their own use.

In the second essay, Hilary Rose pursues related themes to those of Noam Chomsky when she discusses the importance of truth claims in the natural and social sciences. As she notes, these matter considerably when sexual violence or levels of radiation pollution are at stake. She traces the history of relativism and its de-politicizing influence in feminism and natural science, and comments on how academic feminists have gained access and advance in universities but have theoretically and politically lost contact with the problems of most women in the world.

The next three essays deal with issues in film, media and cultural studies. Derek Bousé shows how the movement away from empirical, evidence-based research was prefigured in the history of film theory. For thirty years, as he suggests, film studies were largely theory driven and text based and as a result became merely speculative. There were grand conclusions drawn and assumptions made about the relationship of film images with 'the spectator'. This was done without the benefit of studying what actually occurred and sometimes in defiant disregard of what research elsewhere suggested. And as sometimes occurs with poor science, the claims of film theory were immersed in a dense language, in the expectation perhaps that obscurity might been seen as profundity. John Corner in his essay also looks at incoherence and disarray in the field of media and cultural studies. But he also shows how important strands of work are emerging which are empirical, problem based and alert to questions of power. One difficulty as he notes is that some key concepts such as ideology have been disregarded in contemporary work. The importance of such a concept was that it showed why the media mattered. The net effect of its disappearance from media and cultural studies was to displace the very idea of power and influence. Instead there has been a celebration of the popular as 'good' and a focus on aesthetics and pleasure. We invited a contribution from Angela McRobbie on the basis of her being a representative of the cultural studies tradition. In her essay she argues that women, and especially young women, are now central to New Labour's social policy, while in culture and the media they are the focus of neo-liberal attention. This is embodied in notions of 'female success' and the 'TV blonde'.

The two essays which follow extend these arguments to other areas of academic work. Chris Hamnett describes the rise of the 'cultural turn' in human geography. He argues that what counts in much of such writing is the skill with which authors deploy and link concepts, terms and ideas to build ever more elaborate interpretations. This now replaces any contribution to explaining the structure or process of the world in which they live. The approach is also fundamentally dishonest in its claims to examine ideas of difference, otherness and subordination. Under the guise of liberation and giving voice to those hitherto excluded it simply reinforces the privileges of the intellectual elite. Andrew Gamble in his essay analyzes the poverty of contemporary discussions about the economy. The process of globalization is often presented almost as a natural phenomenon, which should not be interfered with, rather than as something which is constructed through choices, beliefs and action. The concepts of power and interest are once again removed and growth is presented as an end in itself. What the world has actually experienced is the intense concentration of capital and power into the hands of a minority. In the USA, as he notes, the economy has grown rapidly but real wages for the majority have stagnated. Jobs have been created but mostly in the low-wage service sector. He contrasts this with the experience of European countries that have sustained social democratic programmes (about which we hear so little in our media). In these countries unemployment has been higher but welfare benefits were relatively generous, while wages for those in jobs have held up. In this way the growth of social exclusion and poverty have been contained. The US approach, in contrast, has been to process over two million people through its penal system.

The two essays which follow by Philip Schlesinger and Barbara Epstein look at how academic work can be linked to the world beyond universities. Philip Schlesinger argues that engaged research and the space for autonomous intellectual activity have been increasingly crowded out by the research priorities of the state and the funding mechanisms used to implement these. He analyzes how the recent growth of a market for the output of the 'thinktankerati', specialist journalists, media consultants and in-house policy units have all contributed to the increasing marginalization of academic media research. Barbara Epstein traces the growth of corporate culture in US universities and the weakening of links with social movements outside. This is partly because of accelerating pressures on academics with heightened competition for jobs and publications – the sense as she says that everyone must keep running. But, as she argues, progressive movements can be helped by contributions by trained researchers, and teaching and writing may also be enriched by involvement in such activity.

In the essay which follows this, Jean Shaoul shows the value of independent analysis in critiques of political policy. Her account reveals some of the mythologies which have been created around the privatization of public assets. The nationally owned industries in Britain had actually made a substantial operating surplus which could be used for public benefit (by reducing prices, increasing investment or paying for other projects such as health). Their privatization enriched the new buyers but represented a huge loss to the bulk of the population. The alleged 'economies' of privatization amounted largely to reducing the work force and she notes that the amount saved on labour costs was approximately equal to the amount work paid out in dividends. Her essay shows the importance of alternative information to criticize the mythologies which are created in the political sphere and in the pursuit of private interest.

The next two essays by James Curran and Danny Schechter relate to practical alternatives in media. James Curran examines how patterns of corporate ownership lead to a concentration of media and political power. The views of low-income groups and alternative politics are excluded and commercial priorities have a strong impact on programme content. He then very usefully analyzes the strengths and weaknesses of different approaches to public service broad-casting across a range of European and Nordic countries. Danny Schechter also argues that media mergers in America have led to a pattern in which fewer voices are actually heard in what looks superficially like a bewildering array of choices. News and information have been dumbed down as news business was integrated into show business. But, as he argues, some media employees are speaking up in defence in the values of journalism and their own integrity. In Los Angeles, a news room revolt forced a news director to resign. Some opinion polls also show a public dissatisfaction with the media's relentless focus on scandal and trivia as in attitudes to the coverage of the Monica Lewinski story. He concludes by outlining a programme for change which involves building awareness of media power and its irresponsibility. He advocates the monitoring of media content and the development of public television, alternative programming and independent media. The last essay is by Hilary Wainwright who looks at the political implications of the current rise in post-modern theoretical obscurity in the social sciences. She reinforces Chomsky's comments in noting that its effect was to draw intellectuals away from the engaged and empirical work needed to identify the possibilities for change in material relationships. Most importantly she shows how the denial of an extra-discursive reality meant that post-modernists could no longer en-gage with movements and practices which had tried to challenge material power.

Finally we would say that we intend this book to be a call for a link between theory and practice. We do not mean it to be negative or to initiate yet more unproductive and obscure academic rhetoric. We want to promote a clear and empirically based social science, which can address the key issues of its own society. Such a science should analyze the consequences of political policy and inform public debate in the face of the misinformation which so often obscures useful knowledge. We know that there are many academics, students and others who share this objective and we hope that they will join with us in trying to achieve it.

# Cultural compliance

## Media/cultural studies and social science

# Cultural compliance

## Media/cultural studies and social science

GREG PHILO AND DAVID MILLER

This chapter examines the content and direction of contemporary media and cultural studies. Our intention is to compare this area of academic work with the social processes and development of the real world in which it is situated. Our concern is that much of what is supposed to be about social communication and culture can communicate little that is critical or relevant to its own society.

We will begin by looking at one of the best known books in this area, *Mass Communications and Society* edited by James Curran, Michael Gurevitch and Janet Woollacott. When this was first published in 1977 it contained an article by Stuart Hall on 'Culture, the media and the ideological effect'. This high-lighted the work of Gramsci and the importance of understanding ideology as the winning of consent by the dominant class. It was also argued that the essence of capitalist ideology was the understanding of the social relations of production and exchange, simply as relations of exchange. In other words the relations of power and exploitation at the heart of the productive system were masked in a society which saw only 'free' relations of exchange between individuals in the market. Individual workers were therefore 'free' to sell their labour to the highest bidder. The individual employer was 'free' to take on labour at the lowest possible price. The power of capital and the inequality of the relations of production were lost in this ideological sleight of hand. The essential individual freedoms were for employers to employ, for workers to be able to sell labour without the 'restrictions' of trade unions and for consumers to be able to buy. In this understanding of free market relations, the power of unions was anathema. Their role in defending the employed against the productive forces of capital is banished from public view. The demand for the right to work is thus transformed into the individual's right to go to work, across picket lines.

This analysis of ideology offers a very pertinent introduction to the plans of the New Right after 1979 and to Mrs Thatcher's famous claim that there is no such thing as society, only families and individuals. In the event, the 1980s saw a ferocious struggle to establish a new dominance for the market. This involved pushing back the restraining influences of the post-war consensus with its commitment to full employment and social welfare. This period was therefore a high point in the development of news management and of state and corporate public relations – the age of spin doctors (Miller and Dinan, 2000; Philo, 1995a, 1995b). Yet strangely it was also during this period that the concept of ideology disappeared from much academic work in media and cultural studies. When *Mass Communications and Society* was reprinted in a new edition in 1991, the article on ideology was left out. The reason given was that the 'field' had changed and that the new book should not remain 'trapped in the models and paradigms of the 1970s' (Curran and Gurevitch, 1991, p. 7). A new set of theoretical questions and issues now preoccupied cultural theorists. We will argue here that much media and cultural studies had in fact wandered up a series of dead-ends which made it socially irrelevant as a discipline and incapable of commenting critically on the society within which it existed. To illustrate this, we will look first at the cultural and material changes which did occur in our society and then at the problems with the new directions taken by media and cultural studies.

## A new market dominance

The rise of the New Right in the 1980s did not signify a new age or a new type of society. The same social relations of production existed (between employers and employed) and the same tendencies of capital to accumulate. It continues to agglomerate into larger and larger units giving greater power in the market. For example, in 1996 the £28 billion merger of Boeing and McDonnell Douglas in America gave them nearly two-thirds of the world's commercial airline market and over half of the US military aircraft production. In the same year, the MCI/British Telecom merger was valued at over £35 billion. (In 1997 BT were supplanted by an even larger offer for MCI, by WorldCom.) Capital also continues to move globally to take advantage of the most favourable conditions. For example, in Mexico adjacent to the US border there has been a rapid and very extensive development of 'maquiladores'. These are internationally owned factories which are situated to take advantage of low wages and the absence of controls on pollution and safety. Within such markets, power is vested in those that own industry. Those who have only their labour to sell can do so if they are able, those who can not may be discarded. The ability of capital to move is a key source of its power and, with the growth of information technology, financial capital can move very rapidly. We have shown elsewhere how this has had a major influence on British electoral politics (Philo, 1995a).

The concentration of wealth within an economic system which propels it to wherever profits are greatest is inherently destabilizing – not just for the global economy and those subject to its rapid expansion and contraction, but also for global ecology. For example Brazil is now planning a new series of 'export corridors' through what remains of the rain forest. As the *Guardian* reported:

> A new internationally financed assault on the Amazon rain forest is under way. European, US and Asian investment agencies are financing dozens of infrastructure mega projects that will rip open the heart of the Amazon basin. Roads, railways, gas and mining operations and hydro-electric dams are being built or planned . . . *The world is full of money looking for such schemes to finance.* (20 August 1997, our emphasis)

It is extremely difficult to limit such developments, since the main global corporations are based in powerful nation states which defend their interests. There is therefore no collective response to these problems as the failure of the last Earth summit illustrated. There was no agreement then on a tax on aviation fuel to cut pollution because 'the US opposed new taxes and OPEC countries feared loss of revenue and the developing world loss of tourists because of increased prices'. As Stephen Nzita, a political party leader from Zaire,[1] commented, 'if this kind of Earth summit circus continues, then the people of Africa will perish' (*Guardian*, 28 June 1997).

The essence of such 'modern' economic relationships is that capital will agglomerate, will move and will do whatever is necessary to secure the conditions of its own existence. The same can be said of mass communication systems. A small number of corporations now control the bulk of all privately owned commercial communications (Herman and McChesney, 1997). Rupert Murdoch's News Corporation empire is often referred to in terms of its influence on political processes (for example the decision to remove the BBC from the Star satellite service in the Far East, following the displeasure of the Chinese government, and the consistent support given in the 1980s by papers such as the *Sun* and the *Sunday Times* for Conservative policies and later, following a private meeting with Tony Blair, for the Labour Party).

Lewis Lapham, the editor of the New York *Harper's Magazine*, has written of how the press in America celebrate the new world order:

> As might be expected, the shining face of the global economy wears its brightest smile in the show windows of the media owned and operated by the same oligarchy that owns and operates the banks. The accompanying press releases predict limitless good news in the world joyfully blessed by open markets, convertible currencies and free trade. The financial magazines make no attempt to quiet their emotions or restrain the breathless tenor of their prose. Behold, men of genius and resolve, – Billionaires! Visionaries! Entrepreneurs! – trading cable systems for telephone lines and telephone lines for movie studios and movie studios for cable systems, buying and selling the wells of celebrity that water the gardens of paradise. (1998, p. 19)

As he argues, the global economy comes at a cost:

that can be expressed in other sets of always larger numbers – the ones about the destruction of the forests and the fish, about the fast-rising slums that engulf the cities of steel and glass, about the dissolution of the ozone layer and the proliferation of sewer rats and nuclear weapons. The rule of law meanwhile loses its hold on the ferocious elites (corporate and predatory, often criminal) that with the force and arrogance of capitalism intimidate the world's parliaments. (1998, p. 19)

The most powerful players in the global market can successfully 'lobby' for their favoured policy in domestic economies.

With the collapse of the East European economies there is little to challenge American dominance globally. But it has also been noted that within the American domestic economy business interests have gained a new ascendancy. Theorists such as Herman and Chomsky have pointed to the role of the media in the production of consent for corporate and state policy (1988; Herman and McChesney, 1997). But it is also interesting to hear the same message from the owner of an American multi-million dollar company. Gerry Greenfield (of Ben and Gerry's) commented in an interview recently that:

Business strongly influences elections with campaign contributions . . . It controls legislation and lobbyists, and it controls the media through ownership. You have car companies lobbying against fuel efficiency standards, against safety standards; you have businesses lobbying against environmental regulations, against health insurance, against the minimum wage. (*Guardian*, 28 December 1996)

In this period we also see a continuation of the tendency for market economies to develop unevenly. The 'tiger' economies of the Far East had until recently much higher growth rates than most Western economies. For example, between 1979 and 1992 manufacturing output in Britain increased by just 4.5 per cent. In the same period in Japan, output increased by over 60 per cent (Central Statistical Office, 1992). At a global level the decline of the British manufacturing economy is essentially a local change. Shipbuilding may largely cease in Britain but the world tonnage of shipping is likely to increase, albeit that the ships are built in South Korea rather than on Tyneside.

In the 1980s the British economy became more orientated towards its financial and service sectors and there were major increases in unemployment. Such a decline in the industrial workforce might also affect the nature of collective responses to market capitalism. But these developments do not signify a new type of world or new society. The same might be said of the growth of information technology. Such growth is largely determined by the structures of power within which such technologies develop. A technology may have the potential to facilitate a more open and democratic society – but – if property rights are challenged, it is unlikely to be developed in this way at least by the powerful. Thus the potential openness of the internet is already being threatened by legal action on intellectual property rights. More importantly, the new information technology will be developed for the *purpose* of establishing the rights of the propertied – i.e. for surveillance and control of ownership and use in the distribution of products. The new technology does mean that it is possible to engage in traditional activities more quickly – such as the global dealing in shares or currencies. But the fundamental relations of accumulation for profit which govern such systems remain the same. What was 'new' about the 1980s and the politicians and theorists of the New Right was that they sought to remove the limits on these processes of accumulation and the power of capital in the market. In this they were in fact looking back to an older society rather than creating anything very new. Their project was to roll back the priorities of the social democratic state with its commitments to welfare, full employment and 'high' taxation to fund these. The role of the state would instead be to remove the 'restrictions' on the free market in labour (union powers, minimum wages etc.), to 'de-regulate' and allow larger units of capital to form (to increase profitability) and of course to reward the 'wealth makers'. To do this they would reduce direct taxation which would in practice be of most benefit to the top 20 per cent of the population. This would allow the market to develop in a more unfettered form, but it would still be a capitalist market and still therefore a 'modern' society. We can look now more closely at the impact of these changes in practice at a national level in Britain and at their effects on the global economy.

## The New Right and free market culture

The first major change was in the ownership of wealth. The most obvious effect of the political programme of the New Right in Britain was to greatly increase the gap between the rich and poor. Between 1979 and 1991 the disposable income of the top 10 per cent of the population rose by 62 per cent, while that of the poorest 10 per cent fell in real terms by 17 per cent. One effect of this was to increase the number of people working as servants. With echoes of Victorian Britain, the rich could now employ the poor for domestic chores (Cox, 1997). John Cassidy has written in *The New Yorker* of parallel changes in the US As he notes:

> It is only in the past two decades that a systematic assault on social democracy has been carried out in the name of 'economic efficiency'. This right-wing backlash has produced a sharp upsurge in inequality. Between 1980 and 1996, the share of total household income going to the richest 5 per cent of families in the US increased from 15.3 per cent to 20.3 per cent, while the share of the income going to the poorest 60 per cent of families fell from 34.2 per cent to 30 per cent . . . In 1978, a typical director at a big US company earned about 60 times what a typical worker earned; in 1995, he took home about 170 times as much. (1997, p. 13)

In Britain there was also a crucial change in the pattern of social ownership. The privatization programme meant that the majority of the population were poorer in the sense that what they formally owned was sold for a fraction of its worth. The loss to the state caused by these discounted sales of the nationally owned industries was estimated at over £20 billion (Hutton, 1995, p. 184). In an industry such as telecommunications the huge profits that were to come from the development of information technology and fax transmissions were no longer the property of the whole population but benefited only those who owned shares. The privatization of public utilities such as gas, electricity and water also signified a second crucial change in the public service ethos of care and security which had been promised by the 'old' consensual politics. What had been seen as public services became merely commodities to be sold. In a free market the social right to have clean water or to be warm could depend on the ability to pay. Policy in this area was no longer to be determined by 'public service' companies but by private industry whose ownership and shareholders were international. To be secure and to have rights in such a system depends on the ability to purchase in the market. Those who cannot do so are deemed to have 'disconnected themselves'. The language of this society revealed the new relationships. On the railways 'passengers' became 'customers' and in inner cities the cardboard box became the symbol of homelessness. Poverty becomes more visible as people sleep on the streets and die from the effects (seventy-four in London alone in the winter of 1995, *Guardian*, 4 January 1997). This was an important cultural change since the British were not accustomed to seeing such overt evidence of destitution in the heart of major cities. It was a reminder of the consequences of failure in a society that no longer cared 'from the cradle to the grave'. The state thus moved away from social priorities and the key commitment of the post-war years to the welfare of all its citizens. This was confirmed by other changes including the reduction of unemployment and social security rights. The net result was the production of insecurity. This was greatly added to by the economic policies of the New Right which relied on interest rate rises to curb inflation. The result was two serious recessions between 1979–83 and 1989–94, resulting in very high and sustained levels of unemployment (as high as 3.75 million people in 1983). This in combination with the reduction of trade union rights very much weakened the position of the workforce in the labour market. Labour was 'casualized' and versions of this, including short-term contracts, spread through the manufacturing, financial and service sectors of the economy. The public sector had once been seen as a source of secure employment, but, between 1992 and 1996, 42 per cent of staff taken on were non-permanent. It was also reported that 40 per cent of the workforce had to move jobs following the 1989 recession (*Guardian*, 10 February 1997). As the power of management increased, it was possible to impose arbitrary changes in work practices, to enforce longer periods of work for the same reward or to engage in simple bullying.[2] Levels of stress associated with work increased and unemployment was also linked to ill-health and suicide. With no minimum wage, weak unions and a demoralized workforce, Britain's private sector was on the way to becoming either the sweatshop of Europe or a 'flexible labour market' depending upon political perspective.

The third key area of change which we look at here is the impact of the new political approaches on the public sector. In the free market society, 'public' comes to mean all those who do not have sufficient private wealth for basic services such as health or education and who therefore rely on the public sector. The minority with sufficiently high incomes have no need for such public provision as they can buy their own private health or education. The public sector was thus intensively disliked by the new Conservatives and free marketeers. On the other hand, the public sector is a key area through which the 'public' can attempt to get back the resources that have been taken from them by the exploitative relations of the labour market. They can do this by insisting that there are taxes on those who can afford them, to pay for public services. The Conservative attack on taxation was thus a crucial ideological move to ensure that the division of property which they have achieved remains untouched. The critique of the public sector is a corollary of this. It was portrayed in New Right demonology as 'bloated' or incompetent and as in need of 'control'. It was to be disciplined by the appointment of layers of managers and accountants who constantly pressured those who were actually providing services, whether they were teachers, civil servants or health workers. This was presented as accountability but is actually a kind of 'punishment by counting'. These groups were constantly made to account for and justify their work as its 'quality' is assessed from above. The true function of the new layers of management is to impose 'efficiency savings' which can amount to enforcing more production for the same or less reward. At the same time levels of bureaucracy increased because of the constant demands for measurement – national testing, league tables, quality assessment, and other variations of 'performance indicators' were extended through the public sector. In the NHS, between 1989 and 1997 the cost of administrative staff doubled to £2.4 billion (*Observer*, 18 May 1997). In practice cuts in funding must be borne while output is expected to increase and the cost of the new bureaucrats must also be met. The public sector becomes intensely pressured and here again levels of stress for staff increased dramatically. A study by Gail Kinman for NATFHE of lecturers in further and higher education showed 72 per cent reporting that they had an unmanageable workload. The survey also indicated extraordinarily high levels of occupational stress and illness linked with this (38 per cent suffering depression and 26 per cent anxiety, with nearly one in ten indicating alcohol dependency). One lecturer gave this account:

> The department in which I work is suffering from an 'epidemic' of stress: two members of staff are on long term stress-related sick leave. One former colleague in his early 40s has taken early retirement; yet another has been transferred to another department because she could not cope with the demands placed upon her. (Kinman, 1996)

The new 'accounting' in the public sector meant that the social values of production for the public were eroded. They were replaced with the processes by which production and 'efficiency' were measured. Teachers spend less time teaching and more on assessment – of their pupils and themselves. Hospitals are measured in terms of the 'throughput' of patients. Social security staff are given 'targets' for the reduction of numbers of claimants rather than having the provision of help as the central goal. In this new market, rewards are given for 'performance'. So in place of a collective commitment to the use and value of what is produced, there is division and competition. Instead of a collective demand for proper funding, individuals and institutions compete with each other for a share of the dwindling resources. Most importantly, the ethos and purpose of activity in terms of social use is lost in favour of simply meeting the formal criteria for the latest performance targets and plans. We become adept at demonstrating on paper how we have performed. But there is little room in such a system for collective discussion about the purpose of what is being done or what social interests are actually being served.

A fourth key dimension in the social development of this period is the transformation of political culture and the reduction of democratic control. The imposition of the new social and economic arrangements required the development of a more extensive range of quasi-autonomous non-governmental organizations (quangos) and the appointment of sympathetic figures to run them. The *Economist* has written of 'the pernicious growth of government patronage that has accompanied the spread of quangos'. Ministers were responsible for over 42,000 posts and in any single year they make or renew about 10,000 of them. In 1992 only 24 of these were advertised (6 August 1994). This centralization and patronage again offers strange echoes of a previous age. The combination of an undemocratic political centre opposed to state intervention in an economy of casualized labour bears some resemblance to early nineteenth-century capitalism.

A fifth major change was the erosion of civil liberties. There were intensified pressures on the public sphere in the form of direct and indirect censorship and secrecy, with a specific impetus from Northern Ireland (Miller, 1994a, 1995c; Robertson and Nicol, 1992). The surveillance of the population increased both at the level of policing dissent and in responding to changes brought about by government policy in other areas such as social security. Definitions of subversion were also tightened, so that the 'enemy within' became a key target, from inner city 'rioters' to striking miners, from new-age travellers to anti-poll-tax protesters and environmental activists (Campbell and Connor, 1986; Hollingsworth and Tremayne, 1989; Hollingsworth and Norton-Taylor, 1988). The police and intelligence agencies were granted increased powers, which even liberally-minded chief constables worried about (Ewing and Gearty, 1990; Hillyard and Percy-Smith, 1988; Northam, 1990).

None of these processes suggests a weakening of the state or the detachment of the 'cultural' from the exercise of state or economic power.[3] They do not suggest a weakening of determining forces or the growth of a 'post-modern' society. They point instead to the centralization of political and economic power.

Finally we want to examine what changes have occurred at the level of ideologies and core social values – specifically how free market culture has a new prominence both in representations and in everyday lived experience. One element of this culture is the celebration of the 'wealth makers', of profit and of the ability to consume. Material values and the struggle for money and inter-personal power are not new and were not invented by the New Right. But the post-war consensus had been founded in part on a critique of profiteering and exploitation. The state-owned industries especially were expected to have some sense of social priorities. By contrast, for the New Right material success and individual enterprise were the key values and in the 1980s were at the centre of promotional campaigns. The government financed very extensive TV advertising on the themes of 'enterprise culture' and the sale of the state industries, promoting the buying of shares and the philosophy of private ownership (Philo, 1995b; Franklin, 1994). Acquisition and material desire are thus officially sanctioned and parts of television (notably the news) took on a public relations function for these key values of the 1980s. But there is another important reason why the products of television begin to change in this period. The opening of the market increased the pressure on television companies for ratings and signified a move away from the traditional concern with quality and 'good taste'. The priority that television should be seen to be popular and to be responding to the demands of its market erodes the original Reithian ideal that it should in some way set and lead standards. It has also been argued that violence is increasingly used on television as a way of attracting viewers and demanding instant attention. Jaci Stephen made this point when she quit after ten years of reviewing TV for the *Daily Mirror*. As she wrote: 'there is nothing ambiguous about a smashed skull' (*Guardian*, 25 March 1996).

Images of violence and power can be compelling if they explore and act as a focal point for the insecurity and fear of an audience. They can also offer the possibility of identification with characters who represent what it is to be cool and totally in control. This does not mean that all contemporary media are consumed with violence. Some popular television and even music in Britain is still family/community oriented and derives from a tradition which includes musicals and holiday camps (from *Noel's House Party* and *Barrymore* on television to the *Smurfs* and the *Birdie Song* as hit records). Some TV drama and soap opera has also offered sympathetic and critical portrayals of issues such as AIDS (Miller *et al.*, 1998), sexual abuse and violence against women. The furore over TV comes partly from the Right, because of their concern with sexual morality and perhaps because attacking television is an easy election issue for politicians. There is less criticism of Hollywood which is a more central provider of images of power and the delights of exercising it.

The key issue in terms of the changes which we are identifying is that the media as a whole struggle for audiences in what has become an intensively competitive market. One tendency is therefore to push back the boundaries on what can be shown or written. A newspaper such as the *Sunday Sport* or magazines such as *Loaded* are interesting examples of this. We are not suggesting that all social values can be 'derived' from, or reduced to, these changing market relationships. The values of sexual consumption, male power and aggression are certainly not new. What is new is that pressure to dominate markets in communication moves such values into mainstream products and removes barriers on their presentation and celebration. The embracing by the BBC of 'laddish' culture is another interesting example of this in the Corporation's dive down market for ratings. Thus a programme such as *Top Gear* can become a celebration of the speed and sexual pulling power of cars. A youth programme on Sunday lunch time can show fighting and drinking as a bit of a laugh. For example, the *Sunday Show* took up the 'violence on TV' debate in December 1996. The programme ended with the presenter saying 'I like a bit of violence, here are my favourite bits (from the year).' This was followed by a sequence of film and video clips of actual street fights, of people being hit and celebrities such as Bjork punching and attacking other people. After this the programme was wound up with the words 'We don't care what you lot are doing now. We are going off to get trolleyed, absolutely plastered' (with motions of drinking from co-host) (BBC2, 12.15 p.m., 22 December 1996).

The new centrality of the market means that its values are promoted in the media and images and commentaries which were previously restricted can now be supplied. But the rise of the market also produces key changes to relationships in the wider society. The market has a crucial role beyond being simply the mechanism through which pre-existing demands are supplied. It is itself a system of values and relationships which exist at an interpersonal level as the competitive struggle between individuals. In a market society individual status can be given by the ability to buy, to demand service and thus to control others. The key commodity in such a society is human labour. People compete to 'sell' and market themselves and the individual struggle for 'success' can undermine collectivist and social responses. The crucial question which this raises is that if the market constitutes a system of values, how are these linked in practice to the development of social beliefs and action? How do changes in the production/exchange of commodities affect the growth of new attitudes, motivations and behaviour and how are these 'market values' contested or rejected? We can also ask how systems of representation in media relate to these values and to cultures of inter-personal power. Media representations can crystallize and express the key moments in relationships which define a period or type of society. In this sense media images grow historically and are located in the material world. But they can also extend, legitimize or comment on such relationships – they can celebrate or criticize. In this they have a crucial role in the winning of consent for a social system, its values and its dominant interests, or in the rejection of them.

How do we explain the development of the social and the personal and how they are represented, and then show how these elements combine to produce changes in belief and behaviour? We can explore this by looking further at the rise of the 'new lad'. The celebration of this (or other cultures of inter-personal success) in part matches and expresses the new dominance of the market and its social relationships of power and consumption. In the laddish cultural variant the key commodities for consumption are cars, women and alcohol. It is thus a mixture of traditional male and market power. Status as 'one of the lads' is given by the level of consumption. The values are not new but they are now offered in a more developed and legitimized form. The Advertising Standards Authority reported that there were more complaints about 'laddish' themes in 1996 than in any previous year (*Guardian*, 30 December 1996). The new prominence of these values is contested by 'social alternatives' from the Left and by the 'moralism' of the Right. The latter had traditionally asserted the need for moral control – for example the confining of sex to marriage – in the name of social order. Against these, the values of the market celebrate a social and material world which is for sale and that is reduced to a mass of commodities. Human relationships and people are 'commoditized'. The millionaire hero of the film *Indecent Proposal* (1993) can afford to buy another person's wife and justifies it with the view that he 'buys people every day'. When the film was first shown on television in 1996 it was advertised on billboards showing a woman in underwear, along with the phrase 'The price is right so they come on down'. This culture both parallels and promotes the commodification of relationships – in which the greatest expression of inter-personal power is the power to buy the person.

## Market values and social behaviour

To understand the relationship between social culture and individual behaviour, we must first see that an action requires both a motive and an opportunity.

Changes in material circumstances may affect what can be done (what opportunities exist) while changes in social values may affect what is seen as desirable (the available motives). We must, therefore, examine how structures of opportunity relate to value systems and possible sources of motivation. The freeing of market relationships gave a new prominence to the values of inter-personal power, the accumulation of wealth and consumption. At the same time the material security of some sections of the population was damaged and there was an intensification of processes which led to the fragmentation of communities. In the 1980s and 1990s, therefore, we see spectacular examples of middle-class crime arising from the obsession with accumulation (e.g. the Guinness, BCCI and Barings scandals). At the same time there is also a rapid increase overall in recorded property crime. Between 1979 and 1995 recorded instances of burglary increased from 549,000 to 1,240,000 (*Observer*, 4 May 1997).

The weakening of community structures was a consequence of political policies which promoted the free market. The uneven development of the capitalist market plus its tendency to rapid expansion and contraction has historically put pressure on community structures and forced the movement or displacement of labour (from the seventeenth-century enclosures in England to the Highland clearances in nineteenth-century Scotland). More recently the destruction of industries such as steel in Scotland or coal mining across Britain and the decline in manufacturing has weakened and depressed working class communities. Jeremy Seabrook writes of the decline of his own community following the collapse of the boot and shoe industry in Northampton. He describes the emergence of the underclass:

> Like an exhumation of the remains of the working class, the skeleton left behind when all those who could leave have gone, abandoning those who might have been perceived as the undeserving and the helpless, but who were also sheltered within the old working class . . . The people we had called Auntie or Uncle were transformed, little by little, into strangers, and malevolent strangers at that. (1997, pp. 135–6)

A report from the York University Centre for Housing Policy analyzes the process of 'reverse gentrification' as it affects council estates. The report notes that only a fifth of residents (heads of households) in these estates now hold full-time jobs (Burrows, 1997, p. 48). As Will Hutton comments:

> What we are witnessing in our cities is the expression in bricks and mortar of the widening inequality in wages and wealth. But on top there is the dynamic unleashed by the policies and forces that stress individualism and market contracting as the new organising basis of our society.

Hutton also points to the link between poor social conditions, some types of illegal drug taking and violent crime. He describes 'sink estates' which are:

deserted by banks, building societies and supermarket chains [which are] chasing ever higher earnings per share – [sink estates] in which a new and ugly sub-culture is developing – incubating, as a side-effect, violence and racism. (*Observer*, 16 February 1997)

We have therefore a society which promotes values of inter-personal power and combines this with social conditions in which power and violence can be seen as the best or only way of surviving. The apparent increase in violent behaviour is thus an important element of contemporary cultural development. Between 1979 and 1997 recorded crimes of violence against the person increased from 95,000 to 246,000 (Home Office figures, *Guardian*, 15 October 1997), a rise which cannot be explained simply by reference to reporting rates or statistical procedures. The increase in violence can be linked to instrumental purposes, i.e. it is used because it works to achieve an end. We can see for example how the growth of violent crime is linked in part to the need for money to supply drug habits (though it is also linked strongly to alcohol). A pressured society with an increase in absolute poverty is likely to produce an increase in violence as people fight for what resources there are or express frustration and anger on the nearest targets. But violence and the enjoyment of its use have a long history in human culture and should not be seen only as a reaction to difficult circumstances. It is certainly true that violence can result from stress in domestic or work relationships and that it can be used as a desperate attempt to establish control. But it must also be said that in a society which celebrates inter-personal power and competition there will be people who identify with the pleasure of exerting control. Violence can be seen as the ultimate way of establishing the self in relation to the weakness of others. In this sense, the social opposition to the use of violence in practice and to its celebration in representational forms (film/television) is part of the long cultural struggle away from barbarism towards the humane.

The social and economic policies pursued in Britain from 1979 created the conditions for both an increase in property crime and violence. Professor John Pitts has compared the changes in British society in the 1980s with those in France in the same period after the election of Mitterrand as President on a left wing platform. He writes:

In 1981, in both Britain and France, approximately 3.5 million offences were recorded by the police. By the end of the decade, the number in Britain was approaching 6 million. In France, between 1983 and 1986, there was a decline to around 3 million, from which the figure rose gradually to around 3.8 million by 1990. In Britain, crime rose fastest in the poorest neighbourhoods; in France it was in the poorest neighbourhoods that the fall was most marked.

He attributes these differences to the policies pursued by the Mitterrand administration:

which channelled educational, training, housing and community resources into high-crime suburbs, subsidised industry to bring jobs, decentralised key ministries and created new forms of democratic participation for the socially excluded and the young. (*Guardian*, 28 May 1997)

In Britain the rise of the New Right undermined both the values and the structures of opportunity which existed in the period of post-war consensual politics. We do not wish to romanticize the period before 1979. It sustained wide-spread inequalities of wealth and power and has been criticized for being 'statist' and overly centralized – i.e. in the sense that the positive role of the state was conceived of as providing welfare from centralized bureaucracies rather than enabling people to decide what they wanted and helping them to help themselves. Nonetheless, the consensual state was committed in its ideology if not always in practice to the reduction of class inequalities and to meritocratic principles in which reward was linked to ability and effort. Some of the rhetoric of the New Right also apparently echoed this commitment, in slogans such as 'rewarding the wealth makers'. However, the release of the market after 1979 produced very rapid and often random transformations in personal fortune. For example, the deregulation of credit in the 1980s meant that very large sums moved rapidly around the economy. A boom in shares collapsed on 'Black Monday' in October 1987 and this was followed by the almost frantic movement of funds into the housing market. In 1988 house prices in the South East more than doubled in value, followed by a collapse in prices from 1989 (Philo, 1995b). Meanwhile, the effect of high interest rates and the free market on manufacturing industries such as engineering had produced increased unemployment and the decline of apprenticeships and training. The anarchy of the market eroded traditional links between reward and effort and undermined values which could make sustained work seem rational. An unemployed sixteen-year-old in the North East of England might question why there are no apprenticeships, while people in the South could at times 'earn' more simply by owning a house than by actually going to work.

The relative calm of the post-war order was thus replaced by a more pressured and individualistic society with higher levels of violence to others and the self. This was very clearly the case for young males who were most likely to be the victims as well as the perpetrators of violence. The involvement of boys aged ten to thirteen in violent crime rose by 50 per cent in the seven years prior to 1995 and for fourteen- to sixteen-year-olds by 30 per cent. Youth unemployment also meant that young people were targeted for cuts in benefits and were pressured to move in search of work. Between 1984 and 1995 the suicide rate of males under 25 increased by 75 per cent (*Observer*, 26 January 1997). Not surprisingly the crisis was also felt in schools with attacks on teachers and pupils. The Ridings School in Yorkshire became notorious in

1996 when teachers demanded the suspension of sixty pupils in order to make it possible to teach. One reason given at the time for the discipline problems of schools was the disruption of patterns of youth recruitment, training and apprenticeships – a pupil's performance in school was irrelevant if it led to nothing and no references were needed for unemployment. The morale of teachers was also low following the imposition of new bureaucratic controls such as national testing and attacks on the profession by the Conservative government for an alleged fall in standards. It is also important to note that the new prominence of market values such as inter-personal power and accumulation is likely to undermine any mystique which had attached to 'social' public sector professions such as teaching. Teachers were seen as underpaid and criticized as incompetent. It is not surprising therefore if they had difficulty in commanding the respect of some pupils. Our own research on children's responses to film violence showed that some who had little interest in school work were near to awe-struck by new cultural icons such as John Travolta (as the cool killer in *Pulp Fiction*). Their teacher was astonished that children who were reluctant to write in class could reproduce pages of the film script from memory (Philo, 1997).

The release of the market had powerful and long-term social effects. The British example shows interestingly that the damage to social life had begun to affect the middle classes. Only the highest income earners could in practice buy their way out of problems through purchasing private health care, private education and ultimately private security. The weakening of state health care and education were very powerful factors in the political arguments against the New Right. We can see this if we look briefly at the situation in a specific school in Glasgow two weeks before the General Election of May 1997. The school is in a middle-class area and we quote here from the minutes of a parents' and teachers' meeting. They record the major problem that two of the most senior and experienced teachers had taken early retirement at short notice in the middle of the school year. This was because of a government-imposed deadline which was an attempt to stem the flow of such retirements. The minutes read: 'Particular note was made of the disruption caused by the retirements – emotional costs/parent/teacher/pupil relationships'. The minutes also record that the school canteen had been closed to cut costs. Meals were now provided from another school. The decision to close their kitchen was informed by the fact that their catering supervisor 'had been on a higher grade than her colleagues in other schools'. Market-driven criteria mean that those being paid slightly more may be dismissed in favour of younger, inexperienced and cheaper people. The food now coming was 'not of a particularly high standard – burnt pizzas and no soup available'. The minutes ominously record that 'it was thought that parents should make their feelings known to the appropriate authorities' (15 April 1997).

In the event people in Scotland did not require many more hints in making their views known to the authorities. Two weeks later in the General Election of the 1 May 1997 no Conservatives at all were elected in that country.

## New Labour, the market and meritocracy

The Conservatives were thus followed in power by the New Labour party of Tony Blair. 'New Labour' is an odd term. With its commitment to free market liberalism, its moral tone, its exhortations to the lower orders to discover the merits of work and its designation of the deserving and undeserving poor, it is actually a version of old fashioned Christian Liberalism. It would certainly have been recognized by nineteenth-century Liberals such as Gladstone. It is odd that is what is now termed 'old Labour' was actually the new politics of the twentieth century and was developed as a rejection of the deep flaws in old Liberalism. In our view, the policies of New Labour share many of these flaws, particularly in their assumptions about morality, meritocracy and the market.

### New Labour morals

We are not dismissing morality and values as political issues. We have argued elsewhere that the move from barbarism and violence to the humane is a cultural struggle which clearly requires decisions to be made between competing value systems (Philo, 1997). Such a change in human society is likely to involve the state, whether it is in attempts to combat physical or sexual abuse in the home or whether it is at the global level in demands for universal human rights. What we are unsure of is how the moralizing and finger wagging of New Labour actually connects with contemporary society.

As we have seen, the decades of Conservatism produced in Britain one of the sharpest divisions in the ownership of wealth of any industrial society. In the face of this, New Labour has declared that class division is now over. But will people who earn less than £4 per hour really see themselves as part of the same social project as those who wear watches which are worth the average yearly income? Put more bluntly, how is it possible to convince excluded, unemployed and alienated young people on broken down estates that they would be better off earning poverty wages on a training scheme or in a succession of McJobs than in selling drugs or ram-raiding? The problem is that the values so encouraged by free market individualism – of material success, interpersonal power and conspicuous consumption – are absorbed by many people across all classes, irrespective of their potential to achieve these goals 'legitimately' (very few people from housing estates ended up as commodity brokers in red braces). Many of the sermons delivered by New Labour owe more to the concerns of the tabloid press than to a rational social analysis. The 'war against drugs', for example does not include the drugs which actually do the most harm – i.e. 40,000 deaths per year from alcohol and 120,000 per year from cigarettes. The vested interests who supply these products are too powerful. So a phoney war is conducted which has criminalized large numbers of young people, increased the prison population and put truly huge amounts of money at the disposal of organized crime. It is now estimated that approximately 10 per cent of the world economy is related to drugs while up to 25 per cent of the British economy is now illegal (including drugs, prostitution and fake designer products; Burton, 1999, p. 10). This is a true triumph of the free market.

New Labour's exhortations to behave properly are now backed with threats and parents will be made responsible for their children. In September 1999, the education secretary promised a doubling of fines for parents who failed to get their children to school. But as Michael McMahon writes, this is hardly a serious threat:

> You can't take money from people who haven't got it, and most of the people he speaks of punishing are at the bottom of the heap; they are no more able to pay such fines than to control their children. The threat has grabbed the required headlines, and can now be forgotten. It is the schools, not the courts, that are once more called upon to contain the underclass. (McMahon, 1999, p. 10)

A more serious issue which he points to is the consequences of trying to force truants back into school. He speaks of an observation that most experienced inner-city school teachers would make, which is that:

> Increasing numbers of children simply can't cope with school. Some, undisciplined through neglect or indulgence at home, lack not only basic social skills but the ability to feel even a glimmer of concern for the effect of their actions on the people around them. Others tending to truant include the youngsters who express their inadequacy passively: the neurotic offspring of drug addicts, drunks, and depressives, perhaps. These children tend to be easily bullied and can be terrified of having to go to school to face imagined or real tormentors. In areas of social deprivation, there are kids like this on every street. Picking on their pathetic, impoverished parents and threatening them with fines is as pointless as it is cruel. Such people need help not punishment. (McMahon, 1999, p. 10)

It must be said that drug dependency, alcoholism and mental illness as well as inter-personal violence can occur across all social classes. But it is also clear that poverty is strongly linked to the exacerbation of all these and can make their resolution more difficult.

### Meritocracy

New Labour's most positive responses to these problems are in its attempts to increase opportunities for the poor through education and in its expressed desire for a meritocracy. But in these it seems simply not to understand how a class society works. The vision which it offers is of individuals grasping opportunities and rising according to talent. But a class structure cannot simply be wished away. Society is not a mass of isolated individuals but is composed of groups who interact and use their command of resources to pursue their own interests. The education system is inextricably linked to patterns of ownership and control of resources and to the income levels which result from these. Suppose that our society is structured like a triangle with a large number of people at the bottom and a small number at the top; then it is not hard to see how the education system matches this in its own organization. The point is that education feeds people into the existing occupational structure. It does not create new jobs. This means for example that if the bottom 10 million of the population, who have the lowest income, were given intensive training in how to be merchant bankers, then these people would not all go off to be 'something in the city'. This is an issue which was referred to by Chris Woodhead, the Chief Inspector of Schools, in a speech at the Conservative Party Conference of October 1999. He criticized Tony Blair's proposal to put 50 per cent of the population into higher education and asked where the jobs were into which these graduates could go (*Guardian*, 5 October 1999). In practice, the educational structure very largely operates to reproduce the existing social structure. The wealthiest of the population pay for their children to attend elite private schools. There are just over 200 of these in what is termed the Headmasters Conference and they account for approximately 4 per cent of school pupils (Walford, 1986, p. 8). Attendance at such a school is very likely to result in access to the elite universities. Between 45 and 50 per cent of those entering Oxford and Cambridge have attended private schools (*Guardian*, 24 November 1998). This figure includes people who have attended less well-known private schools but they still constitute a very small percentage of the population as a whole. It is sometimes argued that entrance to elite occupations is a result of children attending elite schools. But in practice such children are already well connected from the moment they are born. Attendance at schools such as Eton or Harrow functions as a sort of badge to indicate that they already in the upper class. Such a group in effect lives a separate life from the rest of the population. George Walden, a former Conservative Cabinet Minister, comments in his memoirs about how little members of his own class know about how the rest of the population live:

> [I am] amazed at how little members of whatever social class I now belong to, know of their country. The reason is of course that when it comes to health, housing or education, they don't live in it. (Walden, 1999, p. 236).

At the next level of the class structure are the middle classes – the well-paid workers of the professional service sector, such as accountants, lawyers and middle management. In practice the middle classes do the best that they can with the educational resources that are available to them. If they cannot afford to pay for their children's education in private schools, then they focus on the best comprehensives or grammar schools in their area. They also tend to move to areas with the best schools and to deploy whatever resources they have at their disposal to ensure the success of their own children. This can be seen in the use of private tutors. A glance at the local newspapers of middle-class suburbs such as Bromley in South London reveals pages of tutors for hire. These are often teachers from state schools who supplement their income by coaching children for key exams. The ability to pay for such teaching at around £15 per hour will obviously vary. The majority of the population who earn below £20,000 per year are unlikely to be able to afford very much of it, while the middle classes on higher incomes will be able to purchase what they feel is required to keep their children ahead. The point is that the middle classes mobilize whatever is necessary to achieve this end – which of course includes pressurizing their own children, or 'giving them the best start they can' depending on how the process is seen. The result overall is that, at each level of education, parental income is a key factor in the success of the child. For example, the general household survey of 1991 showed that while 32 per cent of the children of professional fathers obtained degrees, only 3 per cent of the children of unskilled workers did so (HMSO, 1993, pp. 206–7). The recent expansion of the university sector has done little to change this pattern of access. This expansion was achieved by 'converting' the old under-funded polytechnics into universities. As Furlong and Cartmel note 'the older universities still tend to be the preserve of children from professional and managerial backgrounds', while children from lower income families are more likely to attend the 'new' institutions (1997, p. 26). A recent survey of employers conducted by Park Human Resources concluded that employers routinely discriminated against students from the new universities (1999, p. 10).

In the 1980s, educational inequality between high- and low-income groups actually increased as a result of the educational reforms brought in by the Conservatives. Their introduction of 'parental choice' for school intensified the process by which the 'best' schools gathered in predominantly middle-class children. As Nick Davies has written, these reforms:

> ... polarised the entire system between schools which gather the brightest children and the most funds and which are effectively grammar schools; and the contemporary equivalent of secondary modern schools, invariably in poor areas, where there is a concentration of disadvantaged children struggling for education on a reduced budget. This has helped the middle class, whose children tend to fill the classrooms of the successful schools, but it has abandoned the poor. (Davies, 1999b, p. 4)

The years of Conservative government also increased absolute poverty and the desolation of the areas in which the poorest and their schools were situated. As Davies comments:

> Poverty in Britain has trebled since 1979 to the point where a third of Britain's children – more than four million of them – now live below the poverty line. This torrent of poor children poured into the classroom at exactly the time as standards of behaviour and achievement slumped. (Davies, 1999a, p. 5)

The link between social disadvantage and lack of educational 'success' is not hard to discern:

> If a school takes in a substantial proportion of children who come from a disadvantaged background – if their parents do not read, if they have no books at home, if they are awake half the night and then half asleep all day, if they have been emotionally damaged by problems in their family or in their community, if they have suffered from an environment which is likely to expose them to drug abuse and violence and alcohol abuse and the collapse of social boundaries, then the school is more likely to fail academically. A school which is based in a disadvantaged community will struggle with its children, while one that is based in a more affluent area will prosper. (Davies, 1999a, p. 4)

But there is an important qualification to be made to this. The fundamental reason why these populations do not all enter middle- and upper-class occupations is not because they are educationally disadvantaged. The reason is that there is simply no room for them all to do so. If the four million children to whom Nick Davies refers did all overcome their educational disadvantage and obtained four A-levels each, then the middle classes would do whatever was required (hire more tutors, have academic pre-schools, drive infants even harder) to make sure that their children obtained five.

What we are describing here are trends and probabilities. In real everyday relationships, the class structure is not absolutely rigid. People do move in and out of social classes. Some middle- or upper-class people can become impoverished – bankruptcy, illness, drug dependency, alcoholism can have catastrophic effects across all classes. Another key issue is that the economy is not static. An expansion in a particular area can create 'space' for new entrepreneurs particularly if those who already control existing capital are unsure how to exploit the new market. The expansion of youth culture, music and leisure since the 1960s would be an example of this. Footballers, rock stars and fashion designers have done well. The illegal economy is of course another area which is likely to draw in people from a variety of social classes. Other areas of rapid expansion have been property speculation, pornography, the 'big bang' in the City of London and internet trading. The apparent openness of such new areas is not likely to stay so for long. Those who own capital and extensive material resources move very quickly to control the new potential for profitable investment. As a recent survey of internet millionaires concluded: 'It is the big brands with distribution, the Tescos, the WH Smiths, the Kingfishers, they'll win out in the end'. The report also noted that this new market is dominated by Oxbridge graduates who had the contacts to raise funds (Teather and Cassy, 1999, p. 2).

The key point on social mobility through education is that it is a possibility for some individuals, but for the mass of the population it is simply not an option. The number of accountants, lawyers, advertising executives, captains of industry and city financiers is in practice severely limited. The meritocratic vision that everyone who has talent and works hard can get to the top through education is impossible in a class society. It could not be so when there is limited access to 'top' positions. It would be like saying that everyone can win a race if they all ran a bit faster. The logical impossibility of the situation does not stop politicians from encouraging everyone else to do the running. They have brought in league tables for schools and standard assessment tests, they pressurize teachers and encourage parents to do the same. The result has been a great increase in stress for teachers, parents and children. A doctor writing in a national newspaper describes the consequences on the ground:

> I am losing count of the number of despairing teachers referred to me in my work as a GP counsellor in recent years . . . The root of the malaise within education lies in ever more overburdened teachers being expected to carry the scarcely containable anxieties and unachievable expectations of the nation's parents – driven in turn by the government-sanctioned illusion that the state can and should impose, control and dictate the learning process for our children. We are witnessing the systematic destruction of the art and vocation of teaching when misguided 'adult-centric' and developmentally inappropriate values are foisted upon our children. (*Guardian*, 4 October 1999)

It may indeed be developmentally inappropriate to force three-year-olds into the early learning of maths skills in the doomed hope that the sooner they start, the sooner they will attain genius levels. But there is another very serious issue here, on what is the vocation and art of teaching. Put simply, what are teaching and education intended to achieve? Are they meant to impart life skills and values, to show children how to live full and purposeful lives, to produce concerned and thoughtful citizens, to appreciate art and culture or more mundanely how to avoid pregnancy and drugs, read bus timetables or count their change? Or is the whole thing intended to prepare people for the workforce? In the face on these complex questions, politicians mostly avoid them and instead grasp at current shibboleths on whatever can look like the quest for academic excellence. Targets are set in areas such as information technology and the matching of international standards on maths skills. The assumption is that this is somehow going to benefit the overall economy. We do not wish to deride the need for basic skills but it is not clear why it matters if, on average, children in Bulgaria are better are solving some maths problems than children in Britain (they were and it doesn't). Current education policy does not make much sense even at the level of preparing young people for work. In modern societies there is a need for some people to have sophisticated maths and computing skills to work in high-tech industries – but in practice this is a tiny proportion of school leavers. Britain has a predominantly service sector economy with an ageing population. As many as a half of all school leavers may in future be required to work in health and care services. What is the point of all our students being driven to attain higher and higher maths and computing abilities? They would be better off learning key skills such as how to work in teams, how to obtain and evaluate information, how to communicate it to others and to make decisions based on evidence and perhaps most importantly how to care for and respect others.

Such priorities are rarely questioned in public life. New Labour politicians (and their Conservative predecessors) like targets that can be set and then claimed to have been met. This is so irrespective of whether the targets have any rational purpose or of how much damage is done to the students and teachers who have to meet the latest quality thresholds. Ultimately, these politicians will be betrayed by the free market which they so admire, as teachers in schools and higher education move out of the sector because of the low morale, low pay and poor conditions with which it is associated.

### New Labour and the free market

We have argued that formal education cannot of itself alter the class structure and that the conflicts which result from class cannot be wished away by New Labour politicians. There is often confusion over the term 'class' because it is sometimes used to mean the remains of aristocratic privilege, such as in the House of Lords or other types of inherited status. In public debate such 'illegitimate' inheritance is then contrasted with a society based on merit which is supposed to be 'classless' (such as the USA). But in our analysis, class is most crucially about the ownership of economic resources, and the use of these to maximize wealth and power. The normal workings of the 'free market' intensify this concentration of wealth because the most powerful corporations take over the weaker and ultimately control large sections of the market. In such a system there is a constant tendency toward monopoly and corporate hegemony. Such intense concentrations of wealth carry with them patterns of status, of personal inheritance, education and privilege. So the class structure constantly renews itself. This is as true of America as it is of Britain and it explains why patterns of social mobility in the USA are not as fluid as the American dream would suggest (Kerckhoff, 1990). It also goes some way to explaining why people from low-income groups such as the Hispanic grape pickers of California or the poor residents of inner cities do not become president. They would of course be eligible to run and could do so if they had the $20 million campaign costs. It also explains why so few of the children from these groups enter the ivy league universities, where fees run into tens of thousands of dollars. As we have said, class structures are not completely rigid. Some movement is possible in some circumstances but the mass of the population cannot radically alter their class position. Economic growth in such a system results in more economic concentration and the benefits largely accrue to a minority. As Robert Sherrill has noted of the recent growth in take-overs and stock market gains in the USA:

Ninety per cent of the stock gains went to the wealthiest 10 per cent of households with 42 per cent of the bounty going to the superrich 1 per cent. So let's hear no more about the growth of your piddling retirement account . . . There have been record numbers of mergers and acquisitions every year since 1994, topping out last year at a value of 2.5 trillion dollars. Drugs companies, banks, high-tech companies, rail roads, paper and utility companies, corporations of every brand . . . A wave of mergers beginning in 1985 left only four [main military contractors] . . . similar dominations exists in the tobacco industry, where three companies have more than 90 per cent of sales sold up. But they can't compare to Microsoft which alone controls 90 per cent of the world personal computer operating systems; or Boeing which, after it bought McDonnell Douglas in 1996, became the only manufacturer in commercial jets in the United States. (Sherrill, 1999, pp. 1–3)

He also points out that the value of Bill Gates's fortune in 1999 ($51 billion) 'was greater than the combined net worth of the 106 million American at the bottom of the pile' (1999, p. 1). We tend to think of this particular fortune as an aberration, but the concentration of wealth into the hands of a very small minority is typical of this system of accumulation. Unless it is limited through public ownership or by controls imposed by national governments, responsible to mass populations, then it is our future.[4]

In Britain this process of the 'normal' concentration of wealth and capital has been accentuated over the last twenty years by privatization, by de-regulation of the City (of share trading and banking services) and by tax concessions to high-income groups. As we noted above, the effect of this was that the top 10 per cent of the population increased their disposable income by 62 per cent. This group now receive as much income as the whole of the bottom half of society together (*Guardian*, 22 September 1999). Put, bluntly, the issue which faces New Labour is whether they are going to redress the balance and take that money back from the wealthiest groups, if only to repair the damage that has been caused to the poorest communities and to the public sector. At present the answer seems to be that they are not. As analysis by Professor David Piachaud of the London School of Economics suggests that at the present rate of progress it will take twenty years to reduce child poverty to the level that it was when the Conservatives came to power in 1979 (*Guardian*, 1 September 1999).

There are at least three reasons why New Labour does not act to redistribute wealth by taxing the top 10–20 per cent of the population. The first is that money now moves very rapidly between economies. In the 1992 election when Labour did suggest a programme of redistributive taxation, it was revealed in the press that extensive plans had been made to move funds out of the country. It was reported that £870 billion, or half of the total personal wealth, was controlled by just 5 per cent of the population and that 'millions of pounds are leaving Britain with every opinion poll that puts the opposition (i.e. the Labour Party) ahead, winging out via electronic transfer systems to all points of the compass' (*Guardian*, 26 March 1992). The movement of a large proportion of this mobile capital abroad would mean a reduction of spending power in the economy and more crucially would produce a run on the pound with an incoming Labour government being pressed into putting up interest rates. This analysis was paralleled by reports in other newspapers who reached the conclusion that interest rates (and therefore mortgages) would rise within days of a Labour government taking power (*Daily Mail*, 7 April 1992). Other versions of such warnings appeared on television news. For example, a city expert was reported as saying 'if Labour were to win, I think people would be worried about public spending, public borrowing and what might happen to the exchange rate' (ITN 12.30, 1 April 1992, quoted in Philo 1995a, p. 193).

It is also extremely difficult to tax the rich – tax avoidance and evasion are something of an industry in Britain. An army of accountants pursue the legal avoidance of tax, through for example the paying of some types of income into offshore accounts. At the same time, very large sums owed in tax are (illegally) evaded. The accountants Deloitte and Touche have estimated that between 1976 and 1996, this amounted to a loss of £2 trillion (i.e. £2,000 thousand million at 1996 prices; Atkinson, 1999, p. 17). Those who own Britain's financial system have benefited from the relatively lax banking and tax regimes. Britain has become a place where is it possible to launder the proceeds of international crime. The government recently expressed concern about this in relation to the Channel Islands, after it was found that £400 billion (equivalent to half of Britain's annual gross domestic product) had been salted away there. A government report showed that some islanders on Sark were directors of more than 2,000 companies (a company must have an island-based director to register there; *Observer*, 15 November 1998).

Given the sums involved, it might appear sensible for a New Labour government to control tax evasion. On average the Inland Revenue in this area turns each £1 of its own spending into £39 of tax. The sections which deals with major corporate enquiries can bring in £107 for every £1 spent. By comparison, investigations into social security fraud yield £5 for each £1 spent (Atkinson, 1999, p. 17). But it is unlikely that New Labour will launch a major campaign to tax the rich. The capacity to move capital resources and personal assets is simply too great and politicians are made aware of this. For example, in the months before the new Parliament in Scotland was elected in May 1999, the Scottish National Party had promoted its future policy of increasing taxation. The largest employer in the Highland Region then announced that an unfavourable tax regime would mean that the company would move its headquarters out of Scotland (*Scotsman*, 24 October 1998).

Such issues are rarely debated in public and there is almost no discussion in the media of the distribution of wealth and who ought to pay for public welfare, schools and hospitals. This is the second key issue which limits the actions of New Labour politicians. The public debate on tax has been largely dominated by the right wing tabloid press. In order to secure their support, New Labour has kept broadly to the tax and spending limits that it inherited from the Conservatives. Michael White has written recently of this 'Faustian bargain' with Rupert Murdoch and his stable of media outlets:

> In every country in which Mr Murdoch operates (and minimises his tax bill) he is a power-broker, speaking power, not truth, unto power through his diverse media outlets. The Blairites have charmed Lord Rothermere and made a Faustian bargain with Rupert. They think they have a good bargain. (*Guardian*, 30 January 1998, quoted in Philo, 1999, p. XI)

The debate has thus been suppressed – the left of the Labour party has remained silent on the key issue on ownership and control of social resources, in order that New Labour can promote itself on 'middle ground' of politics – i.e. persuade voters who might otherwise have supported the Conservatives. This silence is based on the assumption that only the bottom 20 per cent of the population would be interested in issues of deprivation and poverty. But as we have already suggested, the problems generated by the unfettered free market will affect very large numbers of people. It is only a minority (the top 10–20 per cent) who will be able to buy themselves out of the effects of the free market, by purchasing private health, education and security. There are serious problems of deprivation, both relative and absolute, which will affect the bulk of the population. At present well over half of wage earners in Britain learn less that £20,000 per year and over twenty million adults have no pension other than that provided by the state (*Observer*, 29 August 1999). To challenge these structures of power and concentration of wealth would require at least that they be subject to public scrutiny and to a wide political debate. But as we have suggested such debate now scarcely exists in the mass media. There is substantial coverage of the details of political policy, but little on whether a policy will affect key social processes, patterns of ownership or control of resources. Thus the news may report that there will be a 10p increase in the minimum wage, but without indicating how this will (or won't) affect the distribution of property and wealth in the society. There is no analysis of social power or the structures which sustain it. Such fundamental questions have effectively been taken out of political debate and this is a key feature of the rise of New Labour (Philo, 1995a). There is little public knowledge of the parameters of our own society or of key social and economic processes (for example, how much is spent on health and education, compared with total social wealth). We have shown elsewhere how some political stunts and spin-doctoring actually rely for their success on a lack of public knowledge. For example, the 'naming and shaming' of eighteen failing schools when New Labour came to power was successful at level of producing 'good' media coverage. But it relied on most people not realizing how huge the education system is (there were actually 3,000 failing schools: Philo, 1999, p. xii).

There is a third reason why these arguments on ownership and control of resources have been so muted. Some New Labour politicians do apparently believe that the development of privately owned resources in the free market can produce an efficient, progressive society. Tony Blair for example talks of the 'great engine of the market' (*Observer*, 5 September 1999). Our own view is that the workings of what is called the free market do not correspond to what is useful for human societies. The key issue is that those with access to social power and resources use them to sustain patterns of inequality and to secure their own dominance. This much is not new in human history, but what is distinctive about free market capitalism is that it is based on the systematic investment of resources for profit. This has led to the very rapid development of production where it is profitable to do so (and to the laying waste of areas of the globe where it is not). The industrial growth of the first capitalist countries meant that they could very effectively wage war in order to occupy or control all other societies. The relative efficiency of the new system and its continual search for new sources of profit, raw materials and cheap labour produced an extraordinary transformation in the world economy. In a matter of only 300 years all other systems of production were subverted and overthrown – a process which Marx referred to as the internationalization of capital, but which is now fashionably called globalization (meaning simply the transformation of the world into a single capitalist market). But this focusing of resources into the development of what is profitable does not necessarily correspond to what is humanly useful. The priority is to exchange for profit. Money will be attracted to where it can be multiplied which may be in areas such as speculation on the value of currencies or the price of land, food or other commodities. In Hong Kong the most wealthy are property owners who have made fortunes from the scarcity of land. In Britain there have been speculative property booms in the 1970s, 1980s and 1990s. The recent economic crisis in Japan and other tiger economies came partly from speculation in land values, which then collapsed. In practice fortunes are traded in speculation on the future price of commodities (including food) which do not even exist. This is a long way from the rational organization of economic resources for human use. In such an economy high incomes derive largely from being in the right place at the right time to gather in money. For example, salaries in the City of London spiralled in the ten years from 1987 to 1997. A senior exchange dealer in 1987 would have earned approximately £55,000 per year – but by 1997 the expected salary would be £450,000 per year. In 1987 City dealers received £1 billion in bonuses (*Guardian*, 5 December 1997). In practice this means that a dealer could earn more in two weeks than a teacher or nurse would in a year. There is little merit in such a meritocracy.

Our conclusion is that there is no necessary link between the priorities of a system of exchange for profit and properties of human use, either in the rewards which accrue to individuals or in the promotion of different areas of economic production. It is sometimes assumed that the market is simply the expression of human desires – in the free interplay of demand and supply. But what is supplied in the market is clearly affected by the priority of profit. Thus the BSE crisis in Britain arose because the brains of dead sheep were fed to cattle (Miller, 1999). This was done in the pursuit of profit and 'high yields'. There was no question of asking consumers whether this what they wanted to eat. Market priorities can actually prevent the development of what is useful for human health. For example, malaria kills many more people in the world than AIDS and the drugs to treat malaria are becoming increasingly ineffective. Yet the major drug companies do not have this as a priority because malaria affects poor countries and the 'market' to justify expensive research programmes is not there (Hilton, 2000).

## Corporate power, nation states and the free market

In the real world, the free market is not in fact very 'free'. Consumer demand is heavily influenced by the intensive advertising and marketing of a relatively small number of major brands. Some groups, such as children, are subject to extraordinarily effective pressures, which in turn influence the purchasing decision of parents (Philo, 1999, p. 36). For this reason, some countries have put into place limits on advertising directed at children (notably Sweden where the targeting of advertising at children under the age of twelve is now banned).

But there is another important sense in which the market is not free and is in effect rigged for the benefit of major corporations. The key issue here is their sheer size and the impact of decisions which they make on the employment of very large numbers of people. To a large extent, the major corporations have the power to determine where production will take place. This can make it possible for them to enforce the best conditions for their own profitability. In this process, nation states (especially in the developing world) can have little choice but to comply – thus their populations accept pollution, low wages and poor work conditions. At the same time, the most powerful nation states (notably the USA) act to defend corporate interests. Larry Elliott and Dan Atkinson in their analysis of the free market describe the development of a culture in which the operations of the financial and business sectors are underwritten by the sacrifices of ordinary people. When investments succeed, the corporations benefit; when they do not they are underwritten by governments. The new global elite have developed a system by which they cannot lose:

> What happened to Goldman Sachs and the other blue-chip Wall Street houses when their investments in Mexico looked like turning sour in early 1995? Would they lose the billions in 'hot money' they had recklessly lent to the Salinas government to finance Mexico's current account deficit? Of course not. Within days a US-brokered $50 billion IMF package was conjured up to ensure there was no systematic threat to the West's banking system (shorthand for Wall Street losing its shirt). The Mexican people, naturally did not have it quite so easy. They had to learn the errors of their ways via an IMF austerity package that lead to an 8 per cent contraction in the economy, an increase in unemployment of one million and a 40 per cent fall in investment. The country's debt to the IMF and the USA has been repaid, but wages are not expected to return to their pre-collapse level until 2000 and unemployment affects one quarter of the workforce. (Elliott and Atkinson, 1998, p. 224)

They also describe the extraordinary power of multinationals and how national governments can effectively pay them to operate. Seventy per cent of world trade is managed by just 500 corporations and 1 per cent of multinationals own half of the stock of foreign direct investment (Elliott and Atkinson, 1998, p. 223). In the past, capitalist enterprises sought to impose their own low labour costs. Now, the nation state can actually gather in money from the population in the form of tax and give it to the multinational. As they comment:

> Your taxes are subsidising finance and big business, too. Staggering sums are paid in bribes to multinational companies to attract them or keep them in Britain. Ford trousered £71 million to modernise the Jaguar plant at Coventry and about £15 million to renovate Halewood on Merseyside. And not all these bribes are published because they are considered commercially confidential. (Atkinson and Elliott, 1998, p. 9)

There is a growing body of evidence which shows how the world market is organized for the benefit of US corporations. Chomsky gives a detailed account of the consequences of US intervention in Haiti. He shows how the imposition of liberal market reforms damaged the indigenous economy and further impoverished the population. His account begins in 1981 with a World Bank/USAID initiative which was designed to promote assembly plants and agro-export. This had the effect of limiting the use of land for local needs. The World Bank also offered prescriptions for 'expansion of Private Enterprises' while minimizing 'social objectives' such as health and education. As Chomsky notes:

The consequences were the usual ones: profits for US manufacturers and the Haitian super-rich and a decline of 56 per cent in Haitian wages through the 1980s. (Chomsky, 1999, p. 108)

Current policy from USAID involves promoting privatization and more agri-business. As he notes:

Agribusiness receives ample funding but no resources are made available for peasant agriculture and handy crafts, which provide the income of the overwhelming major-ity of the population. Foreign-owned assembly plants that employ workers (mostly women) at well below subsistence pay under horrendous working conditions benefit from cheap electricity, subsidised by the generous supervisor. But for the Haitian poor – the general population – there can be no subsidies for electricity, fuel, water or food; these are prohibited by IMF rules on the principled grounds that they constitute 'price control'. (1999, p. 107)

Before these 'reforms', local rice production supplied virtually all domestic needs, but now only provides 50 per cent. His conclusion is that:

By such methods the most impoverished country in the hemisphere has been turned into a leading purchaser of US produced rice, enriching publicly subsidised US enter-prises. (1999, p. 108)

In a separate analysis of Brazil, Gregory Palast describes how the US treasury manipulated the politics and economy of that country to ensure that a favoured candidate was elected president in 1988. In an article entitled 'How the US seized power in Brazil', he shows how the Brazilian currency was kept from a catastrophic fall by promises by the US of an IMF loan package. But it was made clear to voters that the funds would not be handed over to the opposi-tion Workers Party. Fifteen days after the candidate was elected, the currency collapsed anyway. As Palast notes:

Knowing the currency would go to pieces after the election, the US treasury made sure American banks could get their money out of the country on favourable terms. (Palast, 1999, p. 10)

Palast also makes the point that the Brazilian currency *was* over-valued, but that the collapse could have been prevented through a controlled devaluation. In his view the crisis was intentional, since this increases the pressure to accept free market reforms:

Only in an economic panic can Rubin (the US treasury secretary) and the IMF unleash the Four Horsemen of Reform: kill social spending, cut government pay-rolls, break the unions and, the real prize, privatise lucrative public assets. (Palast, 1999, p. 10)

These analyses offer a bleak image in which concentrations of corporate wealth and power are increasing to a point unparalleled in human history. As Elliott and Atkinson note, in the USA in 1949 1 per cent of the population owned 29 per cent of the wealth. Now 1 per cent own over 40 per cent (1998, p. 244). What can limit such power and its impact on the populations who are subject to it? In the first part of this century following the great depression of the 1930s and the chaos produced by the free market at that time, there was a widespread in public ownership of key economic resources. The public debate over this in recent years has become clouded by ideological claims over whether 'public' or 'private' ownership is more efficient (see Chapter 10 in this volume by Jean Shaoul). There is no reason in practice why public owner-ship should not be efficient but this is not the key issue. The reason why public ownership was seen as crucial was that the populations of the world should not be subject to the voracious forces of the market – the search for profits over people as Chomsky puts it. Such debate as we have said is now muted in Britain following the dominance of the Conservatives in the 1980s and the endorsement of much of their political platform by New Labour.[5] We have yet to see whether this embracing of the market by Tony Blair's party will do anything more than legitimize the distribution of social power and resources achieved by his predecessors.[6] One purpose of the social sciences is to point to such consequences and to insist that public debate is informed by a rational discussion of the outcomes of political and economic policy.

## Research directions and cultural dead-ends

Given the state to which much social life has been reduced, there is no shortage of subjects which a critical cultural studies could address. But some comment-ators have pointed recently to the very limited nature of much academic work in cultural studies and its effect on students. As Ferguson and Golding note:

> on both sides of the Atlantic we found aspiring graduate students emerging from cultural studies programmes able to offer the most elegant and detailed discourses on Derrida or Lacanian theory, yet seemingly unaware of current threats to public-service broadcasting or legislative and industrial trends eroding media plurality and democratic diversity. (1997, p. x)

In practice much work in communications and culture has been confined to speculating about the latest 'popular' tastes. Academics have become culture industry groupies dedicated to excavating the most recent trends in music, fashion or popular culture and mistaking it for 'resistance' or viewing the transgression of boundaries as progressive political practice – cultural studies as a rationale for hanging out with what is cool. Others have examined the 'social relations of media consumption' which could come down to asking people whether they listened to the radio whilst doing the ironing or whether they felt sad when they watched *Eastenders*. Empirical work in the area has often been extraordinarily slight in its concerns or poor in its methods such as guessing what people believe based on reading fan letters. There has been an absence of will to address the real and often brutal power relationships which have transformed our cultural life. For many in cultural studies a series of theoretical dead-ends beckoned instead. We will outline these now. We will look first at post-modernism and at some of its philosophical roots in arguments about reality and language. We have described above the social relationships of power and interest which structure our society as it is. The purpose of social ideologies is to justify and legitimize those relationships. Post-modernism would reject such an analysis of the 'real' structures which form a society. It offers instead a view of individuals as consumers in a sea of images, from which they construct their own meanings about the world. There can be no 'over-arching' narratives (either for the individual in society or the social scientist) about how the world works. One description of it (operating as a 'discourse') is as good as another. We will look first at how post-modernism abandoned concepts such as 'reality' and 'truth'.

## Reality, language and quiescence

Arguments about the relationship of language to the 'real' have a long history in philosophy and have affected many areas of social science. The essence of these arguments is that reality is always constituted for us through language. The meaning of language is negotiated, therefore 'reality' is negotiated.[7] In this schema there cannot be a simple correspondence between an idea or a statement and an external objective reality. 'Truth' therefore becomes a function of how the text (be it a work of art, a written text or any moment of a language) is interpreted by the cognizing mind of the individual or the 'speech community'. In some post-modern accounts truth is entirely relative to issues of textual representation and to the 'textual strategies', 'signifying practices' and 'language games' that are employed to give authority to a particular account.

Bauman traces the history of these arguments from elements of contemporary hermeneutics through to the work of Barthes and Derrida. As Bauman notes, 'the spokesmen for interpretative reason grew bolder by the year' (1992, p. 130). He quotes Barthes as arguing that:

> *Text means Tissue*; but whereas hitherto we have always taken this tissue as a product, a ready-made veil, behind which lies, more or less hidden meaning (truth), we are now emphasising, in the tissue, the generative idea that the text is made, is worked out in a perpetual interweaving; lost in this tissue – this texture – the subject unmakes himself, like a spider dissolving in the constructive secretions of its web. (Barthes, 1975, in Bauman, 1992, p. 130)

As Bauman comments from this it is a small step to Derrida's *intertextuality*, 'an endless conversation between the texts with no prospect of ever arriving at, or being halted at an agreed point' (1992, p. 130), and to Derrida's maxim that 'there is nothing outside the text', i.e. nothing that may claim a status that is more solid than or different from that of the text.

The argument has therefore moved from the assumption that reality is appropriated or 'seen' through language to the assertion that reality 'only' consists for us as what is constituted in language. Claims to objectivity are no more than 'strategic rituals' to assert authority and establish the dominance of one form of discourse. The problem with all such assertions is that they imply a reality of social relationships. Who is playing the language games and for what purpose? Whose authority and power over who else is being established in discourse? As Geras argues, all truth is supposedly relative to its constitution in language. Yet the relativists are working with their own undeclared assumptions about how this social world 'really' works. Other people's work is declared to be economistic or determinist and thus lacking a 'true' knowledge of the social or the 'actual' openness of history etc. As Geras comments, the relativists overtly deny:

> that there is any being-as-such, any in-itself, in terms of which competing discourses might be adjudicated, [but] they install somewhere out of sight a secret tribunal of truth, mysterious in its ways, which allows *them* to judge here: as 'essentialist', hence *wrong about the nature of the world*; as economistic, thus unable to understand the *reality* of the social; as determinist, therefore misconstruing history's *actual* openness etc.; which allows them to employ a language of external reference, of objectivity, of truth . . . which allows them that long, that tireless, that never-ending 'this is how it is' with which the relativist tells you why you cannot say 'this is how it is'. (Geras, 1990, p. 163, emphasis in original)

There is a further problem in the textualist/relativist approach. To assert that truth *is* what is made through textual strategies or signifying practices necessarily involves assumptions about how language 'really' works – that texts really relate to each other, that meanings really are negotiated. It can only be argued that this is really what occurs by pointing to examples of how language is actually used. To argue this is in effect to say that all truth (reality) is constituted in discourse, *except what we just said which really is true*. In this way, the proclamation that 'there is nothing but the text' involves universal truth statements (that there really are texts, that they really relate to other texts).

We can counter these statements with others – that the division between language and reality is a false dichotomy – that language is formed in a world of relationships and objects and is part of the measurable reality of that world – that judgements and expectations about what is true and what occurs are necessarily measured against the flow of actions and events in the world – that observable gaps between prediction and occurrence can undermine beliefs and expectations. If we expect the stairs to be there and they are not, then we trip. Now it may be that some post-modernists and relativists do not accept our statements of the true nature of the world. Then let them provide evidence to refute what we have said and to show what 'really' happens when people use language. We might for example ask for evidence of the view that 'meaning is constituted by the encounter between the reader and the text' (i.e. there are no intrinsic meanings which can be objectively measured). If we take this literally it follows that it is not possible to classify texts or to distinguish between them, as a new meaning is generated with each new encounter. But how could anyone know this except by indicating that there are different encounters with the text (by people from different speech communities) which generate different meanings? These would have to be perceived by the observer as 'objectively' different, albeit that observers generate their own meanings by their encounter with the new texts (of other people's encounters). So the problem the textualists face is, how could they know it is true that meaning is generated in the encounter with the text, except through observation – and if it was true how could they have observed it?[8]

The drift towards relativism and the bracketing off of 'truth' and even 'accuracy' has characterized much contemporary cultural studies. We can pause for a moment and look at one of the new Open University collections for a new course on 'Culture, media and identities' (Hall, 1997b). The introduction to one volume counsels students that:

> We should perhaps learn to think of meaning less in terms of 'accuracy' and 'truth' and more in terms of effective exchange – a process of *translation*, which facilitates cultural communication while always recognising the persistence of difference and power between different 'speakers' within the same cultural circuit. (Hall, 1997b, p. 11)

We see in such a commentary a privileging of the authors' own concepts where the writers describe what is 'really' happening in relation to language and the exchange of meaning. We (and their students) must expect it to be a correct and accurate account. Yet what is being suggested is that all communications (including their own) can be translated or interpreted differently and therefore there is no accuracy/truth. What then is the basis for the claims made here about power or anything else? Why should we 'always recognize the persistence of difference and power between different speakers'? Is this a true or accurate statement or merely a piece of text which can be 'translated' in various ways? Is this account of power 'real' or is its truth merely 'willed' by virtue of the power of the writer as the OU teacher? Are thousands of OU students destined to repeat the account faithfully (and not retranslate it) by virtue of this power? Or will they by simple processes of logic deduce that the whole enterprise is lost in a relativist muddle? Now read on.

It is an odd phenomenon that those who defend relativism feel able to say categorically what really happens and what other people really do. Thus, in a paper for a 'Discourse and Reflexivity Workshop', Edwards *et al.* complain that realists bang on tables to show what is 'real'. They note that:

> When relativists talk about the social construction of reality . . . their realist opponents sooner or later start hitting the furniture . . . to introduce a bottom line, a bedrock of reality. (1992, p. 1)

Yet they see no problem with their own assertion that people 'really' bang on tables. At one point in their paper they even give a figure for what realists do, saying that '99 per cent of the world's politico-moral disputes [are] conducted exclusively by realists' (1992, p. 15). Is this figure supposed to have any relationship to what actually occurs? Would it make any difference if they had said that 99 per cent of realists believe that the moon is made of green cheese?

It is not clear how textualists *can* offer evidence from within the logic of their own position, i.e. that any claims *they* make are a construct, a mere conjunction of phrases – whose significance is limited to those playing the particular language game (and it is not clear how they would be able to designate the factual existence of other games different from their own). In which case the rest of us will have to get on with analyzing the movements of the real including its language, the production of texts and the measurable relations between them. We will leave behind those who sit resolutely with their arms folded, saying they will only play their own game and do not wish to join in ours.[9]

As Norris argues, the relativist approach to truth also legitimizes political acquiescence (1993). Ideologies cannot be challenged since one definition of the real is in principle as good as another. Norris criticizes Lyotard for posing truth as a function of a multiplicity of language games or 'phrase regimes', each with its own criteria of meaning and validity. According to Lyotard we should seek to maximize the differentials between such narratives. It is necessary to cultivate 'dissensus' or fall into 'totalitarian' phrase regimes with their attempts at closed definitions of reality. As Lyotard puts it 'if the demand to have to establish the reality of the referent of a sentence is extended to any sentence . . . then that demand is totalitarian in its principle' (1988, p. 9). In Lyotard's analysis the rules of one genre of discourse cannot be used to dispute the truth claims of another. Therefore it would be quite wrong to argue with someone who for example denied the existence of concentration camps (least of all by seeking to provide facts or evidence that they really did exist). According to Lyotard names such as the 'Nazis' or the 'death camps' have become so laden with ethical judgements that there is an irreducible conflict of interpretation between the phrase regimes that use them.

It seems odd to suggest that we cannot discuss the facts of what has occurred because the terminology has become so charged. We might stand this on its head and argue that a word such as Auschwitz is charged because of the actual horror which it represents. The reason why Nazi apologists have such an uphill struggle to establish their 'narrative' is because of all the cultural work which has been undertaken to display and report the true consequences of fascist culture. Do we now simply abandon this work and leave ultra-right propagandists to get on with their account, in case we become 'totalitarian' about what is true? Incidentally it is not clear why it is all right for Lyotard to argue his case using such a charged word as 'totalitarian' while other people's arguments should not be informed by a concern over 'death camps'. The important issue in such political arguments is not whether an academic will ever be able to convince a politician or an ideologue. Political ideologies are not constructed for the benefit of academics. They are developed and promoted to win the consent of populations. It is here that the battles are fought to dominate opinion and belief. The powerful will not abandon this terrain simply because academics withdraw and say they do not want join in. Arguments over empirical evidence are crucial since they are central in the legitimation of political power. Thus in the 1980s in Britain there were a series of controversies over the use of statistics by the Conservative government (Philo, 1995b). The core of the political argument was over both unemployment figures and levels of health spending. In January 1989 a Channel Four documentary showed how the figures had been misused. It began with news clips of speeches by Conservative politicians at a Party Conference:

> *Journalist*: Statistics do not just help you win the argument, they give you power.
> *Mrs Thatcher* (on platform): It's time we took the credit for some of the things we have achieved – the 8 million patients treated in hospital each year . . .
> *Journalist*: Power to write the history of the past.
> *Norman Fowler* (Employment Minister): Since the election, unemployment has come down by 650,000, the biggest fall in unemployment for over 40 years . . .
> *Journalist*: And power to decide the policy of the future.
> *Kenneth Clarke* (Health Minister): We will provide to the health authorities another £98 million of tax payers' money to carry out our obligations. (*Dispatches,* Channel Four, 18 January 1989)

The programme then showed how government claims about new spending on health actually included money from the sale of assets. In other words if a hospital was knocked down and the land sold, this was counted as 'new money' being spent on health. The programme described such sales:

> In the looking-glass world of health statistics, this site counts £29 million towards total government spending on the health service. It is not a hospital that is being built on this site either but luxury canal-side flats. Just two years ago on this site was

a hospital with 157 beds and 20 wards employing 400 staff treating 45,000 patients a year. It was pulled down to make way for the private developers. (*Dispatches*, Channel Four, 18 January 1989)

As the journalist notes: 'with this use of figures, if the Government sold the entire Health Service to private developers, it could claim to be spending more than ever before on the Health Service' (*Dispatches*, Channel Four, 18 January 1989).

It is interesting that television journalists could pose the issue of political power and the use of information so acutely, just as media studies were moving away from the analysis of ideology and propaganda. Issues of truth have been treated as passé in favour of speculation about the possible meaning of texts. The focus of study moved to the generation of meaning rather than the content of media and its possible relation to audience beliefs.

## Relativism in media studies

The distinctive influence of relativism in media studies is that the real is bracketed off – one interpretation of a text is in principle as good as another. This can also legitimize the move away from empirical work. From the heights of left bank theory such investigation can be deemed merely empiricist. Baudrillard's work is an example of the move away from the empirical, legitimized by a theory which dissolves events in the world into their representations. In this account the current state of the media universe means that we now live in a 'hyper-reality' of pure floating images (Baudrillard, 1988). The media's world of hyperinformation claims to enlighten but all it does is 'clutter up the space of the representable' (Baudrillard, 1994, p. 114). The masses 'have no opinion and information does not inform them' (1994, p. 115). The media are therefore 'a marvellous instrument for destabilising the real and the true' (1994, p. 118). A meaningless spectacle of images thus replaces the real. Crucially for Baudrillard, there is no difference between the image and what it supposedly represents. The 'simulacrum' to which he refers is an 'imploded' concept – the virtual and the real become another order of reality. As he writes of the Gulf War:

> the war itself reaps its havoc at another level by trickery, hyperreality, simulacra and by the entire mental strategy of deterrence which is played out in the facts and in the images, in the anticipation of the real by the virtual, of the event by virtual time, and in the inexorable confusion of the two. (1995, p. 67)

The result according to Baudrillard is that 'everyone' is trained in the 'unconditional' reception of broadcast simulacra. As he writes:

> The complement of the unconditional simulacrum in the field is to train everyone in the unconditional reception of broadcast simulacra. Abolish any intelligence of the

event. The result is a suffocating atmosphere of deception and stupidity. And if people are vaguely aware of being caught up in this appeasement and this disillusion by images, they swallow the deception and remain fascinated by the evidence of the montage of this war with which we are inoculated everywhere: through the eyes, the senses and in discourse. (1995, p. 68)

Thus there is no intelligence of the actual event and everyone 'swallows the deception'. Everyone, apparently, apart from Baudrillard who can see through the hyper-reality and understand its effects on everyone else. Here again we see the tendency of those who have abolished reality to make clear statements about what 'actually' happens. It is not clear how he does know this since his essays on the Gulf War contain no study of either media content or audience responses. Our own study of the Gulf War actually showed that some parts of the media became very critical of government policy, having been initially very supportive. Some journalists openly criticized information control (Philo and McLaughlin, 1995). Two very senior BBC journalists had the following remarkable exchange of comments while reporting on the war:

> *David Dimbleby*: Don't you get the feeling that there is slightly too much pulling of the levers of public psychology on this?

To which his colleague replies:

> *Mark Mardell*: I always get that feeling to be perfectly honest. (BBC1, 10.00 p.m., 23 January 1991, in Philo and McLaughlin, 1995, p. 154)

Much of the tabloid coverage did glorify the war. But in our audience studies we have found people who were at least as critical of such media accounts as Baudrillard. One respondent (a middle-class accountant) told us that he was so incensed by the Gulf War coverage that he now tended to believe the opposite of what was said in the media. He had applied this to other areas of media coverage such as news accounts which linked mental illness to violence and was now very critical of such reports (Philo, 1996, p. 98).[10] Other studies by the Glasgow Media Group have shown how audience members can use logic to question media accounts. In the 1984/5 miners' strike, TV coverage had focused on images of violent pickets. While many viewers had accepted the view that most picketing was violent, others argued that it could not be true given the sheer numbers of people involved. This was said even where the respondent was not sympathetic to the strikers (Philo, 1990, p. 108). Other viewers contested the news account by citing their direct experience. Everyone who had actually been to a picket line (police and pickets) was scornful of the television portrayal. Yet the strike and its images had a deep impact and everyone interviewed could describe visual moments or events which were especially significant to them. This study was conducted a year after the strike had ended, yet many interviewees were able to reproduce from memory key sections of news dialogue and headlines which directly paralleled those in actual news bulletins. Other Media Group studies produced comparable results in areas such as the media portrayal of AIDS (Kitzinger, 1993; Miller *et al.*, 1998), mental illness (Philo, 1996) and Northern Ireland (Miller, 1994a, b). This does not suggest at all that TV is a 'meaningless spectacle'. In the areas of TV output which we have analyzed there is little relation between Baudrillard's theory and either the actual content of television or its influence on the audience.

Baudrillard's work has been influential in media and cultural studies, providing as it does a sophisticated rationale for avoiding all the hard work of finding out what is actually happening in the world and comparing it with what is said in the media. Even theorists such as Fiske and Morley who might be expected to have their feet more on the ground and their heads less in hyperreality have explored some elements of Baudrillard's work with apparent approval. Morley for example notes the apparent difficulties which the theory raises for the analysis of objectivity or bias in television coverage. As he writes:

> Over the last 30 years or so, one of the staples of media analysis has been work considering the coverage of real events (elections, strikes, etc.) by television, asking questions about the degree of objectivity or bias in the coverage etc. The problem with work of this type is, of course, that it presupposes that there is, first of all, a thing such as 'a general election', for example, and *then* a representation, the coverage of it on TV. Now that is a distinction that is, in some ways, rather difficult to sustain. Contemporary elections in the west are *principally* 'TV events'. They have their principal existence in and through the medium of TV. (Morley, 1996a, p. 63)

Morley also argues that military campaigns can be planned as media events. As he notes:

> In a similar way, when President Reagan bombed Libya, he didn't do it at the most effective time of day, from a military point of view. The timing of the raid was principally determined by the timing of the American TV news; it was planned in such a way as to maximise its televisual impact. It was timed to enable Reagan to announce on the main evening news that it had 'just happened' – it was planned *as* a TV event. (Morley, 1996a, pp. 63–4)

John Fiske develops a similar theme in an account of Margaret Thatcher's television persona. There is no reality to represent since what is represented is a construction for television:

> Margaret Thatcher smiling into the TV camera and making an off-the-cuff remark for the microphone as she walks between the helicopter and the waiting car is not a piece of reality whose image is transmitted to our television screen. She is her own image. Her hairstyle does not pre-exist its TV image and seeing it 'live' is no more authentic an experience than seeing it on the screen. The smile, the hairstyle and the comment would not be there if the TV cameras were not, if the viewers were not.

The smile, the hairstyle and the comment exist simultaneously and similarly on the TV screen and on the helipad, there is no difference of ontological status between them, nor is there any way in which one could be said to precede or reproduce the other. Each is as real or as unreal as the other. (1996, p. 55)

There are a number of points to be made about these two accounts. The first is that the authors seem very clear that the 'TV events' – the special hairstyle, the timing of the bombs – did actually happen. So it is a good job that someone did some empirical research (or did they just read about them in the papers?). A second issue is the audience responses to these media events. The public relations elements of the American action were conspicuously unsuccessful in Britain where 70 per cent of the population opposed the bombing. This was perhaps related to the real consequences of dropping the bombs which were shown prominently on British television. The Conservative Party was so angered by the coverage that its chairman, Norman Tebbitt, issued a special report, criticizing the BBC and making specific suggestions about how the news bulletins should have been organized (Philo, 1990, p. 200). This again suggests an intense contest over how meanings are established, because of their potential power in relation to audiences.

There is a deeper problem with Baudrillard's theory apart from the lack of any empirical support for the claims that are made. The difficulty is that the division between television images and the 'real' is based on a false dichotomy which parallels the one we have already seen between language and reality. In this case the dichotomy allows the image to be spoken of as if it is not part of the real world. It is then argued that because the 'real' is altered for the image, there is no essential difference between the two. On the contrary, a media image is a measurable part of the real in its own right and the processes by which it is manufactured can be analyzed and exposed. The exposure of how this part of reality has been constructed can have an impact on beliefs about the validity of the descriptions which are being offered. This can be done by television itself. The construction of the Thatcher image and that of many other politicians has been a frequent subject for analysis within the media. Michael Cockerell for example made programmes for the BBC on the marketing of Mrs Thatcher. He describes the changes made to her voice and hair style and satirizes the process by showing her being filmed eating fish and chips. He then interviews an irate customer who has been displaced by the media circus:

*Michael Cockerell*: Mrs. Thatcher's chief media advisor is Gordon Reece. He gave her humming lessons to lower her voice on television. 'Think low' he told her. He changed her hairstyle and her clothes and advised her to be filmed for television in ordinary situations like eating fish and chips [shots of Thatcher in restaurant eating] to appeal to the voters.

*Customer*: Well that's one vote she's lost today.

*Michael Cockerell*: From you?

*Customer*: Definitely!

*Michael Cockerell*: But the whole thing is organized so there are pictures taken of the Prime Minister . . .

*Customer*: The media at the moment is a total nonsense with this election. It doesn't allow the average guy to make up his own mind. It's overkill, the whole thing.

(BBC2 *Saturday Review*, 9 June 1984)

This does show how wrong Fiske is to suggest that there is no difference between the television image of Mrs Thatcher and the reality. The customer is perfectly clear what the difference is and, thanks partly to Cockerell's programme, very many other viewers can see along with him the real process by which the image was constructed. One of the reasons for audience dissatisfaction and rejection of messages is exactly the cynicism with which such media events are manufactured for politicians and other interest groups. It is indeed possible for both television audiences and television researchers to identify the difference between a 'chip shop' and 'an attempt at constructing a chip shop event'. The fact that images are manufactured does not preclude in any way the analysis of the news with concepts such as balance or ideology (as a perspective linked to the development of a specific interest). The purpose of such studies is to measure the legitimacy accorded to different perspectives. If television in its own presentation undermines this legitimacy (by revealing media hype) then this in itself can be measured. A researcher could then ask, does television take an equally jaundiced view of the public relations strategies of all groups? Which assumptions are challenged and which are accepted or endorsed by the journalists themselves? These can all be key areas of content analysis.

As we have shown, it is also possible to analyze the processes by which audiences accept or reject messages. Audience members can and do distinguish between media hype and what are judged to be more authentic accounts. They can use processes of logic or more often their own direct experience to criticize the content of media. Where no such experience is available the potential power of media to convince increases. But this is a long way from saying that 'everyone is trained in the unconditional reception of broadcast simulacra'. It is even further from saying that there is no difference between an image and what it supposedly represents. Put simply, if Baudrillard altered his appearance by dressing up to look like Napoleon, then an image of him as this would not show the real Bonaparte. The time has surely come to say that this particular emperor is sartorially challenged.

## Discursive practice and the real

Some theorists have gone over the edge into the twilight world where only discourse is real while others hover on the cusp of the real and the discursive.

In the former camp, Hartley has argued that there is no such thing as an empirical audience:

> in no case is the audience 'real' or external to its discursive construction. There is no actual audience that lies beyond its production as a category . . . audiences are only ever encountered . . . as representations. (Hartley, 1987, p. 125; see also Hartley, 1996)

Some less consistent constructivist theorists still want to retain some notion of an external reality. For them one key advance made by Michel Foucault is that his notion of discursive practice acknowledges that the real exists, but maintains that since reality is only appropriated through discourse, it is discourse which is important. Anything we (really) do in the world must (to have meaning) be a discursive practice. So even real events and actions become discursive. For writers such as Hall this appears to be the contemporary position (Hall, 1992, 1997a). Hall is keen to maintain his belief in a real world outside discourse, but argues that language helps to constitute reality:

> My own view is that events, relations, structures do have conditions of existence and real effects, outside the sphere of the discursive; but that only within the discursive, and subject to its specific conditions, limits and modalities, do they have or can they be constructed within meaning. Thus, while not wanting to expand the territorial claims of the discursive indefinitely, how things are represented and the 'machineries' and regimes of representation in a culture do play a *constitutive*, and not merely a reflexive, after-the-event, role. (Hall, 1992, pp. 253–4)

The real world can thus only intervene via the process of meaning making, because we have no access to the truth outside discourse. 'Reality' is seen as an effect of discourse. It is only through discourse that we can give meaning to the world. This approach makes use of Foucault's notion of 'regimes of truth', whereby truth is the product of a particular discursive formation or way of looking at the world. 'Regimes of truth' are considered as hermetically sealed and are not regarded as being amenable to critique via the use of evidence. Thus any critique of a regime of truth comes from the perspective of another regime of truth. We can also find theorists such as Morley criticizing the radical constructivist position such as that of Hartley (1987) as having gone too far. Morley writes:

> Naturally any empirical knowledge which we may generate of television audiences will be constructed through particular discursive practices, and the categories and questions present and absent in these discourses will determine the nature of the knowledge we can generate. However, this is to argue, contra Hartley, that while we can only know audiences through discourses, audiences do in fact exist outside the terms of these discourses. (Morley, 1997, p. 135)[11]

However, if we can only know through discursive practice and the questions we ask 'determine' our results, then any piece of empirical research is as good as any other and is not 'evidence' for or against a particular proposition. Furthermore, it becomes impossible for researchers from different traditions to share evidence or to build on each other's work since they are sealed off in their own discursive bubble. Such approaches are also unable to explain the way in which discourses change or evolve under pressure from new information or experience or in new material circumstances. Their position doesn't allow for the possibility of mutually held evidence. For example, bank managers and trades unionists might agree about the tendency of capitalism to increase inequalities but differ in their assessments of its justification. This approach also tends to deny that the material world might exert some influence on what is or can be argued.

In fact, the meaning of events is not indefinitely negotiable. The history of failed political slogans points to the way in which 'discourse' can be undermined when it comes up against changed material realities and public disbelief. The 1980s 'discourse' of 'trickle down' theory to justify rewarding the wealth makers lost credibility as people were seen living in cardboard boxes. Political (and other) ideologies are re-negotiated to take account of changing material circumstances – they must constantly close the gap between on the one hand the promotion of relationships of power and inequality as being necessary and desirable, and, on the other, the actual consequences of these relationships for the mass of the population. The re-negotiation and fine-tuning of ideologies, by politicians, spin doctors and media is evidence of the constant need to dominate in the struggle over how the world is to be understood. But without an analysis of changes in social process and material conditions, a textualist has trouble in explaining why a discourse might have to be altered. Hartley, for example, concludes absurdly that the constant investment in mass persuasion is merely evidence that it doesn't work. If it did work, he says, there wouldn't need to be any re-investment as everyone would (apparently for all time) carry on believing what they were told. It would be difficult to find a better example of someone who has lost touch with historical and material process:

> My own sense of it is that if advertising, propaganda and mass manipulation actually worked, we wouldn't need any of it, because everyone would in fact be buying, doing and believing what they were told. The continual investment in mass persuasion is the strongest evidence that it doesn't work. (1996, pp. 8–9)

Hartley presents us with a society in which nothing changes, where the slogans of yesterday could be equally as effective in the different historical circumstances of today, as if the contempt we have today for Chamberlain's 1938 'peace in our time' speech did not relate to the outbreak of war against Hitler very soon afterwards. The reason that the Conservative Party does not continue to campaign on the 1979 slogan 'Labour isn't working' is not because it was not effective at the time, but because it would be manifestly unsaleable in the current climate. Our point is that the potential success of political advertising and public relations must be understood in relation to prevailing social and economic circumstances. We indicated how this produced difficulties for the accounts which the Conservative press sought to give about the poll tax. In practice the press tread a line between how they invite their readers to understand the world and the actual material conditions and experience of those who buy the papers (Philo, 1995b, p. 221).

Finally, the key difficulty with the 'discursive practice' approach is, as we have argued above, that discourse is itself a part of the real world which can be judged in the same way as the rest of reality through experience and evidence about how it really works. Experience and evidence place limits on what we can say about the operation of language and how we can 'constitute' any other area of reality. Let us suppose for a moment that three cultural theorists (two exponents of discursive practice and one constructivist) find themselves in a darkened attic. They have been unable to change the light bulb and are discussing the location of the hole in the floor which is the exit. The first two agree that the hole is just in front of them. In this sense 'reality' is constituted for them by discourse, which has real consequences on the direction of their steps. The constructivist, meanwhile, true to his radical constructivism, subverts the preferred meanings offered by the other two and wanders around randomly in another part of the attic. The other two theorists' assessment of where to walk is, however, immediately revised when they hear the shout and thud which the constructivist makes as he falls through the (real) exit and hits the floor. As we will show in more detail later the construction of what we take to be reality can be constantly revised in relation to experience.

## Post-modernism in public debate

It is extraordinary that the 'post-modern' account of media and audiences has been accepted so readily. Few arts pages or television critics can now apparently function without the word. But with reality safely bracketed off, any amount of uninformed speculation is now possible. The audience is presumed to have no contact with the real – while the cultural critic, afloat in a world of images and discourses, has no need of empirical work. Here are two examples from the *Guardian*. The first speaks of the television audience. The writer notes that there is now apparently a

> blurring of lines between what's real and what's not real, between society and popular culture, between *Casualty* and the *Nine O'clock News*. (5 December 1996)

Actually the news enjoys a high level of credibility with audiences. In our own research we have also studied the impact of the hospital dramas including

*Casualty* on audience beliefs about what a 'real' casualty department is like. Their perception of casualty departments as being 'scary', 'smelly', 'hectic', 'morbid' and 'dirty' came from their own direct experience. They rejected television images of staff having time for leisurely chats and romantic interludes. As one person commented:

> When I think of Casualty I think of the Mayday (her local hospital). I don't think of the *Casualty* programme. (interview 19 November 1996)

The second example discusses the rise of spoof chat shows on television which satirize traditional celebrity interviews. These it is said:

> were perfect creations for the ironic, let's-baffle-you-because-nothing-has-real-value-and-nothing-really-exists, post-political, post-modern early 90's. In an age obsessed with fame, gossip and voyeuristic titillation, they usurped the celebrity interviewer's chair. (*Guardian*, 24 December 1996)

Such programmes can certainly satirize a culture which is obsessed with fame, but by this definition they could not be said to emerge from a society which has no values or in which nothing really exists. The obsession with fame is exactly what has emerged from such a society. This *Guardian* commentary is interesting since it both expresses the post-modern vision and shows what is wrong with it. It poses a world in which there are no overarching social narratives or determining structures – a world of consumers submerged in a sea of images. Resistance consists of refusing to consume or in ironic commentary. As Sivanandan refers to it there is a shift 'From changing the world to changing the word' (1990, p. 49).

The problem with post-modernism is that it mistakes developments in market capitalism and public responses to it for an absence of defining structures. But as we have already noted the market is itself a structure and constitutes a system of relationships and values in its own right. The counter-attack of the new conservatives and monetarists on social democratic capitalism together with the collapse of the Soviet system has given the market and its values a new prominence. A key value is exactly the obsession with fame and interpersonal success to which the *Guardian* example above refers. We can see this by looking at some developments in contemporary television culture. The desire to be 'seen' is central in a society obsessed with fame and glamour (the state of being envied as John Berger (1975) puts it). It produces the widespread desire to work in television (or films) or simply to be seen on television. To attract attention, to be the focus of other people's gaze, is a mark of success and a form of power. In a media-saturated society, some will do anything to get on television, even if it means being humiliated. Thus in contemporary television, people who were once merely members of the audience appear as 'guests' on shows where they are encouraged to eat worms

(*The Word*, Channel 4) or are paraded merely because they are ugly as in the Chris Evans show with its 'ugly bloke' feature (*TFI Friday*, Channel 4). Mike Presdee has written of 'humiliation television', citing programmes such as *Blind Date*:

> Here we have young people persuaded to divulge to the viewing public the inner-most secrets of their partner for the week. Not acted out but in 'real life'. What are their weaknesses, how can we laugh at them. How can we strip them of their dignity. Embarrassment and humiliation is the name of the game and participants play it with a vengeance to the enjoyment of the crowd . . . and now violence, crime, humiliation and cruelty are being created especially for consumption through the various media outlets of television, video and radio. Chris Evans has the ability to reduce people to tears and still be immensely popular . . . Humiliation television has arrived and cruelty has become a commodity. (*Observer*, 6 April 1997)

To take pleasure in violence is certainly not new. What is different is that the 'liberation' of the market makes possible the promotion and sale of violence as just another commodity. It is then legitimized by libertarian appeals to the ideology of the market – the freedom to watch, the freedom to buy. In providing such programmes, TV companies are appealing to elements of human desire and values which would previously have been ruled out on grounds of quality or taste. The intensification of market pressures and deregulation affect their own commercial priorities. This is not an 'a-political' process, but is an exact consequence of political and economic arrangements. The driving force in the market is to attract – the priority is the ratings.

The growth of the market changes both individual relationships and corporate priorities. It signifies that we are not 'post' the period of modernism but rather are locked into a most vicious form of it. There are many different social responses to this. Some are traditional and collective such as the contemporary growth in trade union membership in the United States. In Britain, the impact of the new insecurity, stress at work and fear of unemployment have produced a situation in which approximately 5 million people who are non-unionized are now 'keen' to join a trade union (NOP Poll, *Guardian*, 15 March 1997). Other collective responses include the green movement and new types of ecological politics such as the protests against road building. Other responses, in contrast, celebrate the new individualism, inter-personal power and the definition of self by the capacity to consume. These responses are prominent in a popular media which constantly manufactures images of glamour, style and status. Some elements of media such as alternative television comedy can satirize free market culture and relate to public resentment at the effects of popular capitalism in everyday life. But this multitude of social responses including the growth of consumption and fragmentation of styles does not signify a new type of society. Without understanding this there is little that media studies or social science can offer that is critical of the society which we do have. Reducing social critique to ironic commentaries does not remove the social structures which position and limit us as we are – it simply reduces our ability to do anything about them. The inability to address the real and change it is implicit in the post-modern vision – what is its resort to irony, other than the gallows humour of the politically impotent.

## How it happens

How could so much social thought move so far away from examining the actual conditions of the society in which it exists? It cannot be explained simply by saying that a wrong analysis led towards speculation and irrelevant theorizing. As Weber and other sociologists have noted it is not ideas that produce social movement but ideal and material *interests*. Nick Garnham has suggested that post-modernism was perfectly suited to contemporary academic life as an ideology of cultural workers since it privileged their activity and legitimized unsubstantiated speculation. He notes that the tendency to focus on the text:

> developed out of literary and film studies and carried its textuality into versions of structuralist and post-structuralist Marxism and on into post-modernism. It took with it the bacillus of romanticism and its longing to escape from the determining material and social constraints of human life, from what is seen as the alienation of human essence, into a world of un-anchored, non-referential signification and the free play of desire. The dionysiac mind-set of this tendency and its deep roots within Western European culture are, I think, clear. It is also perfectly designed as an ideology of intellectuals or cultural workers for it privileges their special field of activity, the symbolic, and provides for cheap research opportunities, since the only evidence required is the unsubstantiated views of the individual analyst. (1990, p. 2)

Furthermore, such approaches tend to be silent on the conditions of existence of the work in which they engage. Apparently all meta-narratives have collapsed. But why has this happened? As Norris argues, such a view could only have taken root to such an extent:

> at a time of widespread disenchantment or retreat on the intellectual left when theory itself had abandoned the ground of oppositional critique and assumed the role of a legitimising discourse with every motive for dissimulating its own material interests and conditions of emergence. In which case we would do better to drop all the glitzy self-promoting talk of 'postmodernism', 'New Times', etc., talk whose sole function – whether wittingly or not – is to offer an escape-route or convenient alibi for thinkers with a large (if unacknowledged) stake in the 'cultural logic of late capitalism'. (1996, p. 214)

The textualists are silent about the material interest which they have in speculation and abstract theorizing. They are also unclear about the philosophical basis of their own work. The focus on the text produces a relativism which founders on its inability to be clear about how *they* can make declarations about what is true and real. There are many contradictions in post-modernism but this one is central. The post-modern account assumes that we are 'post' something – that the old industrial society with its strong cultural positioning has disappeared to be replaced by something else. Yet at the same time the account espouses a philosophical position on language and reality which rejects the identification of any structures as real or determining. As we have argued, post-modernists have mistakenly understood a series of new responses to market relationships as being a new type of society, although how they would demonstrate that an old society is really different from a new one or from anything else is left unexplained.

The post-modern textualists follow the same contemplative paths of those who ask the endless question of how do we 'really' know? (For example, if we know the world is there because of our senses, because we can see it, then how do we know it is still there each time we shut our eyes to blink.) The textualists like many philosophers before them disappear into the never-ending circle of questioning the conditions under which each claim of what *is*, is constituted. Those who tire of such circles can join us in making judgements about the real and trusting in these each time we open our eyes or use our senses. As academics we get on with the work of approximating our perceptions to the events of the world and developing our theories to encompass and explain the range of empirical phenomena which we observe. What we found in our empirical studies is that people in the world outside academia also do this. They can also use logic to alter their beliefs or can revise their expectations or understanding in the light of new information or experience. People do not live in a sealed-off conceptual space and nor can a critical social science.

## The active audience and the politics of pleasure

The encounter with philosophy and post-modern theory has left much cultural/communications studies, and indeed many other areas of social science, struggling with the notion of small groups or individuals 'actively' constructing their own interpretations and the meaning of their world. People can apparently live in what amounts to a sealed space of thought and language creating their own versions of what is taken to be real on the basis of pre-existing beliefs, values, codes or competencies (rather as football supporters are alleged to 'see' only the fouls committed by the other side). There are two key theoretical assumptions in this approach which we want to criticize here: first, the assumption that texts can mean whatever audiences interpret them to mean (and that they only have meaning with each new interpretation); second, the assumption that the producer of a text can describe the world in an indefinite number of ways and that there is no recourse to an agreed reality to evaluate the description. There can be no assessment on grounds of accuracy/truth and there can be no agreed evidence which can be shared or acknowledged between perspectives. Neither is it possible to explain the genesis of the description in real outside interests.

These assumptions appear in different areas of media and cultural studies including studies on pleasure and identity and in the theory of the active audience. This last theoretical approach illustrates many of the problems in academic work which has lost touch with the real world. For an audience to be 'active' could mean simply that people are not cultural dopes who believe everything they are told in the media. We would certainly accept this and our own work suggests clearly that different audiences can understand a media message but can have different responses to it. Some people believe and accept the message, others reject it using knowledge from their own experience or can use processes of logic or other rationales to criticise what is being said.

But some theorists go beyond this to suggest that audiences create their own meanings from the text (i.e. meaning is in the encounter with the text). The suggestion is that a text will mean completely different things to different audiences. This could perhaps happen if the audience literally doesn't speak the language of the message or if there are radical cultural differences between those who produce the message and those who receive it – as for example when European colonists in Africa or Asia appropriated artefacts which were of great cultural or religious significance and thought they would make nice wall decorations.

But our own work on responses to media output suggests that varied audience groups have a very clear understanding of what is the intended message and can reproduce it very accurately. We tested this across a number of different areas of media output and formats – on coverage of Northern Ireland (Miller, 1994a), images of mental illness (Philo, 1996) and the reporting of the 1984/5 miners' strike (Philo, 1990, referred to above).

We asked audience groups to produce their own news accounts and scripts of films and soap operas from memory. They were given a small number of photographs from the particular story to act as a stimulus. In the study of beliefs about the miners' strike we gave small groups of people photographs from news coverage with which they wrote there own 'news story' and they were then questioned about what they actually believed. In the event, the different groups were very clear on what the intended message of news reporting was (i.e. that picketing was violent and miners were blamed for the trouble). They did not interpret the intended meaning of the news differently, i.e. it was not the case that conservative groups saw the news as showing miners 'fouls' while the miners and their supporters saw the news as showing police 'fouls'. There were of course differences between the groups – not over the meaning of the message but on whether or not they believed it. Some of these differences were related to pre-existing beliefs, but even here not everyone remained fixed in their views. Some who were sympathetic to the strike were weakened in their support by what they had seen in news reports. There were clear examples of media influence on belief and opinion. We also found that some people criticized the truth of media accounts using processes of logic and reasoning. This was not confined to people who supported the strike. For example one very conservative person commented that she 'would have shot' the striking miners. Nonetheless she rejected the news message and believed that the strike was mostly peaceful. She argued that this was necessarily so because of the numbers involved, as she put it 'because of the amount who were actually on strike, if you take that into account, it can't all have been violent'. In another group a respondent made a similar point noting that 'if they had been really violent the police couldn't have coped, it would have been the army' (Philo, 1990, pp. 40 and 108).

The use of logic and evidence about what really happened concerned other group members. A group of three solicitors who were very conservative in their views debated the real content of the photograph they were using to write a news exercise. They picked up a photograph of pickets which actually showed people standing around peacefully and sitting on the ground. One then suggested as a text to go with it, 'they drove through the angry mobs'. A second person then commented 'that doesn't look like an angry mob to me'. The first replied, 'Oh, these ones here don't look too happy'. As a result of this exchange the line eventually became 'they drove through the gates' (Philo, 1990, pp. 60–1). The point here is that these participants used a photograph as agreed evidence to give an account which differed from the initial view of 'picket violence'.

In other groups some people used different forms of direct experience to criticize the news message on violence. Two people from Bromley in Kent who again were politically conservative rejected what they had seen in news reports on the grounds that they had met miners and their families while on holiday in the North of England. They had got on very well with them and had refused to believe that they were the sort of people who could be violent (Philo, 1990, p. 114). Our research did not show people effortlessly constructing the meaning of texts on the basis of pre-existing systems of thought. Some who were sympathetic to the miners were influenced negatively by media coverage, while some others who were politically conservative rejected the news coverage on violence. There was also a large group of people who had a limited knowledge of the strike and did not have any direct experience of the events. These were the people who were most likely to be influenced in their beliefs by news reporting . We also showed that people from different perspectives agreed on the meaning of the message and that the accuracy of the message could be evaluated using agreed evidence. Much of this would be anathema to a theory which portrayed audience members as sealed in their own conceptual space, producing their own interpretations of the text. We are not of course the only people to criticize active audience theory. James Curran has termed it a 'new revisionism', as 'old pluralist dishes' presented as new cuisine (1990, p. 281), while John Corner has described it as 'complacent relativism' (1991, p. 151). We will show now how some of the confusions within active audience theory have developed and specifically how they have grown from the use of the 'encoding/decoding' model in media studies.

## From encoding/decoding to television as a toaster

The encoding/decoding formulation was originally proposed by Stuart Hall and there are several different versions of his paper. In the earliest there is a long section discussing media influence in relation to genre using the specific example of the Western and violence (Hall, 1973a, 1974). Here we find an account which is based on a 'semiology which seeks to ground itself in historical realities' and which argues that 'in part what the production of the Western genre/code achieved was the transformation of a real historical west, selectively, into the symbolic of mythic "West"' (Hall, 1973a, p. 6).

In this passage we find a contrast drawn between reality and a mythical/ideological account with the implication that reality is knowable and that a key impact of Westerns might be to mislead audiences about 'historical realities'. This section of the paper was included in the version published in 1974 but left out of the later version (Hall, 1980). In fact reality doesn't make much appearance in the 1980 version. Instead we have an account which rather confusedly stresses that audiences have different understandings of texts. They 'decode' texts in different ways according to a variety of 'decoding positions'.

The model suggests (and crucially has been widely taken to suggest) that it is the meaning of texts which are 'negotiated' rather than meanings about reality. In practice what is being discussed (in the 1973 version and much less so in the 1980 version), behind all the terminology, is that there are conflicting versions of reality which arise from the material fact of conflicting power and interests.[12] Yet the impact of the encoding/decoding model was to shift the attention from contestation over reality and to focus instead simply on the text and its interpretation.[13] There was another key factor in the portrayal of the active audience and its free floating powers of 'interpretative resistance' to media messages. This was the development of research designs which in practice were unable to investigate or find effects. This was because they tended only to examine the interpretation (or 'reading') of texts rather than whether anyone believed them. The move from examining the role of texts in the interpretation of reality to examining the interpretations of texts only thus lost a crucial link with the material world. Research in this tradition was unable to properly conceptualize questions of influence on popular beliefs about the world. Such research did not examine the influence of media on belief or the actual use by audiences of their own real experience in criticizing texts (as opposed to their presumed ability to simply make up another meaning).

The encoding/decoding model was used by Morley in his well known *Nationwide* audience study (1980). This ushered in a large body of work premised on active audience theory. Morley later criticized this use of his results saying that reception studies has been wrongly taken to be 'documenting the total absence of media influence, in the "semiotic democracy" of postmodern pluralism' (Morley, 1997, p. 125). But one of the reasons why Morley's work could be used in this way followed from the original research design. It is a relatively static model which was intended to show whether sub-groups such as trade unionists could 'deconstruct' the preferring strategies of the dominant code in media texts (e.g. by 'seeing through' loaded questions). Morley found evidence that they could. This was then taken as support for the assumption the sub-groups could be safe in their systems of codes and competencies, reinterpreting the dominant code, making their own meanings and pleasures. What was missing from Morley's research design was the capacity to trace the sources of the belief systems of the groups. The analysis was held very largely at the micro level of the decoding moment (see Philo, 1990).

Our own research showed that beliefs can be influenced by new messages from the media and also by the flow of new experience which can itself potentially be used in the rejection or acceptance of new messages (as can other factors including cultural histories, processes of logic etc.). In other words the reception model should be dynamic. Media messages change and so does the flow of experience. The two are crucially related. When political ideologies are developed as political practice, they have consequences in public experience. This means that the systems of ideas which legitimize social and political power must be constantly re-worked. The belief that the capitalist economy was best left to free marketeers was challenged after the collapse of share prices on Black Monday in 1987, followed by the collapse of the housing market after 1988. The free market produced radical and very negative changes in many social lives. In the eighteen years after 1979, the poor really did get poorer, there were increases in inter-personal violence, unemployment and insecurity at work. The message on school meals and on skilled teachers leaving which we referred to above only appears as a text in relation to very specific social and material changes. Political propaganda must therefore be re-formulated to explain/apologize or legitimize new relationships and events (Philo, 1995b). It is exactly because people are not sealed off in conceptual bubbles or positioned indefinitely by static structures of discourse that there is a need to constantly rework social ideas in the relation to the defence of interests. If belief systems were not constantly challenged by new experience and its contradictions there would be no need for political debate. In real societies, there are parties, class fractions and interest groups who contest how the world is to be explained and what is to be understood as necessary, possible and desirable within it. In our work we have analyzed the role of the media in such struggles because of its potential power in reflecting and developing key elements of belief. But with a few exceptions, the content of media messages and their impact on audiences have largely disappeared from media and cultural studies.

The emphasis in recent work has been very much on the use which audiences make of messages. Morley and Lull for example both looked at how television programmes are used by family groups as 'common references' to explain things and to illustrate points which people are trying to make (Morley, 1986, p. 32). As Lull argues:

> viewers not only make their own interpretations of shows, they also construct the situations in which viewing takes place and the ways in which acts of viewing, and programme content, are put to use. (1988, p. 17; see also Lull, 1990)

We have argued elsewhere that the methodologies used in such studies are limited in that their focus is explicitly on audience members' *uses* of television (and often collect data by asking people how they use television). This is likely to neglect changes in belief which result from watching television about subjects where there is no discussion or interchange of ideas within the family. For example, in one family who we interviewed for a study of beliefs about mental illness, the father and mother had opposite views on the degree to which conditions such as schizophrenia were linked to violence. The father was a policeman, the mother a nurse and their understanding related to work experience. Their children all linked mental illness to violence and cited TV/horror films as their source of information. The family were not aware of all these differences in views. It was a 'no-no' area – as they said, simply not something they would discuss. Other 'taboo' areas for 'family discussion' could include politics, sexuality, child abuse etc. (Philo, 1996).

In the work by Morley and Lull texts were no longer of much interest. Instead viewing processes and negotiation in the household were the central focus. Such an approach could not and did not have any interest in questions of influence. However, such work is still used as evidence that media influences are if anything minimal. Another area of investigation has been the uses (particularly the gendered uses) of technologies, revealing for example who had the power to hold the television channel changer (Morley and Silverstone, 1990, 1991; Silverstone, 1990). While such research can be valuable for other purposes (see particularly Cynthia Cockburn's 1992 analysis of gender and technology) it does not tell us very much about the formation of public belief (see Silverstone, 1994). What is special about television and radio is that they are *message-bearing technologies*. They raise issues which make them different from other appliances and from who makes the toast or does the ironing. A television is very different from a toaster.[14]

## Popular culture and power from below

For the exponents of consumer culture and those who celebrate the 'popular' there are two key assumptions: first that there are no means of establishing cultural value and, second, that popular culture is seen to emerge from below. It is apparently not imposed from above, nor do the cultural industries appear to have much to do with the formation and transformation of beliefs, tastes or values. Here we see a regurgitation of the official myth of the cultural industries that they simply follow public tastes (for a review of such positions see McGuigan, 1992). Perhaps more importantly there is no analysis in such theories of how the everyday relations of a 'modern' society produce inter-personal competition, new definitions of what it is to be successful and new 'badges' which declare that success (which are provided and promoted by the culture industries).

Fiske is perhaps the best-known advocate of popular culture, which, for him, is identified with people's culture. He writes that it 'is formed always in reaction to, and never as part of, the forces of domination' (1989a, p. 43). Similarly, we can find Mike Featherstone arguing that popular culture is 'the culture of the poor' and an 'appreciation of the common people' (1991, p. 141). Here, the role of the cultural industries in helping to shape tastes and sell products is at best minimal. The products of advanced capitalism are so efficiently appropriated that no traces of their intended meanings remain. For Fiske popular culture *is by definition* resistance to domination:

> Popular pleasures must always be those of the oppressed, they must contain elements of the oppositional, the evasive, the scandalous, the offensive, the vulgar, the resistant. Pleasures offered by ideological conformity are muted and hegemonic; they are not popular pleasures and work in opposition to them. (1989a, p. 127)

Featherstone also apparently endorses the post-modern view of 'the multi-faceted nature, and bewildering and non-hierarchical disorder of popular cultures' (1991, p. 140). We can also find one of Fiske's followers, James Lull, arguing that:

> Popular culture . . . is empowering. The mass media contribute to the process by distributing cultural resources to oppressed individuals and subordinate groups which they use to construct their tactics of resistance against hegemonic strategies of con-tainment. (Lull, 1995, p. 73)

Lull concludes his book with three 'fundamental axioms', one of which is that 'social actors interpret and use the symbolic environment in ways which advance their personal, social and cultural interests' (1995, p. 174).

We can ask for whom popular culture is empowering? If it is everyone, do Fiske and Lull mean to suggest that it is also empowering for adherents of the Far Right, for child abusers, for racists or for misogynists? If so, does this remain a resistant and oppositional use of dominant culture? As for the suggestion that 'popular' culture is non-hierarchical, tell that to the victims of 'popular' cultures which celebrate power and violence for men, attractiveness and beauty for women and able-bodiedness for all. We are not suggesting that 'popular culture' is not important, nor that it should not be studied. We do think that there is a fateful confusion in the work of the populists, which is that they confuse people's culture with the products provided by capitalist corporations. The uncritical celebration of the products of the system is a woefully inadequate way of studying or understanding the forces which shape our world.

For many cultural theorists ordinary people show an impressive ability to 'resist' or 'subvert' dominant culture. Yet the activities which are said to be resistant are often trivial. As Todd Gitlin has put it:

> First, there is the search for the radical potential in marginal or 'alternative' . . . culture . . . One upshot is the prayer, or conviction, that a sufficiently angry youth culture would constitute, by itself, radical politics – keeping alive a flame that the industrial working class had long let flicker out . . . failing to find radical potential in the politics of parties or mass movements, they exalt 'resistance' in subcultures, or, one step on, in popular styles, or even . . . in the observation that viewers watch TV with any attitude other than devoted rapture. This is the second version of resistance theory . . . the search for signs of political insurgency in mainstream culture . . . At times . . . the unstated operating assumption is that popular culture is *already politics*, and, moreover, some sort of insurgency. (Gitlin, 1991, pp. 335–6)

Gitlin goes on to ask what precisely constitutes 'resistance':

> Resistance, meaning all sorts of grumbling, multiple interpretation, semiological inversion, pleasure, rage, friction, numbness, what have you – 'resistance' is accorded dignity, even glory, by stamping these not-so-great refusals with a vocabulary derived from life-threatening work against fascism – as if the same concept should serve for the Chinese student uprising and cable TV grazing. (Gitlin, 1991, p. 336)

We would also want to argue that it is possible to see the type of activities described as 'resistance' in such work as evidence of the adoption of dominant values.[15] One of Fiske's examples (1989a; see also 1993) of the resistant tactics of popular culture is the shopping mall. Here, 'the young are shopping mall guerrillas par excellence' (Fiske, 1989a, p. 37). Their arguments with security guards and shoplifting escapades are celebrated as resistance in action. In the rush to validate 'popular' culture, analysts such as Fiske come close to suggesting that the ultimate in cultural liberation would be the ability of each of us to 'liberate' the occasional leather jacket. The question they do not ask is, if people feel impelled to steal the symbols of the rich and style-obsessed, is this because they are resisting dominant culture or because they have absorbed its values? Joyriders do not take Morris Travellers, or cars with 'baby on board' stickers. They prefer the SRi and hot hatch-backs (Home Office, 1997).

There is also an irony here which is that the 'popular' is understood as that which sells a lot or is widely watched. Popular culture is defined in terms of commodities.[16] This type of popular is celebrated. But other types of popular culture are simultaneously treated with derision. We can point here to the real and enduring (though evolving) sense of their own identities which are clearly important in individuals' lives and in moving history. Some of these are seen as reactionary and old fashioned and as being the result of essentialist myths of, for example, 'the nation' or of 'ethnicity'. Such 'myths' appear to have become more popular in recent years rather than less (with the emergence of new states and tendencies to devolution). Yet, media and cultural studies has not been in the vanguard celebrating popular attachment to such ideologies. On the contrary, many academics in media and cultural studies are more likely to condemn this type of popular culture. It can certainly be argued that some forms of popular nationalism are not at all politically progressive – from the National Front to ethnic cleansing. Yet, no whiff of criticism of the products of the culture industries can be made for fear of being branded elitist. As Terry Eagleton suggests, the 'landscapes of popular pleasure' seem:

> to boil down for the moment to media, shopping and lifestyle, and . . . those who look for forms of individual self-development other than choosing between fancy brand names [are] slurred as both sexist and elitist. (1996a, p. 5)

## Audience and consumption pleasure

Many audience studies have emphasized pleasure.[17] This approach is a major development of work on the active audience and directs attention to the creative ways in which people (very often women) gain pleasure from popular texts. In most of this work audiences are seen as actively constructing meaning so that texts which appear on the face of it to be reactionary or patriarchal can be subverted. Some of the work also dissolves textual meaning into audience interpretation in similar ways to those discussed above. Much of this represents either a misguided attempt to celebrate the abilities of ordinary people or a search for a replacement for the lost proletariat.

Whether it is the pleasure which housewives get in breaking up their day listening to Noel Edmonds on Radio 1 (Hobson, 1980), or of watching JR and Sue Ellen in *Dallas* (Ang, 1985), pleasure is seen as somehow politically progressive. As Harris remarks:

The seeking of semiotic pleasure becomes the central form of resistance, the appropriation of signifiers the substance of politics, linguistic practice the archetype of all subjective and cultural practice . . . the linguistic now includes every activity, from shopping to fantasising to playing video games. (1992, p. 166)

For Ang, the world of fantasy is apparently the 'place of excess, where the unimaginable can be imagined' (Ang, 1996, p. 106). In a review of Janice Radway's (1984) study of readers of romantic fiction, fantasy and fiction are said by Ang to 'offer a private and unconstrained space in which the socially impossible or unacceptable subject positions, or those which are in some way too dangerous or risky to be acted out in real life, can be adopted' (Ang, 1996, p. 94). 'In fantasy and fiction however, there is no punishment for whatever identity one takes up, no matter how headstrong or destructive: there will be no retribution, no defeat will ensue. Fantasy and fiction, then are the safe places of excess in the interstices of ordered social life' (Ang, 1996, p. 95).

This approach evacuates questions of power and interests from the discussion of fantasy and pleasure. The pleasures gained are seen as fundamentally separate from politics and the real. They are a place of escape. We can note here that, in fact, fictional accounts of romance, love and sex regularly *do* end up with the woman being (often violently) punished (Cameron and Fraser, 1987). Furthermore, audience research on representations of sexual violence (in which Ang has not engaged) has found that women viewers tended not to emphasize 'pleasure, escape and fantasy' but 'relevance and social importance' (Schlesinger *et al.*, 1992, p. 168). The extent to which the space of fantasy is unconstrained is difficult to judge since the fantasies of romance readers to which Ang refers (1996, pp. 98–108, discussing Radway, 1984) are more or less based on the romantic idyll promoted by romance novels. This is so to such an extent that according to Radway's findings (Radway, 1984), which Ang notes, readers will reject novels which do not conform to the classic romance. The adoption by romance readers of 'socially impossible' subject positions is also an interesting concept. Given the actual responses of the readers in Radway's study the socially impossible subject positions which Ang finds so appealing seem to consist of no more than the desire for Mr Right.

There is also a residual sense in which pleasure is seen as politically positive. What we might call the will to romance, should, according to Ang, 'be taken seriously as a psychical strategy by which women empower themselves in everyday life, leaving apart what its ideological consequences in social reality are' (1996, p. 107). Ang of course has nothing whatever to say about ideological consequences and would prefer that such vulgar questions were bracketed off altogether.

Fantasy and pleasure are not innocent of traces of power and the will to it. Would any socially unacceptable 'subject position' from which pleasure was derived be regarded as innocent? Curiously, as Harris (1992, p. 170) notes 'we hear only about the semiotic struggles of the politically correct'. We hear very little of the pleasure of fantasies of power and domination. Such pleasure comes from the exercise of (physical, material or symbolic) power over objects or other beings. We have already alluded to some examples of this in the pleasure of consumption or the pleasure of violence. We can also think of examples of pleasure in subordination, where a bad or intolerable situation is made better by grabbing pleasures where one can or even where some pleasure is taken in being the victim of oppression itself. This is known as masochism. Where are the studies which question such 'pleasure'?

As Harris notes, 'there is no analysis of the interplay between nature and culture in popular bloodsports, nothing on the blissful potential re-entry into nature and jouissant loss of self as the pitbulls clash, or the terriers seize the foxcub' (1992, p. 170). We also note that the pleasure of participating in the 'turkey shoot' of the Gulf War (as an Allied soldier or as a viewer) has not yet been analyzed, nor has the pleasure of the popular pastime of racist abuse and violence, or of sexual harassment and rape. Have we really nothing more to say about popular culture than 'people like it'? (Williamson, 1986, p. 19, cited in McGuigan, 1992, p. 78.)

## Identity, difference and the other

Recently much research has disappeared into the ever-shifting sands of relativism offered by theories on identity, 'difference' and 'otherness'. In many cases these entirely neglect questions of power and interests – as if 'others' are universal constructs of all cultures rather than related to ideal and material interests in specific historical circumstances. Work in this area draws on two of the major themes outlined above. First it emphasizes the active role of people in the construction of identities – that is identities are not determined by socio-economic forces, but are 'creatively' put together. Second there is a strand which stresses the textuality, or linguistic nature, of identity. Identities are seen as an effect of discourse – discourse 'speaks' through us. Although these two approaches seem contradictory, they do coexist in a variety of writings on identity. As Eagleton puts it 'at once libertarian and determinist, [post-modernism] dreams of a human subject set free from constraint, gliding deliriously from one position to another, and holds simultaneously that the subject is the mere effect of forces which constitute it through and through' (Eagleton, 1996b, pp. 28–29). Many theorists want to validate what people do in difficult circumstances, or to find alternative radical movements in feminism, gay rights or, more recently, the environmental movement. But they don't have any empirical account of how people actually construct their sense of self in real social relationships, in the context of competing forces and interests. Instead they see people as inhabiting discourses, or as 'hailing' a passing identity.[18] Both versions share a tendency to slip into cultural and epistemological relativism and therefore suffer from an inability to analyze or discuss the material and historical circumstances in which identities are forged. Consequently they do not properly acknowledge the 'real present day political and other reasons why essentialist identities continue to be evoked and often deeply felt' (Calhoun, 1994, p. 14).

Many contemporary authors (e.g. Hall, 1990, 1992, 1996; Grossberg, 1996; Gilroy, 1997; Rutherford, 1990) have sought to oppose essentialism in conceptions of identity (the assumption that there is some 'essence' in history or biology which determines ethnic, gender, national or sexual identity). As an alternative some have adopted as a mirror image, a form of cultural essentialism, which neglects the specific historical circumstances in which differences are named, thought significant and enrolled in the service of, or opposition to, power. The myth of essential national or racial identity is replaced by these theorists with the myth of the necessary 'other'. Identities are held to be unstable and constantly in formation as opposed to being static and unchanging (as in the allegedly essentialist versions). 'The discursive approach sees identification as a construction, a process never completed – always "in process"' (Hall, 1996, p. 2). The fluidity of identity is not only grounds for optimism, but an indication – again – of the active way in which identities are constructed and put together (as if they were not durable – if changing/evolving – parts of the cultural landscape). Alternatively, where identities are conceived as the positioning effects of discourse (Hall, 1990), our 'activity' is somewhat more constrained. In either version, even where history or reality are specifically noted as important (as in Hall, 1996), it is as if identities could be changed just by thinking about them.

One of the leading theorists in this area is Judith Butler, author of two widely cited books, *Gender Trouble* (1990) and *Bodies that Matter* (1993). Two aspects of Butler's work stand out: her insistence that not only gender but sexual difference itself is discursively constructed;[19] and her theory of performativity – that gender identity is an effect of 'performative speech acts' (Butler, 1997). As Barbara Epstein writes:

> [Butler] argues that not only gender but sex itself, that is, sexual difference, should be seen as an effect of power relations and cultural practices, as constructed 'performatively' – that is, by acts whose meaning is determined by their cultural context. Butler argues that the conventional view of sex as consisting of two given, biologically determined categories, male and female, is ideological, and defines radical politics as consisting of parodic performances that might undermine what she calls 'naturalized categories of identity'. Her assertion that sexual difference is socially constructed strains belief. It is true that there are some people whose biological sex is ambiguous, but this is not the case for the vast majority of people. Biological difference has vast implications, social and psychological; the fact that we do not yet

fully understand these does not mean that they do not exist. Butler's understanding of radicalism shows how the meaning of the word has changed in the post-modernist arena. It no longer has to do with efforts to achieve a more egalitarian society. It refers to the creation of an arena in which the imagination can run free. It ignores the fact that only a privileged few can play at taking up and putting aside identities. (Epstein, 1997)

As other feminist critics have argued, Butler's position reduces feminism to a struggle over representation ignoring the macro (economic, social, political and cultural) structures which contribute to women's secondary status (Fraser, 1981). It also evacuates women from feminist theory since 'woman' as a category is held to be an unstable fiction. This is, as Modleski (1991) has put it, *Feminism without Women* (see the discussion in Segal, 1997). Butler's radical discursive approach to sex results in all manner of tangled reasoning as she both denies our ability to understand the world except through discourse and at the same time insists that she knows how the world really works:

> When people ask the question 'Aren't these biological differences?', they're not really asking a question about the materiality of the body. They're actually asking whether or not the social institution of reproduction is the most salient one for thinking about gender. In that sense there is a discursive enforcement of a norm. (Butler, 1997, p. 236; see also Butler, 1993, pp. 1–23)

If meaning is unstable, it is unclear to us how Butler can 'know' what people 'actually' mean. It might be the case that this is the implication or intention underlying the statement or it might not. Certainly that meaning is not literally encoded in the question. If Butler really does think that there is no difference between making an observation of fact and an avowal of a gender norm, then it is impossible for her to say what is actually the case. Gender 'performances' there certainly are, but it is preposterous to reduce gender identity, sexuality and sexual differentiation to the discursive notion of a perpetually deferred performativity.

Furthermore, performativity as with other post-structuralist positions on identity lacks any sense of agency.[20] Hall does make a valiant effort in this respect to rethink agency and subjectivity in discussing the 'suturing of the psychic and the discursive' (Hall, 1996, p. 16). But this still neglects the material and ideal interests which construct and are expressed in identities. Furthermore, Hall says 'I agree with Foucault' that we do not require 'a theory of the knowing subject, but rather a theory of discursive practice' (1996, p. 2). For Hall and others in this tradition, discourses speak through people, or, at best, we 'inhabit' discursive positions: 'Identities are . . . points of temporary attachment to the subject positions which discursive practices construct for us' (1996, p. 6). As we noted above such positions do not allow for the fact that people make judgements on the world based on their own experience and processes of logic and evaluation. There is no theory of how people inhabit discourse or of the processes by which we select between discourses.[21] It is as if we magically find ourselves preferring democracy over fascism.

Grossberg (1996) similarly attempts to escape the incoherences of identity theory but is held back by not engaging with the material factors which encourage or inhibit the linking of difference to power relations in particular historical periods. For Hall and others in this tradition the question of the formation of identities is posed in such a way as to divert attention from the process by which identities are constructed. According to Hall identities 'actually' involve us in:

> using the resources of history, language and culture in the process of becoming rather than being: not 'who we are' or 'where we came from', so much as what we might become, how we have been represented and how that bears on how we might represent ourselves. Identities are therefore constituted within, not outside representation. (Hall, 1996, p. 4)

It is not clear to us how Hall can really be sure that this is what identity 'actually' involves, since by his own definition we cannot say what has really happened in history or the present or how this might 'actually' construct identities. More fundamentally, this position sees identities as the product of uses of history. History is simply a resource of the mythical to be used in the 'invention of tradition' and the construction of new identities. On the contrary, history provides the real material circumstances in which identities are produced and project towards the future. As Ahmad argues, it is inadequate to deny with the post-structuralists and writers such as Hall and Butler 'the historical reality of the sedimentations which do in fact give particular collectivities of people real civilizational identities' (Ahmad, 1992, p. 11).

## On experience, the missing link

As we showed above, the crucial factor missing from an analysis which emphasizes that reality (or identity) is constituted in discourse (or representation) is that of experience. Experience doesn't feature here. But in the real world, as E. P. Thompson argued, experience:

> walks in without knocking at the door, and announces deaths, crises of subsistence, trench warfare, unemployment, inflation, genocide. People starve: their survivors think in new ways about the market. People are imprisoned: in prison they meditate in new ways about the law. (Thompson, 1981, p. 406)

By contrast the approaches to identity we have been discussing do not explain the process by which people accept ideas or reject them, they do not explain how ideas change or the way in which changing material circumstances occasion changes in thought. The proponents of discursive theory would object to this division between material circumstances and ideas. One such theorist is Joan Scott who has explicitly challenged the 'evidence of experience' (1991). According to her 'we need to attend to the historical processes that, through discourse, position subjects and produce their experiences. It is not individuals who have experience but subjects who are constituted through experience' (p. 779). Later she writes of the need 'to refuse a separation between "experience" and language and to insist instead on the productive quality of discourse' (p. 793).[22]

But language does not create new experiences, and new experience does not only occur if the subject has an appropriate language category with which to name it (this is perhaps why people so frequently say things such as 'I can't make sense of this', 'I can't quite express what I mean'). Scott attempts to address this point in her discussion of agency. She writes:

> Subjects are constituted discursively and experience is a linguistic event (it doesn't happen outside established meanings), but neither is it confined to a fixed order of meaning. Since discourse is by definition shared, experience is collective as well as individual. Experience can both confirm what is already known (we see what we have learned to see) and upset what has been taken for granted (when different meanings are in conflict we readjust our vision to take account of the conflict or to resolve it – that is what is meant by 'learning from experience' though not everyone learns the same lesson of learns it at the same time or in the same way). (1991, p. 793)

But this is not what is meant by learning from experience. This is especially the case when the 'established meanings' do not match up to our experiences of the material world. It is precisely for this reason that new words are coined and new meanings born. Look again at the passage above – 'when different meanings are in conflict we readjust our vision'. The key problem for this account is that it cannot explain how the meanings we now have came into existence and how meanings might change. In the absence of either the flow of material events or human agency meanings could not be created and nor would they have to change. To follow this theory we would have to accept that the meanings which are found in the work of Joan Scott (and other post-structuralists) emerged fully formed with the evolution of the first human and have circulated without change throughout all of human history: *Australopithecus* as the first post-modernist.

Our point is that language is adapted and developed in the ceaseless flow of human activity. These activities create new relationships and possibilities which can be conceptualized and named. New concepts and their description can develop with new relationships. For example, the phrase 'living beyond your means' necessarily presupposes a society with the capacity to develop a surplus, a method of trading it and a system of credit. Without these, in a subsistence economy, people would have their means of surviving and would consume them. It would be inconceivable to 'live beyond' them. This raises the interesting question of how new words and definitions develop and how they are 'worked upon' to be appropriate for specific purposes. This is crucial because our view is that language is purposive and is used by active cognizing subjects. The level of reflection in use and 'work' will certainly vary according to circumstance. But we do not accept the radical de-centring of the subject in contemporary post-modern accounts and the view that subjects merely 'hail' passing discourses and are 'positioned' by them.

In practice people actively make sense of and give meaning to their world and in doing so they use different resources, such as the media or new information from peer groups. Our colleague Jenny Kitzinger has shown how women engage in collective sense making on issues such as male violence. She illustrates how a group of women can re-define and name what they already 'felt' about past experience – but which had in a sense been inappropriately named and defined. She describes a focus group discussion in which women comment upon a poster which had been produced for a campaign against male violence. The poster included the statement that 50 per cent of girls would encounter some form of abuse. At first the women in the group dissented from this but as they discussed the issue they came to the conclusion that they had in fact all experienced some form of sexual contact which was at the very least, 'unwanted' if not outrightly abusive. The discussion ended with these comments from three women:

> f2: All these years I just thought: 'Oh that was the night I lost my virginity.' I hadn't actually took the time to think about what actually happened . . . He forced me. Now I'm thinking, for fuck's sake, when I lost my virginity I was raped. I remember actually thumping him to get him off me and he wouldn't get off . . . I was too young, I didn't want to do it . . . I couldn't physically get him off me. I was beating him and I couldn't get him off. It was all over.
> f1: the first time I got drunk, I lost my virginity. I didn't want to do it either. I was pretty young as well.
> f3: You see, I'm the exact same . . . So that's every single person in this room. (Kitzinger, 1999, pp. 16–17)

The women in this group are not simply 'hailing' another discourse at random nor is their sense of what happened determined by a new (feminist) discourse. They work on the possibility of explaining and giving expression to what they have already felt and experienced. The attempt to force someone off is a real and profoundly felt response but what had happened had not been thought through or clearly defined as an assault. As Thompson suggested, the effect of grim experience is to create the possibility of meditating on new ways of explaining it. It may first be named in a way which is inappropriate or be met with incomprehension. It is not uncommon for people to 'feel' that an existing explanation or definition is not right. They may then have to struggle to adapt words and find new ways of explaining what was only partly identified or understood. This can involve them in making new meanings rather than just being spoken through by the ventriloquism of discourse.

Our final objections to the discursive approach are then its idealism and its consequent inability to relate to material process. It is just so implausibly *neat* in its portrayal of the well-ordered conceptual structures which allegedly organize what can be seen and known. It is not surprising that its theorists rarely attempt to measure or account for public consciousness through empirical work. Such consciousness in practice is very messy – a mass of sometimes half-understood concepts and ideas, bits of information from the media and peer groups, jokes, fears, memories of childhood, school, home and work experiences, judgements about what is true, fair, legitimate, desirable, and what is necessary and what is possible, responses from social and political cultures which often contain quite contradictory beliefs. Within such consciousness it is possible to discern ways of understanding, perspectives and responses which relate to factors such as class, ethnicity or gender and which are formed in relation to social interests. Such ideologies do function to limit what can be understood, but our point is that they are potentially unstable in the flow of material circumstances, they are contradictory and are contested. The manner in which all these different elements of social consciousness develop and change over time can only be established through empirical work. In contrast, the theories of identity (as an effect of discourse) which we have discussed here are simply speculative and are constructed independently of any account of how people think and act in the world.

## Consumption

The new interest in how audiences 'consumed' media was paralleled by a wide growth of interest in social science in other areas of consumption (see e.g. Daniel Miller, 1995a; Brewer and Porter, 1993; Keat *et al.*, 1994; Lury, 1996). The work we discuss here also drew on arguments about the instability of meanings and the variable way in which meanings could be interpreted or subverted by consumers. As a result questions of power and the influence of both systems of production and representation were evacuated from the research agenda or turned on their heads in the celebration of alleged consumer power as in Daniel Miller's account of consumption as the 'vanguard of history' and the consumer as the 'global dictator' (1995b).

Issues of identity and lifestyle were closely connected with much of this work. Indeed it has been suggested that 'special emphasis tends to be placed on those theories that relate consumption to issues of identity, and within this, to those that represent consumption as an activity which conveys information about the consumer's identity to those who witness it' (Campbell, 1995, p. 111). This has tended to mean that serious examinations of consumption in the context of both what influences it and the influences that it has have been displaced by a celebration of the 'free' choices of consumption behaviour and identity formation or a proclamation of the power of the consumer.

This preoccupation again tends to emphasize the 'active' role of 'consumers' in constructing their own identities. There are two aspects to note about this. First, products are seen to be 'chosen' and second the meanings attached to those products are also chosen (or more accurately in post-structuralist versions – meanings from the available discourses are adopted or inhabited). Of course this approach tends to exclude the material systems of production which actually produce the goods in question and importantly the promotional machinery which go with them (Fine and Leopold, 1993). These are accorded minimal theoretical importance and there is little empirical investigation of them. We accept that the meanings associated with consumption in general or with particular products should be examined, but the entire process of the production, distribution, retailing and consumption of goods must be analyzed *as a whole* if we are to properly understand the particular characteristics of parts of the cultural circuit.

Instead active choices are seen simply as one of the keys to the 'authority of the consumer' (Keat *et al.*, 1994). Choice in consumption is seen as a 'good thing'. In fact under the banner of 'new times' some theorists went so far as to argue that commodified consumption heralds the 'deep democratization' of culture. Stuart Hall asked 'Have we become so bewitched by who, in the short run, reaps the profits from these transactions and missed the deep democratisation of culture which is also a part of their hidden agenda? Can a socialism of the twenty-first century revive, or even survive, which is wholly cut off from the landscapes of popular pleasures, however contradictory a terrain they are?' (1988b). In an earlier (1984) formulation Hall argues that 'The left was not incorrect in seeing the massive manipulation, the advertising hype, the ballyhoo, the loss of quality, the up- and down-market division, which are intrinsic to commercial consumerism. The difficulty was that this manipulative side was all that was seen' (reprinted in Hall, 1988a, p. 214). Quite so, but the difficulty with subsequent formulations and the tendencies we are describing is that concerns with 'manipulation' were displaced and the 'landscapes of popular pleasures' became the only horizon visible.

There is little recognition of the limitations in the range of consumer goods available and the limited abilities of consumers to choose (limited/partial information about products, limited access to types of shops and limitations of resources). For example, if one wants to select soft drinks which are not tainted by the products of the sugar and sweetener industry, supermarkets are not a great place to shop. And if one wants not to eat the by-products of the petrochemical industry or the scrapings of the abattoir, choices are heavily constrained. Choice in this context has to be seen in a highly qualified way (on food choice see Macintyre *et al.*, 1998; Fine and Leopold, 1993; Fine *et al.*, 1996).

More important, however, is the question of the meanings associated with particular products and how these are integrated into the social world of the 'consumer'. For many contemporary theorists the process of constructing identity via lifestyle requires us to reject accounts which stress the importance of production and the power of advertising, marketing and public relations and instead to affirm the activity, creativity and resistance with which consumption is now associated. Furthermore, in some accounts the active role of creating identities presages the end of fixed status groups and even, as one sceptical commentator puts it, the coming irrelevance of 'previously existing social divisions and forms of social inequality' (Lury, 1996, p. 250; see also Featherstone, 1991). This latter position is most closely associated with Baudrillard (see Bocock, 1993). In reality, however, there are very notable limits on consumption. Given the extent of contemporary inequality between the rich and poor world and within the rich countries, the ability to consume to even a basic level is not assured and has become less so for many over the last twenty years.

There have also been theoretical arguments advanced about the use of products in the creation of identities and the subversion of meaning when consumer products are appropriated by sub-groups. There are two points that we want to make here. First, to the extent that people do choose between products for a variety of reasons, then they might be said to be 'active' in the sense that they make a more or less considered choice. This is by itself a relatively banal proposition. But it is much less clear that these 'active' choices subvert the meanings of the products available or combine them in new ways with other products. In fact most products (from food and drink to consumer durables) are not the subject of either branded advertising (Fine and Leopold, 1993) or of much meaning beyond their use-value. Moreover, there is little evidence that the meanings promoted by corporations selling branded products *are* widely subverted.

Second, and most importantly, for our argument, is the question of what happens as a result of consumption. What are the outcomes of the alleged active selection, appropriation and subversion of commodities? Are the responses politically progressive or even relatively harmless pleasures?

We can examine these questions in relation to Marie Gillespie's (1995) *Television, Ethnicity and Cultural Change*. This book is unusual in the area in that it is based on extensive empirical research in Southall, London. In addition Gillespie is also sceptical of some of the more speculative and free-floating accounts of consumption:

This book does not set out to celebrate consumer creativity any more than consumer culture itself. But following de Certeau (1984), it does take the view that consumption, despite its overdetermination by the market and the unequal distribution of access to economic and cultural capital . . . is not a passive process but an expressive and productive activity. In de Certeau's terms, the 'powerless' as consumers of representations take some control over their lives by employing 'tactics': through 'the silent, transgressive, ironic or poetic activity of the readers', the 'strategies' of the powerful are resisted. (Gillespie, 1995, p. 13)

Gillespie's book is then both empirically based and shows an awareness of the limitations of the more free-floating versions of post-modernism often found in writings on consumption. When discussing the consumption of Coca-Cola and of fast food at McDonald's, she argues that people actively create their own identities. But from the evidence quoted it is not clear that the meanings promoted by Coke or McDonald's have been subverted. For example, she writes of why people like McDonalds:

When asked why McDonald's beefburgers are so appealing, the response was formulated in terms of the slogan, 'Well, it makes your day', and 'it's just a feeling you get'. The nature of the 'feeling' becomes apparent when notions of 'freedom', 'choice' and financial independence are related to the ability to eat what you want. But the 'feeling' is also associated with a trip to McDonald's capturing a moment of 'freedom' outside Southall: freedom from the watchful eye of parental culture and freedom to participate on the 'teenage scene'. (1995, p. 200)

Noting the lack of images on British and 'Asian' TV and video with which to identify Gillespie notes that:

McDonald's . . . and Coca-Cola . . . are seen to represent an alternative. These brands connote, both through the suggestions conveyed by the imagery, songs and slogans of their ads, and through the particular place assumed by their consumption in local life, an ideal 'freedom' which transcends boundaries. (1995, p. 204)

The repetition of the McDonald's advertising slogan as a reason for liking McDonald's is noteworthy as is the notion of 'freedom' associated with Coke. This is not dissimilar to the meanings promoted by the Coca-Cola corporation in their advertising and marketing campaigns.

Is the argument that the desire to breach boundaries is always progressive? Is it always the case that 'parental cultures', for example, are obstacles to social progress? Apparently so:

The aspiration towards cultural change among Southall teenagers takes its most emphatically positive form from images (and sounds) designed to market the products of US-based transnational corporations such as Coca-Cola and McDonald's. This utopian 'teen dream' might easily be dismissed as gullibility. But when the responses to these ads invoke a hoped for transcendence of ethnic – and other – difference, in a setting of consumerist freedom, they define an ideal arena, an imaginative space, within which the construction of new identities becomes possible as a real project. [Visiting McDonald's] is an entirely real 'escape' into a new social and communicative space, in which young people can actively redefine their culture. (Gillespie, 1995, p. 206)

Here we are being asked to accept that the transcending of cultural and material boundaries is good in general and in particular that boundaries are specifically reactionary compared with the dreams of consumer freedom promoted by McDonald's and Coke. We can see the argument that for some oppressed groups any 'free' space might be better than none. But there are other issues that should be addressed.

The most important point for us is the narrow treatment of outcomes. The impulse is to celebrate the choices and identifications of research subjects. In such a scenario, evidence of a desire for transcendence of ethnic, class and cultural hierarchies is treated as a prototypically progressive outcome. But in the haste to show that ordinary people are not 'gullible',[23] larger questions are sometimes ignored. First, what are the consequences of engagements with the worlds of Coke and McDonald's for beliefs and actions? Second, what are the consequences in terms of buying products? Third, what are the consequences for social inequality or the profit margins of transnational corporations of the purchasing decisions, political beliefs and actions of 'consumers'? It is rare for such questions to be addressed in cultural studies. Daniel Miller makes a partial reference to them when he discusses the 'greatest marketing blunder of the century' faced by the Coca-Cola corporation when it introduced a new formula Coke to compete with arch rivals Pepsi. The new formula was apparently rejected by consumers and the old one re-introduced. Miller describes this as 'surely one of the most explicit examples of consumer resistance to the will of a giant corporation' (1997a, p. 33). However, it might be argued that the rejection of the 'new' Coke is in fact evidence of the previous success of Coke in attracting and holding consumer loyalty. The impact on Coca-Cola was at most a cut in profit margins. Do the limits of consumer power amount to the occasional ability to influence the range of sweet fizzy drinks between which we can 'choose'? This is hardly evidence of a significant countervailing power to that of transnational corporations.

The examples of Coca-Cola and McDonald's are particularly strong since they are products which are physically as well as mentally consumed in the act of eating. We can point to various relevant issues in the production and consumption of both sugared drinks and burgers. There have been many questions raised on whether corporate advertising and marketing lead to misperceptions of the quality of products and whether a diet heavy in such foods is harmful to 'consumers' health (Yudkin, 1986; Cannon, 1992; Dibb, 1993). While the consumption of sugar from the bowl in Britain has decreased, following public health advice in recent years, the overall amount of sugar in

British diets has remained the same, largely through increased sales of carbon-ated drinks (Fine *et al.*, 1996). The McLibel case (the longest running court case ever heard in England and Wales) highlighted the role of multinational giants such as McDonald's in employment practice, nutrition, animal rights and advertising. The judge in this case (who sat without a jury) concluded that McDonald's:

> does pay its workers low wages, thereby helping to depress wages for workers in the catering trade in Britain . . . are culpably responsible for cruel practices in the rearing and slaughter of some of the animals which are used to produce their food . . . have pretended to a positive nutritional benefit which McDonald's food, high in fat and saturated fat and animal products and sodium and at one time low in fibre, did not match . . . [and] exploit children by using them, as more susceptible subjects of advertising, to pressurise their parents into going to McDonald's. (Justice Bell, 19 June 1997)

But exposure of this type of 'cultural practice' is not a major theme in media and cultural studies.[24] Instead it is mostly activists and journalists who produce accessible, critical and useful material (in this case see the account by Vidal, 1997).

## Outcomes

The question of outcomes or consequences is one of the key problems with the bulk of the work reviewed here. In Hall's essay on encoding/decoding the circuit of mass communication depends in the end on the moment of 'repro-duction' as a further stage which cannot be guaranteed by the previous stage of 'distribution/consumption'. Reproduction refers to the reproduction of dominant ideology which is thought to ensure the continuation of capitalism. The term 'reproduction' does suggest a unidirectional and functionalist type of media influence, in that the media are assumed always to have a system supporting effect, but at least this approach was concerned with macro level outcomes. In much of contemporary audience or consumption theory, repro-duction or outcomes are barely mentioned. Asking about how people interpret texts cannot of itself answer questions about the influence of the media on ideology or belief. Such questions need to be asked directly. Furthermore, there are a series of highly complex moments between 'belief' and the repro-duction of modern society which have been very sparsely investigated by this tradition and are hardly visible as research questions in contemporary media and cultural studies (Miller, 1997).[25]

There is a need to examine the relationship between beliefs about the world and the political conclusions drawn by the public, the relationship between political conclusions and taking political action, and between public action protest and political change or continuity. Do people, as a result of viewing

*Neighbours*, *The Word* or *Newsnight*, believe that the sun always shines in Australia, people will do anything to get on TV or that inequalities are necessary for the functioning of the economy? As a result of any of these, do they then make a cup of tea, refuse to do the ironing, join the Conservative Party or burrow under Manchester Airport? And what difference does public belief or action make to corporate or government decision making? Do governments respond to public opinion? On which occasions? Are corporations or governments able to resist concerted and organized public opposition, and in which circumstances? Do consumers actually subvert the meanings of commodities? If the meanings of products are subverted is capitalism in any way inconvenienced? Does the 'subversion' lead to a critique of the system that produced the commodities? Do people actually buy the products? How do public knowledge, belief and purchasing trends affect corporate and state planning and regulation? These and associated questions ought to be, but are not, central to the agenda of media and cultural studies.

## The irrelevance of academic writing

Many of the accounts above lead out of political critique and any relevance to the society in which they were produced. Let us consider as an example some of the changes in feminism and where it has left feminist critique and politics.

The new 'cultural feminism' is usefully contrasted with 'old' feminism. Apparently old fashioned feminism was simply interested in gender equality – a goal which has now been surpassed (Hermes, 1995a). Old fashioned feminism of the liberal, radical or socialist variety also subscribed to a transmission model of meaning, which is rejected by cultural feminism since texts, it is argued (in the manner we have seen above), do not have fixed or clear meanings and may be interpreted in varying ways. For the new feminists these familiar arguments include an emphasis on the active audience and their pleasures. Furthermore, it is alleged that old style feminism adhered to 'a conceptualisation of gender as a dichotomous category with a historically stable and universal meaning' (Zoonen, 1996, p. 33), which means that women are seen as having similar interests and experiences as women. Thus, arguments about positive images and combating bias and ideology in gender representations were attacked[26] for assuming an essential or at least undifferentiated model of women's interests, experiences and identities, which could replace the 'negative' images provided by the media. Hermes gives a clear statement of the concerns of the 'new feminism' which she endorses:

> Critics who do not stop at equality but adopt a different approach stress the ambiguity of texts and raise new questions, including some about the pleasure that stereotyping and conventional media texts apparently offer women. The central issue is not social inequality but the popular text itself. (Hermes, 1995a, p. 58)

**71**

Let us examine what the 'new' feminist theorists recommend in the area of cultural politics. First, at the level of methodology and conceptualization, feminists should 'have respect for the wishes of women and thus also for any pleasure that they derive' from the media (Hermes, 1995a, p. 56). Feminism's 'overriding motivation should be to respect women and women's genres, and to demand respect for them from the world at large' (Hermes, 1995b, p. 151). Not only does this approach rule out any investigation and conceptualization of the media as helping to construct choices, pleasures and responses, but more fundamentally is a radical scaling down of feminist aims and demands. Far from such approaches surpassing concerns with equality, they stop well short of even the most modest conceptions of women's liberation.

Second, Hermes suggests that there is some terrain left: 'The division between high and low culture, the neglect of everyday media use and the eternal putting down of women's media are all strategies of domination that define us, as users of those genres and even as their researchers. Those definitions ultimately designate the battlefield for feminist cultural criticism' (1995b, p. 151). Elsewhere, Ang and Hermes want to go further, arguing that 'a flexible and pragmatic form of criticism might be more effective than one based upon predefined truths, feminist or otherwise' (1996, p. 342). The problem with this formulation is that their writings are entirely devoid of criticism of the role of the media, preferring to reject the approaches of feminists who have criticized and tried to challenge gender inequalities.

Third, van Zoonen has a more conventional proposal when she asks 'Would it still be inappropriate to expect a decent and ethical representation, of, for example, feminist issues and the women's movement?' (1996, p. 49). However, given Zoonen's argument that 'we don't know how audiences will use and interpret texts' and that 'one interpretation is not by definition better or more valid than another' (1996, p. 48) then there are no grounds whatever for insisting that the news change its representation of 'women's' issues. Moreover, it is a further downward revision to want to change only the representations of gender issues in relation to 'women's issues' rather than in the whole range of factual (and fictional) output. The closest Hermes gets to a practical question is as follows:

> Would I . . . be happier with women's magazines that were more or less the same but included lesbians, males of different persuasions, models, interviewees and columnists in all sorts of colours? (1995b, p. 9)

Astonishingly, her only answer is: 'That is difficult to say'.

Finally we are left with van Zoonen's other suggestion that strategies to develop the 'pleasures of discovering multiple and sometimes contending constructions in a text' are a logical step (1996, p. 49). Perhaps women could or should learn to find pleasure in programmes which excuse, justify or promote male sexual violence? If so we might well question whether the new cultural feminism is actually feminist in any meaningful sense of the word. As Terry Eagleton has written:

> If we encountered someone who called herself a feminist while forcing as many women as she could into sweated labour, then we would conclude that she was not in fact a feminist even though she thought she was. We would not take her at her word. (1996b, p. 103)

One result of the new cultural feminism is quietism. As Kitzinger and Kitzinger have argued:

> Feminists struggled for decades to name 'sexism' and 'anti-lesbianism'. We said that particular images of women – bound and gagged in pornography magazines, draped over cars in advertisements, caricatured as mothers-in-law or nagging wives in sitcoms – were oppressive and degrading. The deconstructionist insistence that texts have *no* inherent meanings, leaves us unable to make such claims. This denial of oppressive meanings is, in effect, a refusal to engage with the conditions under which texts are produced, and the uses to which they are put in the dominant culture. (1993, p. 15)

This has meant a silence on crucial issues from media and cultural studies. It is extraordinary that it should take a journalist such as Julie Burchill to denounce the celebration of paedophilia in popular culture. As she writes:

> These are the days in which the most obscenely oppressive images are not challenged, but actually celebrated as some sort of liberation. (1997, p. 3)

Angela McRobbie has also criticized cultural feminist approaches to the issue of consumption (1997). She argues that they neglect questions of exclusion, power and class:

> Recent scholarship on consumption has been weakened by an inattention to questions of exclusion from consumption and the production of consumption. Income differentials as well as questions of poverty have dropped off the agenda in this debate. Attention instead has been paid to the meaning systems which come in to play around items of consumption . . . this process gives rise to no awkward questions about how much the shop assistant is being paid, or how, having purchased the weekly shopping, we will get through to the end of the month. Consumer culture is instead an arena of female participation and enjoyment. This runs the risk of inducing a sense of political complacency. (1997, pp. 73–4)

As she notes, cultural feminism neglects relations of power and divisions of class between women:

> The structures which produce and reproduce these divisions (between women) and the consequences these have for relations of power and powerlessness tend to be marginalised. Consumption is extrapolated from the broader sociological context in which purchasing is only one small part of a whole chain of productive activity. (1997, p. 74)

Her conclusion is that there are glaring political problems with cultural feminism and that it jeopardizes feminist scholarship, which was founded upon issues of gender inequality and subordination.

## Critical journalists and silent academics

The abdication of responsibility by many academics can mean that it is left to a small number of critical journalists to do the hard work of uncovering the truth and revealing corruption and abuses of power. Many of the most penetrating critiques of developments in areas such as government information management, the new PR and promotional industries and political corruption, state secrecy and surveillance, journalistic practice, editorial control, censorship and news reporting of conflict, the tabloid press, media empires and satellite broadcasting, the problems faced by women in the news media, gendered politics and culture, on racism and on children, childhood and youth have been written not by academics, but by journalists. (See: on government information management, Cockerell *et al.*, 1984; Cockerell, 1989; Foot, 1990; Harris, 1990, Jones, 1995; on surveillance, secrecy and deception, Campbell and Connor, 1986; Hollingsworth and Norton-Taylor, 1988; Hollingsworth and Tremayne, 1989; Leigh, 1980; Norton-Taylor, 1985, 1995; Norton-Taylor *et al.*, 1996; on the new PR and promotional industries and political corruption, Hollingsworth, 1991, 1997; Leigh and Vulliamy, 1996; on journalistic practice, editorial control, censorship and news reporting of conflict, Harris, 1983; Jones, 1986; MacArthur, 1993; Pilger, 1986, 1991; Thomson, 1991; on the tabloids, Chippendale and Horrie, 1990; on media empires and satellite broadcasting, Bower, 1991; Chippendale and Franks, 1991; on women in the media, Sebba, 1994; Dougary, 1994; on gendered culture, Campbell, 1987; on racism, Kohn, 1996; Malik, 1996; on children and youth, Campbell, 1986, 1993.)

Post-modern/textualist approaches have had a pervasive influence on many areas of social science beyond media and cultural studies. In geography, for example, the approaches were recently satirized in an article by Neil Smith arguing that ' "sleep" was a vital site of unexplored oppositional possibility'. The 'counterconscious creativeness of sleep' had apparently been ignored because of the 'totalising megadiscourses of economism and historicism' (Smith, 1996, p. 505). Chris Hamnett in an editorial in *Environment and Planning* refers to the article and comments on the state of his discipline:

Under the banners of postmodernism, postimperialism, discourse, narrative, deconstruction, textuality and the like, a language, a set of concepts, and a mode of writing have permeated human geography, which bear an increasingly tenuous relationship to social relations and social practices as they are lived and experienced by many people . . . Unfortunately, given current academic politics and the fear of putting a foot wrong, some younger scholars may lack the confidence to point to the weaknesses inherent in some contemporary writing and may feel the need to sprinkle their work with the requisite terms . . . the piece was intended to prick the balloon of post-modern theoretical vacuity and social irrelevance. (Hamnett, 1997, p. 127; see also Chapter 6 in this volume)

In the subject area of history, Neville Kirk has pointed to the problems of post-modern approaches. He argues that they:

effectively dissolve reality/being into the processes of thought and language. In doing so, they preclude, by definition, any real engagement between language, politics and the 'social'. We are left simply with idealist engagements between discourses of politics, discourses of society and discourses of the economy. There is no way off this discursive merry-go-round, apart from the option of making and breaking concepts against evidence, the 'real' fact of social history. (1994, p. 237)

Kirk advocates a materialism in the tradition of E.P. Thompson, which as he says:

points to the existence of a reality beyond consciousness and simultaneously explores the dialectic between on the one hand agency and consciousness . . . and on the other hand, the unintended, unrecognised and material determination of life. (1994, p. 222)

In concluding this section we can point to six major problems with recent work. The first is the dearth of empirical research and the preoccupation with theoretical abstraction divorced from practice (Mills, 1959). The second is that much of what currently passes for wisdom is unable to describe the real world because it is lost in language games in which the real is just another discourse. Third is the problem of agency. Subjects are conceived as constructed by or temporarily inhabiting discourses. Discourses in effect speak through people. Human agency seems to have no role in constituting or reproducing culture and society. The key problem with this formulation is the inability to show how cultures emerge and how they change. It is as if the 'first' play or book ever written involved only the 'speaking' of pre-existing discourses. We ask where did the discourses come from, how do they change and how do they relate to experience and the development of social interests? Fourth is the evacuation of notions of material and ideal interests and power to be replaced with words such as 'choice' and 'activity' or with cultural essentialist terms such as 'the other'. Fifth is the problem of outcomes. There is a deafening silence in media and cultural studies about the consequences of popular culture and the media. We mean this both in the more familiar sense of consequences in terms of public belief and also, more fundamentally, in the sense of the consequences in terms of the distribution of power and resources and the reproduction or transformation of cultures and societies. Sixth and finally is the consequent problem of politics. Much of this work leads out of politics altogether and certainly out of progressive politics. If the point is to change the world, then such work is pointless.

## Obfuscation and abstraction

There are other reasons why much of social science including media and communications studies has been unable to address or interest wider public audiences. The inability to write clearly in accessible language has frequently been commented on – from C. Wright Mills (1959) to more recent criticisms by Todd Gitlin (1991). We accept that there are some issues which are intrinsically difficult and which require complex reasoning. Nonetheless it does seem that academics in common with other professional groups can retreat without good reason into private languages. These are used to secure the status of the author and perhaps disguise the slightness of their contribution to public debate. As Gitlin comments:

> One thing that has rent theory and criticism asunder is the self-insulation of professional social science. And no factor has contributed to that self-insulation more than the quality, if that is the right word, of academic writing. Which raises the question of why academics write routinely, hermetically, in clotted prose, ridden with jargon and the passive voice, even enthusiastically crossing the line from complexity to obscurity. (1991, p. 329)

Peter Golding has also pointed to the twin problems in media research of under-theorization and over-theoreticization. By the first he means mindless description and calibration and the 'endless landscale of meaningless numerical data'. For the second he refers to the problems we have already raised – the construction of theory divorced from the real problems of a real world:

> On the other hand, we find the threat of over-theoreticisation, turning our backs on the real problems of a real world in the mistaken belief that they are trivial. It does not help any cause to attempt the legitimation of our field by constructing an impenetrable architecture of grandiose constructs totally detached from the material reality which is our object of study. (Golding, 1994, p. 15)

The everyday practice of academic work often consists of developing theories about theories or discussing how models relate to other models. Whole literatures are spawned on the conceptual formations of past great theorists and where later work is situated in relation to these. Such academic practice on the nuances of models and theories can proceed without reference to why any of it matters in relation to real activity in the world.

## What can be done

We have already noted that research and academic work is driven not by a natural progress of ideas but by socially derived interests. There are four groups of such interests to which we can point. In our view academics can usefully ask where their own work stands in relation to these. First, there are those of government/state research designed to further the interests of policy. Funding from research councils and other bodies has been increasingly directed to follow such interests. Second we may note commercial research designed for the interests of powerful players in the market and the 'generation of wealth'. The power of the New Right in the 1980s and the attacks on critical disciplines such as sociology and universities in general focused much new research into the first two areas. The production of wealth was put firmly on the research agenda and the media were to be examined as 'competitive industries', 'commercial enterprises' and 'corporate organisations'. The corporations themselves were not slow to see the potential of new perspectives in media research. Global media business was now heroic and worries about ownership and power over audiences were now irrelevant. Andrew Knight, the Executive Chairman of News International, spelt this out in a speech to the Institute of Directors:

> For heavens sake, let's get over our hang-ups over who owns what. The future landscape of the media, means that the perception (and it is only a perception – not a fact) of the mighty media mogul will belong to the past.

As he explained, the viewer is now sovereign:

> I am talking about the life building dynamic of images and information where nobody is a sole provider, because the thinking, articulate emancipated viewer is the only king in his or her sovereign individualist millions. (Knight, 1993, pp. 3–4)

It does not therefore matter if in future all communications are controlled by three or four corporations. We can relax in our armchairs as sovereign individuals enjoying our semiotic democracy. Ownership of course does have its privileges. Mr Knight wrote his speech before *The Sun* (owned by News International) was told to change its political support for the 1997 General Election. As the largest paper in Britain, *The Sun* had previously supported the Scottish National Party in Scotland and the Tories in its English editions. It was now converted to the cause of Tony Blair and Labour. Such support can of course be revoked if governments look like threatening the global success story of media corporations.

## Academic interests and public interests

The third impetus for academic work is that generated from professional interests within a specific discipline. Academics debate with each other and such arguments are often conducted as discussions about the work of past great theorists or as a series of what amounts to fashionable arguments within a particular area – 'the debates' at any given moment. These as we have said tend to spiral off into abstract theorizing and professional languages which only the initiated can follow. Terry Eagleton recently gave what he termed the 'jaundiced'[27] view of the Birmingham Centre for Contemporary Cultural Studies and its relentless championing of all that is chic in theory:

> the Centre for Contemporary Cultural Studies at Birmingham University moved in the Seventies from left-Leavisism to ethnomethodology, flirted half-heartedly with phenomenological sociology, emerged from a brief affair with Levi Straussian structuralism into the glacial grip of Louis Althusser, moved straight through Gramsci to post-Marxism, dived into discourse theory and teetered on the brink of Post-Modernism. (1996a, p. 3)

The fourth area is what we might term public issue research which focuses on the concerns and problems of the wider public. We might include in these problems the consequences of 'popular capitalism' which we have outlined above. Such research must also include the analysis of how public issues are defined as important since it is entirely possible that powerful interests might seek to set the agendas of public concerns. That said, there are a series of questions which a critical social science should address. It should at least evaluate and show the consequences of political and economic policy and should question the accuracy of statements which are developed to justify new policy and social arrangements. It should refute what is false and explore the range of options and policies which can address key social issues. We cannot argue from first principles 'which way' a society ought to go, but it is possible to show the consequences of different forms of social organization. Such critical analysis should be developed as far as possible through empirical research. All such work presupposes a theoretical understanding of the key elements which compose a society and create movement within it. A critical social science must therefore analyze the key relationships which generate public issues and how these relationships can affect public understanding of the issues and the manner in which they can be resolved. It must analyze the ideological struggles over what is understood to be necessary, possible and desirable. The development of public belief and understanding is thus a central concern for public issue research.

In writing this review it was not our intention to dismiss the whole of media and cultural studies. Some important work has been done, but it is our view that much in these areas and much else in social science has drifted towards irrelevance. At the beginning of this report we noted that in the late 1970s ideology was a major concern for critical media studies. Stuart Hall referred to it in a major essay as the 'return of the repressed' (1982). We can compare that with the content of the most recent Open University course on 'Culture, Media and Identities' which is accompanied by six textbooks of which Hall is series editor (du Gay *et al.*, 1997; Hall, 1997b; Woodward, 1997; du Gay, 1997; Mackay, 1997; Thompson, 1997). One indication of how much has changed in media and cultural studies is that class and ideology do not feature as the subject of a single chapter in any of these books, nor is there any discussion of government information management, the production of factual or fictional broadcast or press output or even the impact of the media on public beliefs.[28]

We will finish by noting two sets of statistics which highlight the grim nature of the modern world into which academics and the rest of humanity are locked. The first is that the richest ten individuals in the world now have assets greater than the bottom forty-eight countries combined (United Nations, 1997). The second come from three separate reports from international agencies predicting a global ecological crisis within fifty years, threatening the lives of literally billions of people. They show that three billion people would be severely short of water. The reports were published in January 1997 and were reported on page 4 of the *Guardian* (28 January 1997). On the *front* page of the paper and that of most of the national press was a story about a man in red braces resigning from Channel Four Television. Would contemporary media and cultural studies even notice such a juxtaposition, see its significance or write about it?

Our point is that a large part of humanity is being obliterated by the social, material and cultural relationships which form our world. It can be painful and perhaps professionally damaging to look at such issues and to ask critical questions about social outcomes and power or about the truth of what politicians say or the media report. It is perhaps easier to focus on consumption, pleasure and cultural fashion, discussed in impenetrable private debates. But for academics to look away from the forces which limit and damage the lives of so many, gives at best an inadequate social science and at worst is an intellectual treason – just fiddling while the world burns.

## Notes

1 Now Democratic Republic of Congo.
2 A very extensive study undertaken by the University of Manchester Institute of Science and Technology found that one in four employees were subject to bullying, the highest incidence in Europe. The study linked this to the growth of long hours, job insecurity and the effects of 'downsizing' on workloads (*Guardian*, 15 February 2000, p. 7).
3 Such a separation is suggested by post-modern theorists as well as by some liberal sociologists (e.g. Abercrombie, 1996; Abercrombie *et al.*, 1980, 1986, 1990). For a critique of this position see Miller, David (1997).
4 It is sometimes argued that pension funds and insurance companies invest heavily in the stock market and that this ensures a wider formal 'ownership' of capital. There is some truth in this in the sense that these institutions represent a wider body of (mostly middle-class) interests. But these organizations very much follow the logic of the market

in their investment policies – i.e. the search for profit with the resultant concentration of resources and power of the corporations in which they invest.

5 It is interesting that even the public media in Britain can now assume that what the world needs is Thatcherism mixed with Tony Blair. The Social Democracies of Europe are the main forces standing against the effects of the unfettered capitalist market. Yet in a report on the German economy a BBC journalist commented without qualification that:

> The Germans pay themselves too much in work and too much out of it in benefits and pensions – they are living beyond their means . . . Schroeder's (the German Social Democratic Chancellor) core supporters are rather old Labour – they want the rich to pay . . . the fact is that Germany has not been down the sober road of economic re-structuring. Mr Schroeder has to be his nation's Mr Blair and Mrs Thatcher rolled into one. (BBC1, 9.00 p.m., 27 September 1999)

In such a statement the views of 'old Labour' come close to being derided and the BBC comes down firmly on the side of economic re-structuring.

6 This is not to say that New Labour policy is identical to that pursued by the Conservatives. It has been argued that their 'ethical foreign policy' has some real substance as for example in the funding of mine clearance and in the moves to cancel Third World debt (though most of this was in practice unrecoverable). In trade, however, Britain has continued the policy of supplying arms to countries such as Indonesia, Saudi Arabia and Turkey (*Observer*, 24 October 1999).

7 Put another way, what is taken to be 'real' can be shown to be produced or constructed through the exchange of meanings (the language and definitions used in specific situations). This perspective has been very important in social science in for example explaining the practice of the legal system and the organization of justice. Aaron Cicourel has shown how definitions of 'guilt' amongst juveniles may owe much to assumptions of what they look like, e.g. to 'body motion, facial expressions, voice intonations'. These provide the basis for some inferences and judgements by police officers, instead perhaps of what we imagine as 'hard evidence' about what was actually done. Cicourel also shows how other offenders who were 'neatly dressed' were processed in a lenient fashion. As he notes, in these cases 'the issue was not to establish guilt but to deliver a "lecture" on the evils of criminal acts' (Cicourel, 1968, p. 124). Such work has important implications in social science. It would mean for example that officially recorded crime rates would be suspect as objective measurements of what has actually occurred. But, as we show, these useful insights have now been overtaken by a move to relativism in the work of some theorists. Reality is seen as a mere effect of language and there is no way of establishing truth by evidence (in a law court or anywhere else).

8 Derrida encounters the same problem in trying to explain his own theories. He argues that language can never express absolutely what is immediate or real, because to work as a system of meaning it must make sense when the speaker is not present or not even alive. The words 'I see' may suggest immediate presence but according to Derrida they also imply the possibility of being understood by other people, elsewhere, perhaps much later (so the words also include the possibility of absence and their meaning is constantly deferred – hence 'différence'). Yet in order to explain this, Derrida has to fall back on the formula of saying what is really happening, in order to distinguish between someone being 'really' present and someone who is not. Thus he writes: 'Let us consider the extreme case of "a statement about perception". Let us suppose that it is produced at the very moment of perceptual intuition: I say "I see a particular person by the window" while I really do see him' (1973, p. 92).

As Raymond Tallis notes, Derrida's assertions are a reformulation of traditional concerns about 'agency' – the view that even in apparently voluntary actions we are not fully the agents of what our actions mean (Tallis, 1988, p. 229). As he suggests: 'Derrida denies that the speaker is present in his speech act – or indeed in any signifying or even significant act – because, like so many philosophers before him, he will accept nothing less than an absolute coincidence between voluntary acts of consciousness and meaning' (1988, p. 227). Tallis effectively derides this view by applying it to analyzing the process of walking. When we walk we are part of a collective culture of walking – with a future and a past (I carry traces of other walks – I may walk like my father). We may forget what we are doing, whilst walking, our intending selves may temporarily absent themselves. But does this mean that when I walk to the pub, I am not intending to do so, or if I arrive somewhere else, I would not notice? (1988, p. 217).

Tallis also argues that the view of reality and meaning as being an effect of language derives from a fundamental misreading of the work of Saussure. He notes for example that Saussure distinguished between 'natural' motivated signs and arbitrary conventional ones. A natural sign might be that clouds indicate rain. The interpretation of this sign depends on experience in the natural world. Such experiences do not owe their meaning to their place in a closed system of language. This is the obvious difference between 'clouds' meaning clouds and clouds meaning rain (1988, p. 85). Tallis also makes the important point that words are produced and used in relation to patterns of reality. So while in the system of language any given word may be arbitrarily assigned, its use is not random. To call a 'dog' by that word is arbitrary, but to say 'that dog is barking' relates to a specific real event. To see language as an entirely closed system thus loses the distinction between langue (the language system) and parole (its use in practice) (1988, p. 76).

9  We are not the only ones to conclude that academics should continue producing academic work. To paraphrase Morley's account of the post-modern philosophical debate: it seems that having decided there is a problem with 'realist epistemologies', the philosophers finally grasp that the only truly post-modern way of dealing with this is by not writing ('graphic silence'; Morley, 1997, p. 132). Since this is not much of an alternative for professional writers, they decide, after millions of words on the deconstruction of texts, on truth as perspective and culturally produced knowledge, that they *will* carry on writing but will henceforth be a bit more self-reflexive and will watch out for rhetoric and metaphors.

10 In February 1998, both the British and US governments made major efforts to argue for a renewed assault on Iraq. They met an ambivalent response. In the US a poll showed only 18 per cent of Americans favouring a limited air strikes policy and 39 per cent wanted continued diplomacy (*Guardian*, 24 February 1998).

11 Morley argues that we have failed 'to recognise currents of cultural studies work which are sceptical of the claims of both postmodernism and relativism' (1998, p. 486). As can be seen from this section, we do explicitly make a distinction between exponents of discursive practice such as Hall and to some extent Morley and the more textualist approach of Hartley and others. However, we are also sceptical of some of the currents which are not post-modernist or (consistently) relativist such as the work of Morley and particularly Hall.

12 In another paper dated a month later in 1973 Hall (1973b) does discuss the fact that differential readings 'arise from the fact that events are interpretable in more than one framework or context: different groups or classes of people will bring different explanatory frameworks to bear, depending on their social position, their interests, place in the hierarchy of power and so on' (1973b, p. 14) In this passage (pp. 13–15) it is clearer that Hall is talking of readings of events and not of texts. Nevertheless, there is a confusion in his work from this which has been resolved in audience research (and in Hall's subsequent work) in favour of the interpretation of texts.

13 This was also the direction in which Hall himself moved as can be seen from an interview (about the encoding/decoding model) given by him in 1989 (Hall, 1994).

14 Morley objects to this description of his work. He writes that we see research on the domestic consumption of television as the 'sad and mistaken' result of the 'long journey from the (apparently now halcyon) days of the encoding/decoding model' (p. 487). But we do not see the encoding/decoding model in such positive terms. Indeed, as we argue above, we see some of the problems of audience research and its flight from both the real and the text as originating in the model.

Morley goes on to argue that 'the whole point of my own research into the domestic context of reception was not to "abandon" questions of media power, textuality (or indeed ideology) but rather to complement that perspective on the "vertical" dimension of media power, with a simultaneous address to its "horizontal"/ritual dimension' (1998, p. 487). It may well be that case that Morley did not intend to abandon questions of media power and ideology, and it may also be the case that we haven't read enough of Morley's work, but we can't find any evidence in any of his audience work from 1986 onwards of an engagement with such questions, except to minimize their importance.

15 Seaman (1992) makes a similar argument in relation to work on the social uses of television in his critique of the 'active audience'.

16 'a set of generally available artefacts: films, records, clothes, TV programmes, modes of transport, etc.' as Hebdige (1988) puts it. The popular, then, is determined by virtue of market research techniques which the same theorists otherwise deride as being simply discourses (Ang, 1991). This concentration on the products of consumer capitalism as coterminous with popular culture is widespread. It is endorsed by Strinati (1995) and appears to inform the new Open University course on 'Culture, media and identities'. There it is the production of meanings associated with the Sony Walkman which is the focus of cultural analysis (du Gay *et al.*, 1997).

17 In some analyses the pleasures of media consumption are assumed to be equally available to all. But there are some more sophisticated versions which discuss choice and pleasure in popular culture in terms of cultural competence, drawing on the work of Bourdieu (1984). Bourdieu's influential work on class hierarchies in cultural tastes focused on the process whereby members of the middle class became 'educated' into 'appreciating' high culture. Taste in Bourdieu's analysis was a marker for class. Contemporary audience theorists have adapted this work and argued that rather than middle-class people having a monopoly on cultural 'competence' it was preferable to see people as simply having different competences (e.g. Brunsdon, 1981; Hobson, 1982; see also Moores, 1997). Thus 'the competences necessary for reading soap opera are most likely to have been acquired by those persons culturally constructed through discourses of femininity, the competences necessary for reading current affairs television are most likely to have been acquired by those persons culturally constructed through discourses of masculinity' (Morley, 1992, p. 129). In this type of argument competence is equated with pleasure and choice. People like and choose what they can understand, as if whatever people can understand will immediately be what they like. This seems to exclude the possibility that people make judgements about what they like. Such judgements are likely to betray all sorts of traces of cultural contexts and processes of socialization, but we cannot explain public tastes and choices by saying that people cannot understand what they don't like and don't like what they cannot understand. It is perfectly possible to 'understand' the work of artists such as Damien Hirst, for example (or even the work of writers such as Baudrillard or Lyotard), but to judge it pretentious and irrelevant (and in the latter case, also inaccurate and obfuscatory). On the basis of the notion of cultural competence we would have to agree with Conservative spin doctors that the Conservative Party was rejected at the 1997 election because people didn't understand them, rather than because they made judgements on their record and policies.

18 An example of the problems of working with a contradictory notion like this can be found in the work of Ang. As we have seen above she has argued that audiences actively

make meaning and resist the meanings promoted by the media. Yet she also subscribes to a 'post-structuralist' theory of subjectivity which she describes as follows:

> subjectivity is not the essence or the source from which the individual acts, thinks and feels; on the contrary . . . it is through the meaning systems or discourses circulating in society and culture that discourse is constituted and individual identities are formed. Each individual is the site of a multiplicity of subject positions proposed to her by the discourse with which she is confronted; her identity is the precarious and contradictory result of the specific set of subject positions she inhabits at any moment in history. (Ang, 1996, p. 93)

Defending herself against the criticism that the notion of the active audience implies at best a weak notion of media power, Ang argues that on the contrary the proliferation of broadcast media channels means that 'active choices' are now the key way in which the media exert power over audiences:

> the figure of the 'active audience' has nothing to do with 'resistance', but everything to do with incorporation: the imperative of choice *interpellates* the audience as 'active'! (Ang, 1996, p. 12)

Here Ang attempts to use the discursive notion of the subject to defend the 'active audience'. There is a sense here in which we don't make choices, but choices make us. If so, then Ang's arguments about resisting media meanings, or the creative seeking of pleasure, immediately collapse under the heavy determination of discourse. In the post-structuralist account the concept of agency (if it figures at all) is rendered devoid of any manifestation of human deliberation and decision making. Joan Scott insists that 'subjects do have agency' but their 'agency is created through situations and statuses conferred on them . . . Subjects are constituted discursively' (1991, p. 793). Human agency in other words is an effect of discourse and the choices we make are entirely confined within the range of meanings 'proposed to us' by discourse. This is agency without an agent.

19  Such approaches can be found fairly widely in cultural studies. See for example Ros Brunt's argument athat sex is 'socially and culturally constructed' (1988). See also Laclau and Mouffe's (1985) account that political and class identities are discursively constructed. As Epstein writes:

> [Laclau and Mouffe] argue that all political identities or perspectives are constructed, that there is no particular relation between class position, for instance, and political stance. In support of this, they argue that workers are not automatically socialist or even progressive: often they support right-wing politics. Laclau and Mouffe are of course correct that there is no automatic connection between class and politics, or between the working class and socialism, but this does not mean that there is no connection between the two, that all interpretations or constructions of class interest are equally possible and equally valid. (Epstein, 1997)

20  According to Butler 'it is important to distinguish performance from performativity: the former presumes a subject, but the latter contests the very notion of a subject' (1997, p. 235).

21  Subjects are seen as effects of discourse. To imagine otherwise is to pose what Spivak (1987) in her 'pretentiously opaque' (Eagleton, 1999) style describes as a 'metalepsis':

> that which seems to operate as a subject may be part of an immense discontinuous network . . . of strands that may be termed politics, ideology, economics, history, sexuality, language, and so on . . . Different knottings and configurations of these strands, determined by heterogeneous determinations which are themselves dependent upon myriad circumstances produce the effect of an operating subject. Yet the continuist and homogenist deliberative consciousness symptomatically requires a continuous and homogenous cause for this effect and thus posits a sovereign determining subject. This latter is, then, the effect of an effect, and its positing a metalepsis, or the substitution of an effect for a cause.

If we suspend the critical faculties which come with consciousness and assume for a second that all of this is true, the question remains what happens then? What do people actually do with all the myriad of discourses swirling around in their heads? The problem is that seeing subjects as effects of discourse eradicates decision making and human action from its explanatory framework. This is true even of those approaches (e.g. Hall, 1996, 1997a; Nixon, 1997) which attempt to struggle out of the impasse of the 'decentred subject' by pointing to Foucault's later work on 'technologies of the self' (Foucault, 1988) which describes the 'specific techniques or practices through which subject positions are inhabited' (Nixon, 1997, p. 322). The problem remains that none of these technologies is thought to involve matters of human evaluation, will or judgement.

22 Scott also writes: 'what could be truer, after all, than a subject's own account of what he or she has lived through? It is precisely this kind of appeal to experience as uncontestable evidence and as an originary point of explanation . . . that weakens the critical thrust of histories of difference' (p. 777).

We are not suggesting that experience provides incontestable access to truth and nor did authors such as E. P. Thompson who are criticized by Scott. Furthermore, the use of the concept of experience does not preclude an examination of the emergence of categories for describing and analyzing the world. These can include categories such as those pertaining to gender or ethnicity or more transient ones such as the emergence of political slogans. The analysis of the creation of such categories can only be meaningfully pursued if we analyze the interaction of the symbolic and the material.

Furthermore, there are some things which are true about the world which cannot be wished away by claiming that experience of the world is only a linguistic event or that use of terminology like observation or seeing is only a metaphor. For example, there are biological differences between men and women. These can be seen as more or less significant or worthy of comment, but they nevertheless exist and can be observed (in the sense of seen, demonstrated – i.e. observation is not (as Butler argues) a metaphor; it is a description which can be more or less accurate). But to say this does not mean (or not necessarily), as Judith Butler (1997, p. 236) has claimed, that the 'social institution of reproduction' is the 'most salient' issue in thinking about gender.

Similarly Scott argues that reclamation histories (in the manner of Sheila Rowbotham's (1973) classic *Hidden from History*) are important strategically in giving the 'lie to hegemonic constructions of social worlds' (1991, p. 776), but they 'weaken the critical thrust of histories of difference' (1991, p. 777):

> Presenting the story in this way excludes, or at least understates the historically variable interrelationship between the meanings 'homosexual' and 'heterosexual'. (p. 778)

The most obvious problem is how does she know that the meanings associated with sexual identity have changed historically if not by proposing a foundationalist basis for history? The most problematic part of the argument though is the way in which taking the experience of the powerless seriously is seen as helping to maintain inequalities of power and resources. Using the concept of experience is to 'naturalise categories such as man, woman, black, white, heterosexual and homosexual by treating them as given characteristics of individuals' (1991, p. 782). As with other post-structuralist theorists the category woman is seen as essentialist and as imposing false unity on the differing interests of women. Scott criticizes Downs' (1993) article 'If "woman" is just an empty category, then why am I afraid to walk alone at night'. Downs argues that women do have certain experiences in common such as fear of male violence. Scott maintains that this fear is 'the effect of a certain feminist discourse' (1993, p. 2). So fear of violence is not to do with women's real concrete experiences of violence but is created and amplified by feminism. In the real world women do face male violence, and this is not altered if any given woman rejects feminism and/or thinks of herself as not being a woman. In this sense, then, identity and subjectivity are not (or not only) effects of discourse.

In the end the activities of real thinking, acting humans are regarded with little more than contempt by the post-structuralists. Their attempts to change the world (and not just the word) are derided as primitive and unsophisticated. It is not only history that needs to be rescued from the 'enormous condescension' (Pickering, 1997, p. 244) of post-structuralism, but hope, agency and indeed humanity.

23 It seems to us that gullibility is not an appropriate description for the thousands of us who by virtue of lack of apparent alternatives (in products, or information) 'choose' falsehoods, myths or products which damage us.

24 Morley (1998, p. 486) takes exception to our argument here. He writes 'Gillespie's failing, in their eyes, is that she does not address either McDonald's low wage policies, or their relation to questions of animal welfare'. Certainly these are important issues, but they were not what Gillespie's study was about. Nor was it what our critique was about. As can be seen we were pre-eminently concerned with the question of outcomes.

25 Favoured concepts in the indexes of books on audiences include consumption, reception, reading. Terms like public opinion, belief, response and influence do not occur (e.g. Ang, 1996; Moores, 1993; Morley, 1992; Seiter *et al.*, 1991; Alasuutari, 1999).

26 For an early example of this see Mandy Merck's (1979) allegedly 'socialist' argument.

27 Eagleton also notes the more 'charitable' version which accepts that 'Hall helped to fashion many of the trends he conformed to. If he had the air of a camp-follower, he had usually pitched a fair bit of the camp himself' (1996a, p. 3).

28 The course work on representation and media functions very largely as a paean to constructionism. There are mentions of criticisms, but each is used to build towards the grander project. There is no mention of realist critics who have sought to demolish the enterprise. (See Eagleton (1996b), Geras (1990), Norris (1993, 1996), Sivanandan (1990) and Tallis (1988).)

Stuart Hall did, of course, produce explicitly political critiques of the New Right and was specifically associated with coining the phrase 'Thatcherism' (Hall and Jacques, 1983) and later with 'New Times' and post-Fordism. In our view, the work on Thatcherism overestimated its ideological/political coherence as well as its success in reforming the machinery of the state and in capturing public opinion. Because Thatcherism had a 'project', it was concluded that the left needed one too. This, it was argued, meant a long and difficult reform of the left on the 'hard road to renewal' (Hall, 1988a). But the results of this in 'New Times' (Hall and Jacques, 1989) and 'post-Fordism' involved the jettisoning of many of the critical analyses of left thought (for critiques see Harris, 1992; Rustin, 1989; Sivanandan, 1990). Indeed the journey from 'New Times' to New Labour has been seen by some commentators as but a short step. As Decca Aitkenhead has written, *Marxism Today* 'fetishised and feted the core essentials of Thatcherism – individualism, the market, private ownership, consumer culture. As the issues progressed, the magazine moved on from flirtation with Thatcherism to a preparation of the ground for Blairism. Almost every fundamental of New Labour can be found in the pages of *Marxism Today*'s back issues. Rights and responsibilities, community and citizenship, love of modernisation, they were all dressed up rather unconvincingly as a "progressive" take on Marxism' (1998).

Hall's political writings shared some of the problems that we have raised with cultural studies. They have the same resigned attitude in relation to the social and material changes brought about by the unleashing of the market in the 1980s. At the same time they were overly optimistic about the new territory for the left opened up by such changes, especially in relation to consumption. There was also the same absence of empirical analysis of social structures and how to change them. In the political advocacy of consumerism and consumer power associated with the 'New Times' project, the key to progressive political change appears to be the radicalizing experience of consumer refusals and boycotts. As Harris writes:

In the advocacy of consumerism, the 'new times' project is seen at its weakest theoretically. It offers a position that regresses to a point before the work of Durkheim and Mill, let alone Althusser and Marx. It seems that in their demoralised flight from serious politics, the Labour Party and the British Communist Party discourage the reading of not only Marxism but even bourgeois sociology and the radical bits of British liberalism. (1992, p. 190)

# References

Abercrombie, N. (1996) *Television and Society*, Cambridge: Polity.

Abercrombie, N., Hill, S. and Turner, B. (1980) *The Dominant Ideology Thesis*, London: Allen and Unwin.

Abercrombie, N., Hill, S. and Turner, B. (1986) *Sovereign Individuals of Capitalism*, London: Allen and Unwin.

Abercrombie, N., Hill, S. and Turner, B. (1990) *Dominant Ideologies*, London: Unwin Hyman.

Ahmad, A. (1992) *In Theory: Classes, Nations, Literature*, London: Verso.

Aitkenhead, D. (1998) 'These aged teenagers at *Marxism Today* guiltily shuffling their feet', *Guardian*, 23 October, http://www.guardianunlimited.co.uk/Archive/Article/0,4273,3785863,00.html

Alasuutari, P. (ed.) (1999) *Rethinking the Media Audience*, London: Sage.

Ang, I. (1985) *Watching Dallas*, London: Routledge.

Ang, I. (1991) *Desperately Seeking the Audience*, London: Routledge.

Ang, I. (1996) *Living Room Wars: Rethinking Media Audiences for a Post-Modern World*, London: Routledge.

Ang, I. and Hermes, J. (1996) 'Gender and/in media consumption', in Curran, J. and Gurevitch, M. (eds) *Mass Media and Society*, 2nd edition, London: Arnold.

Atkinson, D. (1999) 'The pie in the sky nightmare', *Guardian*, 4 February.

Atkinson, D. and Elliott, L. (1998) 'Anxious?, Insecure? You'll get used to it', *Guardian*, 6 June: 9.

Barthes, R. (1975) *The Pleasure of the Text*, New York: Hill and Wang.

Baudrillard, J. (1988) *Selected Writings*, Cambridge: Polity Press.

Baudrillard, J. (1994) 'The masses', in *The Polity Reader in Cultural Theory*, Cambridge: Polity Press.

Baudrillard, J. (1995) *The Gulf War Did Not Take Place*, Sydney: Tower Publications.

Bauman, Z. (1992) *Intimations of Post-Modernity*, London: Routledge.

Berger, J. (1975) *Ways of Seeing (Advertising)*, London: BBC Enterprises.

Bocock, R. (1993) *Consumption*, London: Routledge.

Bourdieu, P. (1984) *Distinction*, London: Routledge.

Bower, T. (1991) *Maxwell*, London: Mandarin.

Brewer, J. and Porter, R. (1993) *Consumption and the World of Goods*, London: Routledge.

Brunsdon, C. (1981) '*Crossroads*: notes on a soap opera', *Screen*, 22(4) 32–7.

Brunsdon, C. and Morley, D. (1978) *Everyday Television: 'Nationwide'*, London: BFI.

Brunt, R. (1988) 'Bones in the Corset', *Marxism Today*, October.

Burchill, J. (1997) 'Death of innocence', *Guardian G2*, 12 November, pp. 2–3.

Burrows, R. (1997) *Contemporary Patterns of Residential Mobility in Relation to Social Housing in England*, York: University of York Centre for Housing Policy.

Burton, J. (1999) Report of Social Market Foundation, *Guardian*, 5 July.

Butler, J. (1990) *Gender Trouble: Feminism and the Subversion of Identity*, New York: Routledge.

Butler, J. (1993) *Bodies That Matter: On the Discursive Limits of 'Sex'*, New York: Routledge.

Butler, J. (1997) ' "Gender as performance: an interview with Judith Butler" by Peter Osborne and Lynne Segal for *Radical Philosophy*', in Woodward, K. (ed.) *Identity and Difference*, London: Sage in association with the Open University.

Calhoun, C. (1994) 'Social theory and the politics of identity', in Calhoun, C. (ed.) *Social Theory and the Politics of Identity*, Cambridge: Blackwell.

Cameron, D. and Fraser, E. (1987) *The Lust to Kill*, Oxford: Polity.

Campbell, B. (1986) *Unofficial Secrets*, London: Virago.

Campbell, B. (1987) *The Iron Ladies: Why Do Women Vote Tory?*, London: Virago.

Campbell, B. (1993) *Goliath – Britain's Dangerous Places*, London: Methuen.

Campbell, C. (1995) 'The sociology of consumption', in Miller, D. (ed.) *Acknowledging Consumption*, London: Routledge.

Campbell, D. and Connor, S. (1986) *On the Record: Computers, Surveillance and Privacy*, London: Michael Joseph

Cannon, G. (1992) *Food and Health: the Experts Agree*, London: Consumer's Association.

Cassidy, J. (1997) *The New Yorker*, reprinted in *Independent on Sunday*, 7 December 1997, p. 13.

Central Statistical Office (1992) *Economic Trends*, February, London: HMSO.

Certeau, M., de (1984) *The Practice of Everyday Life*, Berkeley, CA: University of California Press.

Chippendale, P. and Franks, S. (1991) *Dished: The Rise and Fall of British Satellite Broadcasting*, London: Simon and Schuster.

Chippendale, P. and Horrie, C. (1990) *Stick it Up Your Punter: the Rise and Fall of the Sun*, London: Heinemann.

Chomsky, N. (1999) *Profit over People: Neoliberalism and Global Order*, New York: Seven Stories Press.

Cicourel, A. (1968) *The Social Organisation of Juvenile Justice*, New York: John Wiley and Sons.

Cockburn, C. (1992) 'The circuit of technology: gender, identity and power', in Silverstone, R. and Hirsch, E. (eds) *Consuming Technologies: Media and Information in Domestic Spaces*, London: Routledge.

Cockerell, M. (1989) *Live from Number 10*, (2nd edn) London: Faber.

Cockerell, M., Hennessy, P. and Walker, D. (1984) *Sources Close to the Prime Minister*, Basingstoke: Macmillan

Corner, J. (1991) 'Meaning, genre and context: the problematics of public knowledge in the new audience studies', in Curran, J. and Gurevitch, M. (eds) *Mass Media and Society*, London: Edward Arnold.

Cox, R. (1997) 'Domestic servants', paper for the *Royal Geographical Society Conference*, Exeter University, January.

Curran, J. (1990) 'The new revisionism in mass communications research: a reappraisal', *European Journal of Communication*, 5(2/3): 135–64.

Curran, J. and Gurevitch, M. (eds) (1991) *Mass Media and Society*, London: Edward Arnold.

Curran, J., Gurevitch, M. and Woollacott, J. (eds) (1977) *Mass Communications and Society*, London: Edward Arnold.

Curran, J., Morley, D. and Walkerdine, V. (eds) (1995) *Cultural Studies and Communications*, London: Edward Arnold.

Davies, N. (1999b) 'The fatal flaw at the heart of our education system', *Guardian*, 14 September.

Davies, N. (1999a) 'How a Tory political group bred educational disaster', *Guardian*, 16 September.

Derrida, J. (1973) 'Speech and phenomena: introduction to the problem of signs in Husserl's phenomenology', in *Speech and Phenomena on Husserl's Theory of Signs* (translated Allison), Northwestern University Press.

Dibb, S. (1993) *Children: Advertisers' Dream, Nutrition Nightmare?*, London: National Food Alliance

Dougary, G. (1994) *The Executive Tart and Other Myths*, London: Virago.

Downs, L. L. (1993) 'If "woman" is just an empty category, then why am I afraid to walk alone at night', *Comparative Studies in Society and History*, 35(2): p. 414–37.

Eagleton, T. (1996a) 'The Hippest', *London Review of Books*, 7 March, pp. 4–5.

Eagleton, T. (1996b) *The Illusions of Postmodernism*, Oxford: Blackwell.

Eagleton, T. (1999) ' "In the Gaudy supermarket", review of *A Critique of Post-Colonial Reason: Toward a History of the Vanishing Present* by Gayatri Spivak, Harvard', *London Review of Books*, 21(10), 31 May, http://www.lrb.co.uk/review.htm.

Edwards, D., Ashmore, M. and Potter, J. (1992) 'Death and furniture; the rhetoric, politics and theology of bottomline arguments against relativism', paper at the 15th Discourse and Reflexivity Workshop, Loughborough University.

Elliott, L. and Atkinson, D. (1998) *The Age of Insecurity*, London: Verso.

Epstein, B. (1997) 'Postmodernism and the Left', *New Politics*, 6(2) (new series), whole No. 22, Winter, http://www.wilpaterson.edu/~newpol/issue22/epstei22.htm.

Ewing, K. and Gearty, C. (1990) *Freedom under Thatcher: Civil Liberties in Modern Britain*, Oxford: Clarendon.

Featherstone, M. (1991) *Consumer Culture and Postmodernism*, London: Sage.

Ferguson, M. and Golding, P. (1997) 'Preface', in Ferguson, M. and Golding, P. (eds) *Cultural Studies in Question*, London: Sage.

Fine, B. (1995) 'From political economy to consumption', in Miller, D. (ed.) *Acknowledging Consumption*, London: Routledge.

Fine, B. and Leopold, E. (1993) *The World of Consumption*, London: Routledge.

Fine, B., Heasman, M. and Wright, J. (1996) *Consumption in the Age of Affluence: the World of Food*, London: Routledge.

Fiske, J. (1989a) *Understanding Popular Culture*, London: Unwin Hyman.

Fiske, J. (1989b) *Reading the Popular*, London: Unwin Hyman.

Fiske, J. (1993) *Power Plays, Power Works*, London: Verso.

Fiske, J. (1996) 'Post-modernism and television', in Curran, J. and Gurevitch, M. (eds) *Mass Media and Society*, 2nd edition, London: Arnold.

Foot, P. (1990) *Who Framed Colin Wallace?*, Basingstoke: Macmillan.

Foucault, M. (1988) 'Technologies of the self', in Martin, L., Gutman, H. and Hutton, P. (eds) *Technologies of the Self: a Seminar with Michel Foucault*, Amherst, MA: University of Massachusetts Press.

Franklin, B. (1994) *Packaging Politics*, London: Arnold.

Fraser, N. (1981) 'Foucault on modern power: empirical insights and normative confusions', *Praxis International*, 1(3), October: 272–87.

Furlong, A. and Cartmel, C. (1997) *Young People and Social Change*, Milton Keynes: Open University Press.

Garnham, N. (1990) *Capitalism and Communication*, London: Sage.

du Gay, P. (ed.) (1997) *Production of Culture/Cultures of Production*, London: Sage in association with the Open University.

du Gay, P., Hall, S., Janes, L., Mackay, H. and Negus, K. (eds) (1997) *Doing Cultural Studies: the Story of the Sony Walkman*, London: Sage in association with the Open University.

Geras, N. (1990) *Discourses of Extremity; Radical Ethics and Post-Marxist Extravagances*, London: Verso.

Gillespie, M. (1995) *Television, Ethnicity and Cultural Change*, London: Routledge.

Gilroy, P. (1997) 'Diaspora and the detours of identity', in Woodward, K. (ed.) *Identity and Difference*, London: Sage.

Gitlin, T. (1991) 'The politics of communication and the communication of politics', in Curran, J. and Gurevitch, N. (eds) *Mass Media and Society*, London: Edward Arnold.

Golding, P. (1994) 'Media research and the new communications map', *Nordic Communications Review*, Special Issue No. 1, pp. 7–16.

Gray, A. (1999) 'Audience and reception research in retrospect: the trouble with audiences', in Alasuutari, P. (ed.) *Rethinking the Media Audience*, London: Sage.

Grossberg, L. (1996) 'Identity and cultural studies – is that all there is?', in Hall, S. and du Gay, P. (eds) *Questions of Cultural Identity*, London: Sage.

Habermas, J. (1983) 'Systematically distorted communication', in Mattelart, A. and Siegelaub, S. (eds) *Communication and Class Struggle*, Volume 1, New York: International General.

Hall, S. (1973a) 'Encoding and decoding in the television discourse', paper for the Council of Europe Colloquy on *Training in the Critical Reading of Televisual Language*, Centre for Mass Communications Research, Leicester University, September.

Hall, S. (1973b) 'The "structured communication" of events', paper for Obstacles to Communication Symposium, UNESCO, *University of Birmingham Centre for Contemporary Cultural Studies Stencilled Occasional Papers*, Birmingham: CCCS.

Hall, S. (1974) 'The television discourse: encoding and decoding', *Education and Culture*, 25, Unesco: 8–14.

Hall, S. (1977) 'Culture, the media and the ideological effect', in Curran, J., Gurevitch, M. and Woollacott J. (eds) *Mass Communication and Society*, London: Edward Arnold.

Hall, S. (1980) 'Encoding/decoding', in Hall, S., Hobson, D., Lowe, A. and Willis, P. (eds) *Culture, Media, Language*, London: Hutchinson.

Hall, S. (1982) 'The rediscovery of "ideology": return of the repressed in media studies', in Gurevitch, M., Bennett, T., Curran, J. and Woollacott, J. (eds) *Culture, Society and the Media*, London: Methuen.

Hall, S. (1988a) *The Hard Road to Renewal: Thatcherism and the Crisis of the Left*, London: Verso in association with *Marxism Today*.

Hall, S. (1988b) 'Brave new world', *Marxism Today*, October, pp. 24–9.

Hall, S. (1990) 'Cultural identity and diaspora', in Rutherford, J. (ed.) *Identity: Community, Culture, Difference*, London: Lawrence and Wishart.

Hall, S. (1992) 'New ethnicities', in Donald, J. and Rattansi, A. (eds) *'Race', Culture and Difference*, London: Sage.

Hall, S. (1994) 'Reflections upon the encoding/decoding model: an interview with Stuart Hall', in Cruz, J. and Lewis, J. (eds) *Viewing, Reading, Listening*, Oxford: Westview.

Hall, S. (1996) 'Introduction: who needs "Identity"', in Hall, S. and du Gay, P. (eds) *Questions of Cultural Identity*, London: Sage.

Hall, S. (1997a) 'The work of representation', in Hall, S. (ed.) *Representation: Cultural Representations and Signifying Practices*, London: Sage in association with the Open University.

Hall, S. (ed.) (1997b) *Representation: Cultural Representations and Signifying Practices*, London: Sage in association with the Open University.

Hall, S. and du Gay, P. (eds) (1996) *Questions of Cultural Identity*, London: Sage.

Hall, S. and Jacques, M. (eds) (1983) *The Politics of Thatcherism*, London: Lawrence and Wishart in association with *Marxism Today*.

Hall, S. and Jacques, M. (eds) (1989) *New Times*, London: Lawrence and Wishart.

Hamnett, C. (1997) 'The sleep of reason?', *Environment and Planning D: Society and Space*, 15: 127–8.

Harris, D. (1992) *From Class Struggle to the Politics of Pleasure*, London: Routledge.

Harris, D. (1996) ' "Jargon basement", review of *Male Matters: Masculinity, Anxiety, and the Male Body on the Line*, by Calvin Thomas (University of Illinois Press)', *Bay Area Reporter*, 13 June, p. 40.

Harris, R. (1983) *Gotcha!*, London: Faber.

Harris, R. (1990) *Good and Faithful Servant*, London: Faber.

Hartley, J. (1987) 'Invisible fictions: television audiences, paedocracy and pleasure', *Textual Practice* 1(2): 121–38.

Hartley, J. (1996) *Popular Reality*, London: Routledge.

Hartley, J. (1999) *Uses of Television*, London: Routledge.

Hebdige, D. (1988) *Hiding in the Light: On Images and Things*, London: Routledge.

Herman, E. and Chomsky, N. (1988) *Manufacturing Consent – The Political Economy of the Mass Media*, New York: Pantheon Books.

Herman, E. and McChesney, R. (1997) *Global Media: Missionaries of International Capitalism*, London: Cassell.

Hermes, J. (1995a) 'A perfect fit: feminist media studies', in Buikema, R. and Smelik, A. (eds) *Women's Studies and Culture: a Feminist Introduction*, London: Zed Books.

Hermes, J. (1995b) *Reading Women's Magazines*, Cambridge: Polity.

Hillyard, P. and Percy-Smith, J. (1988) *The Coercive State: the Decline of Democracy in Britain*, London: Collins/Fontana.

Hilton, I. (2000) 'A bitter pill for the world's poor', *Guardian*, 5 January.

HMSO (1993) *General Household Survey*, London: HMSO.

Hobson, D. (1980) 'Housewives and the mass media', in Hall, S., Hobson, D., Lowe, A. and Willis, P. (eds) *Culture, Media, Language*, London: Hutchinson.

Hobson, D. (1982) *Crossroads: Drama of a Soap Opera*, London: Methuen.

Hollingsworth, M. (1991) *MPs for Hire*, London: Bloomsbury.

Hollingsworth, M. (1997) *The Ultimate Spin-Doctor: the Life and Fast Times of Tim Bell*, London: Hodder and Stoughton.

Hollingsworth, M. and Norton-Taylor, R. (1988) *Blacklist: the Inside Story of Political Vetting*, London: Hogarth Press.

Hollingsworth, M. and Tremayne, C. (1989) *The Economic League: the Silent McCarthyism*, London: National Council for Civil Liberties.

Home Office (1997) *The Car Theft Index*, London: The Stationery Office.

Hutton, W. (1995) *The State We're In*, London: Jonathan Cape.

Jones, N. (1986) *Strikes and the Media*, Oxford: Blackwell.

Jones, N. (1995) *Spin Doctors and Soundbites*, London: Cassell.

Keat, R., Whiteley, N. and Abercrombie, N. (eds) (1994) *The Authority of the Consumer*, London: Routledge.

Kerckhoff, A. (1990) *Getting Started: Transitions to Adulthood in Great Britain*, Oxford: Westview Press.

Kinman, G. (1996) *Occupational Stress and Health Among Lecturers Working in Further and Higher Education*, London: NATFHE.

Kirk, N. (1994) 'History, language, ideas and post-modernism: a materialist view', *Social History*, 19(2): 221–40.

Kitzinger, J. (1993) 'Understanding AIDS', in Eldridge, J. (ed.) *Getting the Message*, London: Routledge.

Kitzinger, J. (1999) 'A sociology of media power: key issues in audience research', in Philo, G. (ed.) *Message Received*, London: Longman.

Kitzinger, J. and Kitzinger, C. (1993) ' "Doing it": representations of lesbian sex', in Griffin, G. (ed.) *Outwrite: Lesbianism and Popular Culture*, London: Pluto.

Knight, A. (1993) 'A British success story – an examination of prospects for the UK media', speech to the Institute of Directors Annual Convention, 27 April.

Kohn, M. (1996) *The Race Gallery*, London: Random House.

Laclau, E. and Mouffe, C. (1985) *Hegemony and Socialist Strategy*, London: Verso.

Lapham, L. (1998) *Waiting for the Barbarians*, London, Verso. Excerpt in *Guardian*, 27 December 1997.

Leigh, D. (1980) *The Frontiers of Secrecy*, London: Junction Books.

Leigh, D. and Vulliamy, E. (1996) *Sleaze: the Corruption of Parliament*, London: Fourth Estate.

Lewis, J. (1990) *The Ideological Octopus*, London: Routledge.

Lull, J. (ed.) (1988) *World Families Watch Television*, Newbury Park, CA: Sage.

Lull, J. (1990) *Inside Family Viewing: Ethnographic Research on Television's Audiences*, London: Routledge.

Lull, J. (1995) *Media, Communication, Culture: a Global Approach*, Cambridge: Polity.

Lury, C. (1996) *Consumer Culture*, Cambridge: Polity.

Lyotard, J. (1988) *The Differend: Phrases in Dispute*, Manchester: Manchester University Press.

MacArthur, J. (1993) *Second Front: Censorship and Propaganda in the Gulf War*, Berkeley, CA: University of California Press.

Macintyre, S., Reilly, J., Miller, D. and Eldridge, J. (1998) 'Food choice, food scares and health: the role of the media', in Murcott, A. (ed.) *The Nation's Diet*, London: Addison Wesley Longman.

Mackay, H. (ed.) (1997) *Consumption and Everyday Life*, London: Sage in association with the Open University.

McGuigan, J. (1992) *Cultural Populism*, London: Routledge.

McMahon, M. (1999) 'How Tracy the truant taught me a lesson', *Observer*, 3 October, p. 10.

McRobbie, A. (1997) ' "Bridging the gap": feminism, fashion and consumption', *Feminist Review*, 55: 73–89.

Malik, K. (1996) *The Meaning of Race*, Basingstoke: Macmillan.

Merck, M. (1979) 'Sexism in the media?', in Gardner, C. (ed.) *Media, Politics and Culture: a Socialist View*, Basingstoke: Macmillan.

Miller, Daniel (ed.) (1995a) *Acknowledging Consumption*, London: Routledge.

Miller, Daniel (1995b) 'Consumption as the vanguard of history', in Miller, D. (ed.) *Acknowledging Consumption*, London: Routledge.

Miller, Daniel (1997) 'Consumption and its consequences', in Mackay, H. (ed.) *Consumption and Everyday Life*, London: Sage in association with the Open University.

Miller, David (1994a) *Don't Mention the War: Northern Ireland, Propaganda and the Media*, London: Pluto.

Miller, David (1994b) 'Understanding "Terrorism": US and British audience interpretations of the televised conflict in Ireland', in Aldridge, M. and Hewitt, N. (eds) *Controlling Broadcasting: Access, Policy and Practice in North America and Europe*, Manchester: Manchester University Press.

Miller, David (1995) 'The media and Northern Ireland: censorship, information management and the broadcasting ban', in Philo, G. (ed.) *The Glasgow Media Group Reader*, Volume II, London: Routledge.

Miller, David (1997) 'Dominant ideologies and media power: the case of Northern Ireland', in Kelly, M. and O'Connor, B. (eds) *Media Audiences in Ireland*, Dublin: University College Dublin Press.

Miller, David (1999) 'Risk, science and policy: BSE, definitional struggles, information management and the media', *Social Science and Medicine* special edition 'Science speaks to policy', 49: 1239–55.

Miller, D. and Dinan, W. (2000) 'The rise of the PR industry in Britain 1979–1998', *European Journal of Communication*, 15(1), January, pp. 5–35.

Miller, D., Kitzinger, J., Williams, K. and Beharrell, P. (1998) *The Circuit of Mass Communication: Media Strategies, Representation and Audience Reception in the AIDS Crisis*, London: Sage.

Mills, C. W. (1959) *The Sociological Imagination*, Oxford: Oxford University Press.

Modleski, T. (1991) *Feminism without Women: Culture and Criticism in a 'Postfeminist' Age*, London: Routledge.

Moores, S. (1993) *Interpreting Audiences: the Ethnography of Media Consumption*, London: Sage.

Moores, S. (1997) 'Broadcasting and its audiences', in Mackay, H. (ed.) *Consumption and Everyday Life*, London: Sage in association with the Open University.

Morley D. (1980) *The 'Nationwide' Audience: Structure and Decoding*, London: BFI.

Morley, D. (1981) 'The "Nationwide" audience: a critical postscript', *Screen Education*, 39: 3–14.

Morley, D. (1986) *Family Television*, London: Comedia.

Morley, D. (1992) *Television, Audiences and Cultural Studies*, London: Routledge.

Morley, D. (1995) 'Television: not so much a visual medium, more a visible object', in Jenks, C. (ed.) *Visual Culture*, London: Routledge.

Morley, D. (1996a) 'Post-modernism: the rough guide', in Curran, J. and Gurevitch, N. (eds) *Mass Media and Society*, 2nd edition, Arnold, London.

Morley, D. (1996b) 'Populism, revisionism and the "new" audience research', in Curran, J., Morley, D. and Walkerdine, V. (eds) *Cultural Studies and Communications*, London: Arnold.

Morley, D. (1997) 'Theoretical orthodoxies: textualism, constructivism and the "new ethnography" in cultural studies', in Ferguson, M. and Golding, P. (eds) *Cultural Studies in Question*, London: Sage.

Morley, D. (1998) 'So-called cultural studies: dead-ends and reinvented wheels', *Cultural Studies*, 12(4), October: 476–97.

Morley D. (1999) ' "To boldly go . . .": the "third generation" of reception studies', in Alasuutari, P. (ed.) *Rethinking the Media Audience*, London: Sage.

Morley, D. and Robins, K. (1995) *Spaces of Identity: Global Media, Electronic Landscapes and Cultural Boundaries*, London: Routledge.

Morley, D. and Silverstone, R. (1990) 'Domestic communication', *Media, Culture and Society*, 12(1): 31–56.

Morley, D. and Silverstone, R. (1991) 'Communication and Context: ethnographic perspectives on the media audience', in Jensen, K. B. and Junporshi, N. W. (eds) *A Handbook of Qualitative Methodologies for Mass Communication Research*, London: Routledge.

Nixon, S. (1997) 'Exhibiting masculinity', in Hall, S. (ed.) *Representation: Cultural Representations and Signifying Practices*, London: Sage in association with the Open University.

Norris, C. (1993) *The Truth About Post-Modernism*, Oxford: Blackwell.

Norris, C. (1996) *Reclaiming Truth: Contribution to a Critique of Cultural Relativism*, London: Lawrence and Wishart.

Northam, G. (1990) *Shooting in the Dark: Riot Police in Britain*, London: Faber.

Norton-Taylor, R. (1985) *The Ponting Affair*, London: Cecil Woolf.

Norton-Taylor, R. (1995) *Truth is a Difficult Concept: Inside the Scott Inquiry*, London: Fourth Estate.

Norton-Taylor, R., Lloyd, M. and Cook, S. (1996) *Knee Deep in Dishonour: the Scott Inquiry and its Aftermath*, London: Victor Gollancz.

Palast, G. (1999) 'How the US seized power in Brazil', *Observer*, 7 March, p. 10.

Park Human Resources (1999) 'New universities "treated unfairly" ', *Guardian*, 27 October.

Philo, G. (1990) *Seeing and Believing*, London: Routledge.

Philo, G. (1995a) 'Political advertising and popular belief', in Philo, G. (ed.) *Glasgow Media Group Reader*, Volume II, London: Routledge.

Philo, G. (1995b) 'Television, politics and the rise of the new right', in Philo, G. (ed.) *Glasgow Media Group Reader*, Volume II, London: Routledge.

Philo, G. (ed.) (1996) *Media and Mental Distress*, London: Longman.

Philo, G. (1997) *Children and Film/Video/TV Violence*, Glasgow: Glasgow Media Group.

Philo, G. (ed.) (1999) *Message Received*, Longman, London.

Philo, G. and McLaughlin, G. (1995) 'The British media and the Gulf War', in Philo, G. (ed.) *Glasgow Media Group Reader*, Volume II, London: Routledge.

Pickering, M. (1997) *History, Experience and Cultural Studies*, Basingstoke: Macmillan.

Pilger, J. (1986) *Heroes*, London: Pan.

Pilger, J. (1991) *Distant Voices*, London: Vintage.

Radway, J. (1984) *Reading the Romance: Women, Patriarchy and Popular Literature*, Chapel Hill, NC: University of North Carolina Press.

Robertson, G. and Nicol, A. (1992) *Media Law*, 3rd edition, London: Penguin.

Rowbotham, S. (1973) *Hidden from History: 300 Years of Women's Oppression and the Fight Against It*, London: Pluto Press.

Rustin, M. (1989) 'The politics of post-Fordism and the trouble with "new times"', *New Left Review*, 175: 54–78.

Rutherford, J. (1990) 'A place called home: identity and the cultural politics of difference', in Rutherford, J. (ed.) *Identity*, London: Lawrence and Wishart.

Schlesinger, P., Dobash, R., Dobash, R. and Weaver, K. (1992) *Women Viewing Violence*, London: BFI.

Scott, J. (1991) 'The evidence of experience', *Critical Inquiry*, 17, Summer: 773–97.

Scott, J. (1993) 'The tip of the iceberg', *Comparative Studies in Society and History*, 35: 2.

Seabrook, J. (1997) 'An English exile', in Jack, I. (ed.) *What Happened to Us*, Granta, 56, January.

Seaman, W. (1992) 'Active audience theory: pointless populism', *Media, Culture and Society*, 14(2), April: 301–12.

Sebba, A. (1994) *Battling for News: the Rise of the Woman Reporter*, London: Sceptre.

Seiter, E., Borchers, H., Kreutzner, G. and Warth, E. (eds) (1991) *Remote Control: Television, Audiences and Cultural Power*, London: Routledge.

Segal, L. (1997) 'Sexualities', in Woodward, K. (ed.) *Identity and Difference*, London: Sage in association with the Open University.

Sherrill, R. (1999) ' "The company picnic", review of Mokhiber, R. and Weissman, R. (1999) *Corporate Predators*, Monroe, ME: Common Courage Books', *The Nation*, 28, June: see www.thenation.com/issue/990628/0628 sherrill.sht.

Silverstone, R. (1990) 'Television and everyday life: towards an anthropology of the television audience', in Ferguson, M. (ed.) *Public Communication: The New Imperatives*, London: Sage.

Silverstone, R. (1994) *Television and Everyday Life*, London: Routledge.

Silverstone, R. and Hirsch, E. (eds) (1992) *Consuming Technologies: Media and Information in Domestic Spaces*, London: Routledge.

Sivanandan, A. (1990) *Communities of Resistance: Writings on Black Struggles for Socialism*, London: Verso.

Smith, N. (1996) 'Rethinking sleep', *Environment and Planning D: Society and Space*, 14: 505–6.

Sokal, A. and Bricmont, J. (1998) *Intellectual Impostures: Postmodern Philosophers' Abuse of Science*, London: Profile Books.

Spivak, G. C. (1987) *In Other Worlds: Essays in Cultural Politics*, New York: Routledge and Kegan Paul.

Spivak, G. C. (1999) *A Critique of Post-Colonial Reason: Toward a History of the Vanishing Present*, Boston: Harvard University Press.

Strinati, D. (1995) *An Introduction to Theories of Popular Culture*, London: Routledge.

Tallis, R. (1988) *Not Saussure: a Critique of Post-Saussurean Literary Theory*, Basingstoke: Macmillan.

Teather, D. and Cassy, J. (1999) 'The cyber slickers', *Guardian*, 4 October, G2, pp. 1–4.

Thomson, A. (1991) *Smoke Screen: the Media, the Censors, the Gulf*, Saffron Walden: Laburnham Press.

Thompson, E. P. (1981) 'The politics of theory', in Raphael, S. (ed.) *People's History and Socialist Theory*, London: Routledge and Kegan Paul.

Thompson, K. (ed.) (1997) *Media and Cultural Regulation*, London: Sage in association with the Open University.

United Nations (1997) *Human Development Report*, Oxford: Oxford University Press.

Vidal, J. (1997) *McLibel: Burger Culture on Trial*, Basingstoke: Macmillan.

Walden, G. (1999) *Lucky George*, London: Penguin.

Walford, G. (1986) *Life in Public Schools*, London: Methuen.

Williamson, J. (1986) 'The problems of being popular', *New Socialist*, September, p. 19.

Woodward, K. (ed.) (1997) *Identity and Difference*, London: Sage in association with the Open University.

Yudkin, J. (1986) *Pure, White and Deadly*, London: Penguin.

Zoonen, L., van (1994) *Feminist Media Studies*, London: Sage.

Zoonen, L., van (1996) 'Feminist perspectives on the media', in Curran, J. and Gurevitch, M. (eds) *Mass Media and Society*, London: Arnold.

# Disciplinary dead-ends and alternative theory

# 1

## What is wrong with science and rationality?

NOAM CHOMSKY

The paper that follows was a contribution to a symposium in which six prominent exponents of post-modernist critical theory presented critiques of 'science' and 'rationality', with three responses. Mine was one, though submitted with reluctance, for reasons explained. My response keeps to explicit quotes. The sources are not identified – frankly, because I was not sure that the authors would appreciate personal identification – but can easily be found in the original publication (http://www.zmag.org/ScienceWars/index.htm). Re-reading the response after seven years, and after having read a good deal more of post-modern, post-structuralist critique, I do not see much to add to these comments. The critiques discussed here have not, to my knowledge, been superseded. Later contributions are subject to essentially the same responses, as far as I am aware.

A great deal of extremely valuable work has been done on the history of science and technology, from its earliest origins to the present. This has become a very lively topic of recent scholarship, a welcome development. Much of that work has been concerned to unravel the social and economic forces and the cultural framework in which the efforts to understand the world have proceeded, and the ways these efforts were distorted and sometimes undermined by prejudice, power relations, irrational belief and other harmful factors. Some of this work has proceeded by the norms of traditional scholarship. Some has adopted post-modernist conventions and phraseology, but in no essential way, as far as I can see. To my ear, at least, the effect is, commonly, to add layers of unhelpful complexity and often obscurantism.

As for the effects on activism and engagement in problems of human concern, that is a highly personal and individual matter. People differ, of course, in what motivates and stimulates them. Perhaps some are inspired by abandonment of the long and hard intellectual and moral struggle to comprehend the world in its various aspects, including the human mental and social world. It is hard for me to see how that course will advance human concerns. And with the best of will, I cannot perceive that any new directions have been proposed within the post-modern framework, or new ways of undertaking the traditional enterprise in a constructive way, or new and more promising alternatives that should be pursued. What was presented in the symposium seems to me a fair sample of the new ideas and approaches that are recommended, often hailed, but without explanation or justification that I can understand. What I have seen, all too often, is that people are being deprived of valuable modes of understanding and insight that they badly need, and that crucial questions about how the world works and how it might be changed are avoided, even ridiculed. While left intellectuals discourse polysyllabically to one another, truths that were once understood are forgotten, history is reshaped into an instrument of power, the ground is laid for the institution of more efficient modes of domination and control, potential activism is diverted and suffering people are effectively abandoned and disempowered.

Perhaps too harsh a judgement, perhaps one based on ignorance or failure to understand. I hope so. But I think it is a judgement that should not be too casually dismissed.

## Rationality/science – from *Z Papers* special issue

This discussion involves people with a large range of shared aspirations and commitments; in some cases at least, friends who have worked and struggled together for many years. I hope, then, that I can be quite frank. And personal, since to be honest, I don't see much of independent substance to discuss. I don't want to mislead, and therefore should say, at once, that I am not all sure that I am taking part in the discussion. I think I understand some of what is said in the six papers, and agree with much of it. What I don't understand is the topic: the legitimacy of 'rationality', 'science', and 'logic' (perhaps modified by 'Western') – call the amalgam 'rational inquiry', for brevity. I read the papers hoping for some enlightenment on the matter, but, to quote one contributor, 'my eyes glaze over and thanks, but I just don't want to participate'. When Mike Albert asked me to comment on papers advocating that we abandon or transcend rational inquiry, I refused, and probably would have been wise to keep to that decision. After a good deal of arm-twisting, I will make a few comments, but, frankly, I do not really grasp what the issue is supposed to be.

Many interesting questions have been raised about rational inquiry. There are problems about justification of belief, the status of mathematical truth and of theoretical entities, the use to which rational inquiry is put under particular social and cultural conditions and the way such conditions influence its course, and so on. These, however, are not the kinds of topics we are to address; rather, something about the legitimacy of the entire enterprise. That I find perplexing, for several reasons.

First, to take part in a discussion, one must understand the ground rules. In this case, I don't. In particular, I don't know the answers to such elementary questions as these. Are conclusions to be consistent with premises (maybe even follow from them)? Do facts matter? Or can we string together thoughts as we like, calling it an 'argument', and make facts up as we please, taking one story to be as good as another? There are certain familiar ground rules: those of rational inquiry. They are by no means entirely clear, and there have been interesting efforts to criticize and clarify them; but we have enough of a grasp to proceed over a broad range. What seems to be under discussion here is whether we should abide by these ground rules at all (trying to improve them as we proceed). If the answer is that we are to abide by them, then the discussion is over: we've implicitly accepted the legitimacy of rational inquiry. If they are to be abandoned, then we cannot proceed until we learn what replaces the commitment to consistency, responsibility to fact, and other out-dated notions. Short of some instruction on this matter, we are reduced to primal screams. I see no hint in the papers here of any new procedures or ideas to replace the old, and therefore remain perplexed.

A second problem has to do with the allusions to 'science', 'rationality', etc., throughout these papers. These targets are sharply criticized, but they are not clearly identified. True, they are assigned certain properties. But these are either irrelevant to the issue raised or unrecognizable to me; in many cases, the properties attributed to rational inquiry are antithetic to it, at least as I have always understood this endeavor.

Perhaps my failure to recognize what is called here 'science', etc., reflects personal limitations. That could well be, but I wonder. For some forty years, I've been actively engaged in what I, and others, regard as rational inquiry (science, mathematics); for almost all of those years, I've been at the very heart of the beast, at MIT. When I attend seminars, read technical papers in my own or other fields and work with students and colleagues, I have no problem in recognizing what is before me as rational inquiry. In contrast, the descriptions presented here scarcely resemble anything in my experience in these areas, or understanding of them. So, there is a second problem.

With regard to the first problem, I'm afraid I see only one way to proceed: by assuming the legitimacy of rational inquiry. Suppose that such properties as consistency and responsibility to fact are old fashioned misconceptions, to be replaced by something different – something to be grasped, perhaps, by intuition that I seem to lack. Then I can only confess my inadequacies and inform the reader in advance of the irrelevance of what follows. I recognize that by accepting the legitimacy of rational inquiry and its canons, I am begging the question; the discussion is over before it starts. That is unfair, no doubt, but the alternative escapes me.

With regard to the second problem, since what is called 'science', etc., is largely unfamiliar to me, let me replace it by 'X', and see whether I understand the argument against X. Let's consider several kinds of properties attributed to X, then turn to the proposals for a new direction; quotes below are from the papers criticizing X.

First category. X is dominated by 'the white male gender'. It is 'limited by cultural, racial and gender biases' and 'establishes and perpetuates social organization [with] hidden political, social and economic purposes'. 'The majority in the South has waited for the last four hundred years for compassionate humane uses of X', which is 'outside and above the democratic process'. X is 'thoroughly embedded in capitalist colonialism' and doesn't 'end racism or disrupt the patriarchy'. X has been invoked by Soviet commissars to bring people to 'embrace regimentation, murderous collectivization, and worse'; though no one mentions it, X has been used by Nazi ideologists for the same ends. X's dominance 'has gone unchallenged'. It has been 'used to create new forms of control mediated through political and economic power'. Ludicrous claims about X have been made by 'state systems' which 'used X for astoundingly destructive purposes . . . to create new forms of control mediated through political and economic power as it emerged in each system'.

Conclusion: there is 'something inherently wrong' with X. We must reject or transcend it, replacing it by something else; and we must instruct poor and suffering people to do likewise. It follows that we must abandon literacy and the arts, which surely satisfy the conditions on X as well as science. More generally, we must take a vow of silence and induce the world's victims to do likewise since language and its use typically have all these properties, facts too well-known to discuss.

Even more obviously, the crafts and technology should be utterly abolished. It is surprising that several of these critiques appear to be lauding the 'practical logical thinking' of 'technologists' who concentrate on 'the mechanics of things', the 'T-knowledge' that is 'embedded in practice' and rooted in 'experience'; that is, the kind of thinking and practice which, notoriously, have been used for millennia to construct tools of destruction and oppression, under the control of the white males who dominate them (I say 'appear to be', because the intent is not entirely clear). The inconsistency is startling, though admittedly, if consistency is to be abandoned or transcended, there is no problem.

Plainly, what I've reviewed can't be the argument; these cannot be the properties of rational inquiry that lead us to abandon (or transcend) it. So let us turn to a second category of properties attributed to X.

X is 'E-knowledge', 'obtained by logical deduction from firmly established first principles'. The statements in X must be 'provable'; X demands 'absolute proofs'. The 'most distinctive component of Western E-knowledge' may be its 'elaborate procedures for arriving at acceptable first principles'. These are among the few attempts here to define or identify the villain.

Furthermore, X 'claims to a monopoly of knowledge'. It thus denies, say, that I know how to tie my shoes, or know that the sky is dark at night or that walking in the woods is enjoyable, or know the names of my children and something about their concerns, etc.; all such aspects of my (intuitive) knowledge are far beyond what can be 'obtained by logical deduction from firmly established first principles', indeed well beyond the reach of rational inquiry now and perhaps ever, and are therefore mere 'superstition, belief, prejudice', according to advocates of X. Or if not denying such knowledge outright, X 'marginalizes and denigrates' it. X postulates dogmatically that 'a predictable end point can be known in advance as an expression of X-achieved truth', and insists upon 'grounding values in [this] objective truth'. It denies the 'provisional and subjective foundations' of agreement in human life and action, and considers itself 'the ultimate organizing principle and source of legitimacy in the modern society', a doctrine to which X assigns 'axiomatic status'. X is 'arrogant' and 'absolutist'. What doesn't fall 'within the terms of its hegemony . . . – anger, desire, pleasure, and pain, for example – becomes a site for disciplinary action'. The varieties of X are presented as 'charms to get us through the dark of a complex world', providing a 'resting place' that offers a 'sure way of "knowing" the world or one's position in it'. The practitioner of X 'screens out feeling, recreating the Other as object to be manipulated', a procedure 'made easier because the subjective is described as irrelevant or un-X'. 'To feel was to be anti-X'. 'By mid twentieth century the phrase "it works" came to be enough for X-ists', who no longer care 'why it worked', and lost interest in 'what its implications' are. And so on.

I quite agree that X should be consigned to the flames. But what that has to do with our topic escapes me, given that these attributions scarcely rise to the level of a caricature of rational inquiry (science, etc.), at least as I'm familiar with it. Take the notion of 'E-knowledge', the sole definition of science presented here. Not even set theory (hence conventional mathematics) satisfies the definition offered. Nothing in the sciences even resembles it. As for 'provability', or 'absolute proofs', the notions are foreign to the natural sciences. They appear in the study of abstract models, which are part of pure mathematics until they are applied in the empirical sciences, at which point we no longer have 'proof'. If 'elaborate procedures', or any general procedures, exist 'for arriving at acceptable first principles', they have been kept a dark mystery.

Science is tentative, exploratory, questioning, largely learned by doing. One of the world's leading physicists was famous for opening his introductory classes by saying that it doesn't matter what we cover, but what we discover, maybe something that will challenge prevailing beliefs if we are fortunate. More advanced work is to a large extent a common enterprise in which students are expected to come up with new ideas, to question and often undermine what they read and are taught, and to somehow pick up, by experience and co-operative inquiry, the trick (which no one begins to comprehend) of discerning important problems and possible solutions to them. Furthermore, even in the simplest cases, proposed solutions (theories, large or small) 'outrun empiricism', if by 'empiricism' we mean what can be derived from experience by some procedure; one hardly has to move to Einstein to exhibit that universal trait of rational inquiry.

As for the cited properties of X, they do hold of some aspects of human thought and action: elements of organized religion, areas of the humanities and 'social sciences' where understanding and insight are thin and it is therefore easier to get away with dogmatism and falsification, perhaps others. But the sciences, at least as I am familiar with them, are as remote from these descriptions as anything in human life. It is not that scientists are inherently more honest, open or questioning. It is simply that nature and logic impose a harsh discipline: in many domains, one can spin fanciful tales with impunity or keep to the most boring clerical work (sometimes called 'scholarship'); in the sciences, your tales will be refuted and you will be left behind by students who want to understand something about the world, not satisfied to let such matters be 'someone else's concern'. Furthermore, all of this seems to be the merest truism.

Other properties are attributed to X, including some that are presumably intended as caricature: e.g. that practitioners of X claim 'that seventeenth-century Europe answered all the basic questions of humankind for all times to come . . .'. I've tried to select a fair sample, and apologize if I've failed. As far as I can see, the properties assigned to rational inquiry by the critics fall into two categories. Some hold of human endeavour rather generally and are thus irrelevant to the issue (unless we mean to abandon language, the arts, etc., as well); they clearly reflect the social and cultural conditions that lead to the outcome that is properly deplored. Others do not hold of rational inquiry, indeed are flatly rejected by it; where detected, they would elicit internal critique.

Several writers appear to regard Leninist–Stalinist tyranny as an embodiment of science and rationality. Thus 'the belief in a universal narrative grounded in truth has been undermined by the collapse of political systems that were supposed to [have] produced the New Socialist Man and the New Postcolonial Man'. And the 'state systems' that 'used positive rationality for astoundingly destructive purposes' were guided by 'socialist and capitalist ideologies' – a reference, it appears, to radically anti-socialist (Leninist) and anti-capitalist (state-capitalist) ideologies. Since 'scientific and technological progress were the watchword of socialist and capitalist ideologies', we see that their error and perversity is deep, and we must abandon them, along with any concern for freedom, justice, human rights, democracy and other 'watchwords' of the secular priesthood who have perverted Enlightenment ideals in the interests of the masters.

Some of the commentary is more familiar to me. One contributor calls for 'plural involvement and clear integration in which everyone sits at the table sharing a common consciousness', inspired by 'a moral concept which is linked to social trust and affection in which people tell what they think they see and do and allow the basic data and conclusions to be cross examined by peers and non-peers alike' – not a bad description of many seminars and working groups that I've been fortunate enough to be part of over the years. In these, furthermore, it is taken for granted that 'knowledge is produced, not found, fought for – not given', a sentiment that will be applauded by anyone who has been engaged in the struggle to understand hard questions, as much as to the activists to whom it is addressed.

There is also at least an element of truth in the statement that the natural sciences are 'disembedded from the body, from metaphorical thought, from ethical thought and from the world' – to their credit. Though rational inquiry is rife with metaphor and (uncontroversially) embedded in the world, its intent is to understand, not to construct doctrine that accords with some ethical or other preferences, or that is confused by metaphor. Though scientists are human, and cannot get out of their skins, they certainly, if honest, try to overcome the distortions imposed by 'body' (in particular, human cognitive structures, with their specific properties) as much as possible. Surface appearances and 'natural categories', however central to human life, can mislead, again uncontroversially; we 'see' the sun set and the moon illusion, but we have learned that there is more to it than that.

It is also true that 'Reason separates the "real" or knowable . . . and the "not real"', or at least tries to (without identifying 'real' with 'knowable') – again, to its credit. At least, I know that I try to make this distinction, whether studying questions that are hard, like the origins of human knowledge, or relatively easy, like the sources and character of US foreign policy. In the latter case, for example, I would try, and urge others to try, to separate the real operative factors from the various tales that are spun in the interests of power and privilege. If that is a fault, I plead guilty, and will compound my guilt by urging others to err in the same way.

Keeping to the personal level, I have spent a lot of my life working on questions such as these, using the only methods I know of – those condemned here as 'science', 'rationality', 'logic' and so on. I therefore read the papers with some hope that they would help me 'transcend' these limitations, or perhaps suggest an entirely different course. I'm afraid I was disappointed. Admittedly, that may be my own limitation. Quite regularly, 'my eyes glaze over' when I read polysyllabic discourse on the themes of post-structuralism and postmodernism; what I understand is largely truism or error, but that is only a fraction of the total word count. True, there are lots of other things I don't understand: the articles in the current issues of math and physics journals, for example. But there is a difference. In the latter case, I know how to get to understand them, and have done so, in cases of particular interest to me; and I also know that people in these fields can explain the contents to me at my level, so that I can gain what (partial) understanding I may want. In contrast, no one seems to be able to explain to me why the latest post-this-and-that is (for the most part) other than truism, error or gibberish, and I do not know how to proceed. Perhaps the explanation lies in some personal inadequacy, like tone-deafness. Or there may be other reasons. The question is not strictly relevant here, and I won't pursue it. Continuing with my personal quest for help in dealing with problems to which I have devoted a large part of my life, I read here that I should recognize that 'there are limits to what we know' (something I've been arguing, in accord with an ancient rationalist tradition, for many years). I should advance beyond 'panopticized rationality' (which I might happily do, if I knew what it was) and should not be 'transferring God into knowable nature' (thanks). Since 'it is now obvious' that its 'very narrow and surface idea of rationality and rationalism' has undermined 'the canon of Western thought', I should adopt 'a new notation system which laid out moral and historical propositions' in a 'rationality [that is] deepened' (thanks again). I should keep to 'rebuttable axioms', which means, I take it, hypotheses that are taken to be open to question – the practice adopted without a second thought in all scientific work, unless the intent is that I should drop *Modus Ponens* and the axioms of arithmetic; apparently so, since I am also to abandon 'absolutism or absolute proofs', which are unknown in science but, admittedly, sometimes assumed with regard to the most elementary parts of logic and arithmetic (a matter also subject to much internal controversy in foundational inquiries).

I should also follow the lead of those who 'assert that there is a common consciousness of all thought and matter', from human to 'vegetable or mineral', a proposal that should impinge directly on my own attempts for many years to understand what Hume called 'the secret springs and origins, by which the human mind is actuated in its operations' – or might, if I had the slightest idea what it means. I am also enjoined to reject the idea that 'numbers are outside of human history' and to regard Gödel's incompleteness theorem as 'a situation of inability' of the twentieth century, which to my old fashioned ear sounds like saying that the irrationality of the square root of two – a disturbing discovery at the time – was 'a situation of inability' of classical Greece. How human history or the way rationality 'is presently defined' impinge on these truths (or so I thought them to be), I again fail to see. I should regard 'Truth' not 'as an essence' but 'as a social heuristic', one 'predicated on intersubjective trust and story telling whether through narrative or numbers and signs'. I should recognize that 'scientific endeavor is also in the world of story and myth creation', no better or worse than other 'stories and myths'; modern physics may 'have more funding and better PR' than astrology, but is otherwise on a par. That suggestion does in fact help solve my problems. If I can just tell stories about the questions that I've been struggling with for many years, life will indeed be easier; the proposal 'has all the advantages of theft over honest toil', as Bertrand Russell once said in a similar connection.

I should also 'favor particular directions in scientific and social inquiry because of their likely positive social outcomes', thus joining the overwhelming mass of scientists and engineers – though we commonly differ on what are 'positive social outcomes', and no hints are given here as to how that issue is to be resolved. The implication also seems to be that we should abandon 'theories or experiments' favoured 'because of their supposed beauty and elegance', which amounts to saying that we should abandon the effort to understand the mysteries of the world; and by the same logic, presumably, should no longer be deluded by literature, music and the visual arts.

I'm afraid I didn't learn much from these injunctions. And it is hard for me to see how friends and colleagues in the 'non white world' will learn more from the advice given by 'a handful of scientists' who inform them that they should not 'move on the tracks of western science and technology', but should prefer other 'stories' and 'myths' – which ones, we are not told, though astrology is mentioned. They'll find that advice a great help with their problems, and those of the 'non white world' generally. I confess that my personal sympathies lie with the volunteers of Tecnica. In fact, the entire idea of 'white male science' reminds me, I'm afraid, of 'Jewish physics'. Perhaps it is another inadequacy of mine, but when I read a scientific paper, I can't tell whether the author is white or is male. The same is true of discussion of work in class, the office or somewhere else. I rather doubt that the non-white, non-male students, friends, and colleagues with whom I work would be much impressed with the doctrine that their thinking and understanding differ from 'white male science' because of their 'culture or gender and race'. I suspect that 'surprise' would not be quite the proper word for their reaction.

I find it depressing, frankly, to read learned left discourse on science and technology as a white male preserve, and then to walk through the corridors at MIT and see the significant results of the efforts to change that traditional pattern on the part of scientists and engineers, many of them very remote from the understanding of 'positive social outcomes' that we largely share. They have dedicated serious and often successful efforts to overcome traditional exclusiveness and privilege because they tend to agree with Descartes (as I do) that the capacity for understanding in the 'profoundest sciences' and 'high feeling' are a common human attribute, and that those who lack the opportunity to exercise the capacity to inquire, create and understand are missing out on some of life's most wonderful experiences. One contributor condemns this humane belief for labelling others as 'defective'. By the same logic, we should condemn the idea that the capacity to walk is a common human possession over a very broad range.

Acting on the same belief, many scientists, not too long ago, took an active part in the lively working-class culture of the day, seeking to compensate for the class character of the cultural institutions through programmes of workers' education or by writing books on mathematics, science and other topics for the general public. Nor have left intellectuals been alone in such work, by any means. It strikes me as remarkable that their left counterparts today should seek to deprive oppressed people not only of the joys of understanding and insight, but also of tools of emancipation, informing us that the 'project of the Enlightenment' is dead, that we must abandon the 'illusions' of science and rationality – a message that will gladden the hearts of the powerful, delighted to monopolize these instruments for their own use. They will be no less delighted to hear that science (E-knowledge) is intrinsically a 'knowledge system that legitimates the authority of the boss', so that any challenge to such authority is a violation of rationality itself – a radical change from the days when workers' education was considered a means of emancipation and liberation. One recalls the days when the evangelical church taught not-dissimilar lessons to the unruly masses as part of what E. P. Thompson called 'the psychic processes of counter-revolution', as their heirs do today in peasant societies of Central America.

I'm sorry if the conclusion sounds harsh; the question we should consider is whether it is correct. I think it is.

It is particularly striking that these self-destructive tendencies should appear at a time when the overwhelming majority of the population regard the economic system as 'inherently unfair' and want to change it. Through the Reagan years, the public continued its drift towards social democratic ideas, while the shreds of what existed were torn away. Furthermore, belief in the basic moral principles of traditional socialism is surprisingly high: to mention merely one example, almost half the population consider the phrase 'from each according to his ability, to each according to his need' to be such an obvious truth that they attribute it to the US Constitution, a text taken to be akin to Holy Writ. What is more, with Soviet tyranny finally overthrown, one long-standing impediment to the realization of these ideals is now removed. With limited contribution by left intellectuals, large segments of the population have involved themselves in urgent and pressing problems: repression, environmental concerns and much else. The Central America solidarity movements of the 1980s are a dramatic example, with the direct involvement in the lives of the victims that was a novel and remarkable feature of protest and activism. These popular efforts have also led to a good deal of understanding of how the world works, again, with very limited contributions from left intellectuals, if we are to be honest.

Particularly noteworthy is the divergence of popular attitudes from mainstream ideology. After 25 years of unremitting propaganda, including ten years of Reaganism, over 70 per cent of the population still regard the Vietnam war as 'fundamentally wrong and immoral', not a 'mistake'. Days before the US–UK bombing began in the Gulf, the population, by two to one, favoured a negotiated settlement with 'linkage' rather than war. In these and numerous other cases, including domestic affairs and problems, the thoughts are individual and private; people have rarely if ever heard them publicly expressed. In part, that reflects the effectiveness of the system of cultural management; in part, the choices of left intellectuals.

Quite generally, there is a popular basis for addressing the human concerns that have long been part of 'the Enlightenment project'. One element that is lacking is the participation of left intellectuals.

However meritorious motives may be, the abandonment of these endeavours, in my opinion, reflects yet another triumph for the culture of power and privilege, and contributes to it. The same abandonment makes a notable contribution to the endless project of creating a version of history that will serve the reigning institutions. During periods of popular activism, many people are able to discern truths that are concealed by the cultural managers, and to learn a good deal about the world; Indochina and Central America are two striking recent examples. When activism declines, the commissar class, which never falters in its task, regains command. As left intellectuals abandon the field, truths that were once understood fade into individual memories, history is reshaped into an instrument of power, and the ground is laid for the enterprises to come.

The critique of 'science' and 'rationality' has many merits, which I haven't discussed. But as far as I can see, where valid and useful the critique is largely devoted to the perversion of the values of rational inquiry as they are 'wrongly used' in a particular institutional setting. What is presented here as a deeper critique of their nature seems to me based on beliefs about the enterprise and its guiding values that have little basis. No coherent alternative is suggested, as far as I can discern; the reason, perhaps, is that there is none. What is suggested is a path that leads directly to disaster for people who need help – which means everyone, before too long.

Originally published in the *Z Papers*. Now available through *Z Magazines'* website
http://www.znetupdates@tao.ca

# 2

# Life after the Science Wars?

HILARY ROSE

When the Science Wars broke out in the mid-1990s I found the binary choice on offer – roughly speaking strong social constructionism or naive realism – theoretically and politically restrictive. In response I wrote what I thought of as a provocation: 'My enemy's enemy is – only perhaps – my friend' (Rose, 1996). What had happened was that many disciplines and social movements either interested in or engaged in confronting science and technology no longer accepted the automatic superiority of natural scientific knowledge over and above all other kinds of knowledge. Having been part of this struggle first as a socialist and then as a socialist feminist I welcomed this weakening of the authoritarianism of natural science. However, this weakening was hostilely received by the natural scientific elite, for such loss of deference constituted a profound challenge to the hegemony of natural science disourse. Having enjoyed this hegemonic position since the birth of modernity the natural sciences still show rather few signs of making space for other newer discourses. Of course within the Anglophone context the problem is compounded, for the Science Wars are here merely an aggressive re-statement of the old cultural assumption which rumbles away beneath the surface that 'science' equals the natural sciences. Any questioning of this self-evident truth is unthinkable. Concepts of *Wissenschaft* or *Vetanskap* which help hold together the whole of systemic inquiry in other cultural traditions are simply not available in an Anglophone context; in consequence tolerance of epistemological pluralism has here long been more precarious. This is not to say that relations between the natural and the social sciences have been downhill all the way, but that over the last quarter century the issue of epistemological difference has first during the 1970s and then in the 1990s become a matter of noisy cultural and political conflict.

Over time the epistemological conflict has been given a number of dichotomizing names which place realism, plain or critical, on one side, with relativism, social constructionism or nominalism on the other. Some academic disciplines developed a relatively inclusive culture and embraced epistemological diversity. Thus sociology departments in the early days of expansion of the 1960s and 1970s rarely hired intellectual clones, instead making sure they included at least one structuralist Marxist, a phenomenologist, an ethnomethodologist and a number-crunching positivist etc. Although at that historical moment it was seen as inevitable that all, or almost all, would be male and pale, given that social uniformity, epistemological pluralism was permitted. But while such epistemological diversity was possible within some of the social sciences and the humanities, within most of the natural sciences – I exclude theoretical physics for reasons I suggest below – there was a deep consensus arounds both methods and the taken for granted necessity of realism.

Outside academia, though many activists were either students or academics, the new social movements of the late 1960s and beyond addressed cultural as much as economic issues. Where the nature of knowledge is not just theoretically crucial as it was to the academics, but politically crucial as it was to the new social movements, epistemological pluralism was not always available. Inevitably because of the plurality of disciplines attracted to the radical science movement and the fact that it was typically natural science and technology which were the target of criticism, it was here that the latent conflict broke out. In Britain the movement was to become bitterly divided. The activists, a melange of natural and social scientists, had cut their teeth exposing the genocidic effects of the herbicides, fragmentation bombs, CS and nerve gas in the Vietnam War. Against the claims posed by the 'military industrial complex', the activists posed realist counter-claims. Mostly these were based on arguments which turned on the chemical and physical properties of the weapons, but sometimes they entailed collecting data on the injuries suffered by non-combatants. In this spirit I recall making a study of refugees from South to North Vietnam who had been exposed to the chemical sprays and a social survey of the Bogside after a major use of CS gas by the British army.

Children of modernity, but morally outraged by this actually existing science, we sought for explanation. Was science neutral, to be used or abused, as the liberal and old left credo had it, or was science inexorably on capitalism's and imperialism's side? We went back to Marx and Marxism with its economic determinism, then explored the neo-Marxism of the Frankfurt School which added a more cultural dimension. In that search for something rather more inclusive than the raced and gendered proletarian science of old left Marxism, most within the radical science movement came to embrace the US slogan of 'science for the people'. The echo of both Galileo and the democratic impulse of the USA served a radical science movement with its multiple strands rather well.

But it was when the movement turned to domestic issues, above all the question of IQ theory and race, that the epistemological issues broke surface (Pustilnik, 1995, pp. 22–43). While the realists fought the IQ theorists on the grounds of bad and biased science which should and could be exposed as mere racist myth-making, the relativists proposed that 'science is social relations' (Young, 1977). Within a capitalist and racist context the claim that science 'is' rather than the more modest 'is shaped by' (or some other qualifying term), which might leave the field some autonomy beyond raw sociological determinism, precluded the possibility of anti-racist scientists winning the argument against their racist counterparts. Doing radical anti-racist science in a capitalist and racist society was declared to be theoretically impossible this side of revolutionary transformation. Some years later the feminist historian of science Elizabeth Fee (1981) was to make the same arguments in considering the possibility of a feminist science. Within feminism's more pluralistic context, the paper did not cause problems among politically engaged feminist natural scientists.

Yet this ability to see the epistemological mote in the eye of the natural scientist was matched by the usual inability to see the similar beam in the eye of the social theorist seer. For the self-same argument could be deployed against the knowledge claims of the radical historian, whether the neo-Marxist Robert Young or the feminist Fee. For if science is social relations, how come history, as part of *Wissenschaft* or systemic inquiry, escapes the charge? Is not history also social relations? Further, if systematic inquiry is social relations, then radical, socialist, feminist, history or for that matter sociology or economics etc. is an epistemological contradiction. The possibility of any reliable knowledge dissolves in the acid of social relations, for if the argument is pushed to the extreme the possibility of knowing in any non-particularist way is precluded. Arguably that was not what Young intended, as elsewhere he claims he wants to reconconcile internalism with externalism (for a useful summary of his work see Bohlan, 1995), but unquestionably at the time he was read as a thoroughgoing relativist (Rose and Rose, 1979). For the natural scientists on the very public barricades of the race issue, this epistemological stance, for all its intellectual radicalism, had singularly few charms. The IQ critics found themselves facing racist science with an outbreak of relativism on their own side effectively removing the ground on which they stood.

The scientific racism debate within the radical science movement was exacerbated in a very direct way by the appearance of strong social constructionism – of the Edinburgh school. With the black civil rights movement and the anti-racist scientists contesting the resurgence of scientific racism, it was singularly painful to find a fellow sociologist of science drawing on what he described as an interest theory of knowledge, to point out that most of the critical biologists were Marxists (Harwood, 1976, 1977). In a still Cold War context such an observation felt more like old style red-smearing than a theoretical or empirical advance. Another Edinburgh sociologist of science spoke in a radio talk of Jensen, the lead US IQ theorist, as a new Galileo, presumably because he was subject to criticism by anti-racists. While this corresponded exactly to the heroic view the scientific racists held of themselves, it was difficult to see that a handful of academic critics and some angry disruptive students quite added up to the historic punitive capacity of the Catholic Church. Even the interest approach was half-heartedly applied, as a number of germane interests were set to one side. For example most of the biologists in the forefront of the debate (e.g. Lewontin, Gould, Kamin, Rose) were Jewish as well as Marxist while the theorists of the new scientific racism were pale non-Jewish males, who for the most part were reluctant to dissociate themselves from extreme right wing and near-nazi journals' use of their work.

Nonetheless what this precursor to the Science Wars did was to make it clear that both the relativist theses of 'science is social relations' and the strong programme in science worked to explain science away. Within academia perhaps it would have been possible to enjoy the radical boldness of the new theses; in a larger context in which conflicts about good science/bad science were in the eye of the political and cultural storm there was no space for epistemological pluralism. The conflict which anticipated the Science Wars by two decades seems only to have surfaced with such intensity in the UK. In the USA the movement was too big, too amorphous to be split so decisively. In continental Europe structuralist Marxism rather than this new philosophical relativism was the dominant current. Moving on from this 'either/or' binary debate to something closer to 'both/and', was as I indicate better managed in the case of feminist science theory, but is still by no means resolved (Rose, 1994).

## Friends and enemies

These epistemological divisions were to be echoed, albeit in low key, in the mainstream research system in the UK during the 1980s. Then an extreme right wing government initiated a counter-revolution in British economy, culture and society. For example there was an entirely serious political attempt to abolish the Social Science Research Council (SSRC) entirely. The Minister for Education, Sir Keith Joseph, one of Mrs Thatcher's intellectual heavyweights, questioned whether there could be a social science, when the entire field was manifestly totally ideological and in the case of sociology more or less the equivalent to socialism. From our civil service friends we heard (we never entirely knew whether the accounts were apocryphal or true) of the Minister ranting around the corridors of power demanding to know whether his department had managed to sack any socialists/sociologists yet. Social science was for Sir Keith, and indeed a number of highly placed natural scientists, an oxymoron. At best he and a number of elite natural scientists would admit to the possibility of social studies, but not social science. It is not without irony that it was an elite natural scientist, Michael Swann, who, as Principal of Edinburgh University, had insisted that his new unit, set up in the early 1970s (and which came to be the Edinburgh school) was to be called the Unit for the Social Studies of Science. For Swann, and later Joseph, that high-status word 'science' had to be reserved for the hard and, as some of us suspected, boys' stuff.

With some linguistic sensitivity, the SSRC was rebranded as the Economic and Social Research Council. The exercise was quietly given support from colleagues from the natural science and engineering research councils. Some part of this new found solidarity was about making common cause in the face of a clever and energetic Philistine, not simply at the university gate, but in charge.

The 1980s saw other alliances against a common enemy. The terrible scourge of AIDS was met by an alliance across disciplines and across epistemologies and movements. The sheer complexity of the challenge posed by the virus and its transmission, and the profundity of our ignorance of sexual practices, demanded multiple approaches. Looking back to those multi-disciplinary multi-epistemological co-operative meetings, certainly facilitated by generous funding, it is difficult to think of anything more different from the vituperative exchanges of either the radical science movement debate or that of the Science Wars which was to follow. It is true that there still are other smaller inter-disciplinary meetings, typically at the interface between science and health care, which recapture the co-operative quality of the AIDS research meetings in the mid-1980s, but they occur in the interstices of an increasingly divided and competitive research sytem.

Maintaining such co-operative conversations became more difficult as the Conservative 'reforms' of both the higher-education and the research system succeeded in constructing a competitive academic environment. The academy, like much else in the UK, began to look and feel much more like that of the USA. What feelings there had been of being part of an academic community were seriously weakened.

## Changing context; changing understandings

But there were other changes taking place. The unquestioning cultural and political support for science and technology, above all in the form of techno-economism which had been embodied in Harold Wilson's 1964 election campaign slogan of 'the white heat of the scientific and technological revolution', was coming under widespread cultural and political questioning. The risk to the environment from science and technology forced itself into public recognition. Within the UK and more broadly within Europe the lead campaigning groups such as the German Greens, Friends of the Earth and Greenpeace, together with the new environmentalist journalists, constructed an argument which built on the realist wing of the radical science movement. They became thorough-going externalists in that they denounced the external economic and political interests which shaped the dominant narrative of science, and they collaborated with those critical scientists, from the 1950s pioneers such as Rachel Carson, Barry Commoner and Alice Stewart, to today's alternative scientists as providers of a robust counternarrative.

Nowhere were these natural science narratives from above and below more evident than in the struggle over nuclear power and weaponry. After 1945 huge resources had been poured into nuclear research and its military and civil technologies. What had been the physicists' war now became the physicists' peace. They devised science policy, ran it nationally and internationally, and with the enthusiastic support of the political classes, allocated themselves the lion's share of resources. Forty years on, the nuclear dream had faded. The myth of almost free clean energy dissolved into an embarrassing saga of cover-ups and half-truths. Gradually, not least through the work of the low-level radiation biologists, the public learnt of accidents at the power plants, the build up of invisible radioactive pollution and perhaps above all the failure to confront the massive problem of safe waste disposal. The official posture that the civil and military nuclear programmes were distinct was finally relinquished. On matters nuclear, governments and their scientists began to establish what was to become a richly deserved reputation for arrogance, secrecy and dishonesty.

Unsurprisingly these disastrous events gave science and scientists' claim that they alone could speak truth to power a distinct loss of credibility. Increasingly publics, as both quantitative and ethnographic studies showed, had a much more analytic approach to science and scientists (Irwin and Wynne, 1996). Far from seeing science as one undifferentiated cultural whole and inevitably on the side of social progress, they trusted government scientists least, then industrial and academic scientists, while scientists working with environmental groups were typically trusted the most.

By the mid-1980s these widely expressed doubts and criticisms of science were beginning to disturb elite scientists. Was science losing its popularity and, although this was rarely spelt out, would this be politically endorsed by cuts in the science budget? To meet the threat the Royal Society established the Committee on the Public Understanding of Science (COPUS) chaired by the geneticist Walter Bodmer. Bodmer himself was a key figure in the rising profile of the life sciences. Director of the Imperial Cancer Research Fund, present at the birth of the Human Genome Project (HGP) he also served as chair of the international Human Genome Organisation. It was obvious to the leadership of the new genetics that, to enter into the era of big science, popular support was crucial. The HGP set aside some 5 per cent of its huge budget to the consideration of the ethical, legal and social implications of the new genetics. The much-cited Bodmer Report (1985) – *The Public Understanding of Science* (or PUS to give it its unlovely acronym) – took a rather different tack. The report sought to overcome what the scientists saw as the loss of popular support, for which opinion surveys showed little evidence, by proposing that a more scientifically literate public would be more supportive. Armed with this deficit model of the citizen's relationship to science, COPUS set itself to increase scientific and technological literacy. A whole battery of science festivals, hands-on experiences for children, prizes for authors of books which enhance PUS, government-supported science engineering and technology weeks for schoolchildren and research awareness for industry were brought into being.

However, while the Bodmer credo that the increased public understanding of science bred trust and thereby support was a matter of faith, both quantitative and qualitative social science studies pointed and continue to point to the association between increased scientific literacy and increased scepticism about science. The trouble, as the thoughtful Wellcome Report on the public views of cloning concluded, was that a scientifically informed public can be even more critical than an ignorant public (Wellcome Report, 1998).

Despite the presence of the Chair of the ESRC on COPUS in its early days, it was rather clear that social science had had a modest impact on the COPUS credo. There was an occasional nod to the relationships of science and the citizen being a two-way street, but the PUS agenda was chiefly characterized by a continuing commitment to the deficit model, and thus to one-way communication. The job of the public is to listen and learn, then, and only then will we (we the non-natural-scientifically qualified public) get the story right. This belief that there is only one true story and that the natural scientists know it dies hard. In February 1999 during the height of the GMO claims and rebuttals, and in the response to the public debate about the claims of Arpad Pusztai to have found that genetically modified potatoes harmed rats, a group of biologist Fellows of the Royal Society wrote a letter to the *Guardian*. In this they still speak of the need for the public to listen to 'independent' scientists. In their anxiety to dismiss Pusztai's claims they conveniently forgot that the Southwood committee had earlier dismissed the so-called maverick claims of Leeds microbiology professor Lacey that BSE could cross species (subsequently proven right). The experience had not taught any modesty. Further, as a number of commentators have noted, such claims rarely indicate what the scientists are to be 'independent' of. Yet what the savvy citizen knows is that increasingly top UK biologists, own, have shares in or are highly paid consultants to biotechnology firms. Such connections, especially if undeclared, could not unreasonably be argued to make scientists less than 'independent' in any Nolan-like sense of the word.

Nor is this change limited to the commercial opportunities opening up for elite biologists; the political economy of the research system has undergone massive changes. For much of the post-war period, the research system was predominantly funded by the state; today the biggest funder is industry. A new production system of scientific knowledge, whether we like it or not, is now firmly in place. Not only has the funding structure changed but so have the priorities. Nuclear, after its long hegemony, has waned and the fields set to dominate the twenty-first century are biotechnology and informatics. Where nuclear had a close relationship to its funder the state, today biotechnology and its close kin informatics are funded primarily by venture capital. Changing funders, however, offers rather modest prospects for increased transparency and accountability. We have moved from one problem with nuclear because of the demands of national security to a new problem over biotechnology and informatics – the demands of commercial secrecy. In both cases it seems hard to shape the technologies subtly and through democratic accountability; only resistance seems to pay off. International citizen opposition to nuclear power, coupled to near and actual disaster, has made building new nuclear power plants an impossibility in any democratic country, though the nuclearphiles have managed to impose such a project on a post-Chernobyl Ukraine.

## Goodbye Marx – hello Darwin

These radical economic and cultural restructurings have had their counterpart in the terrain of social theory. The immense influence of Marxism in the 1960s was sustained by a political culture in which students' and even workers' movements in the West made alliances with Third World liberation struggles and with the Cultural Revolution. This influence was to wane at different speeds in different countries. Thus in France, Marxism and particularly structuralism were caught in the theoretical and political meltdown with what was experienced as the defeat of the May events. In this context of defeat, numbers of the most deeply politically engaged turned to develop new theory, or to find alternative subordinate non-Marxist currents to continue social struggle informed by radically different epistemologies. Some changed sides altogether and were to become New Right theorists. Post-modernism and post-structuralism were born. Both suffer when their own core arguments are pointed against them. Thus post-modernism's insistence that truth is dead and that we are at the end of grand narrative seeks to persuade us that the first proposition is true and the second proposition is itself a grand narrative.

At this point the usual movement of ideas between intellectuals in not dissimilar contexts becomes mixed with the accounts of systematic institutional change and development. Foucault's influence reached across the Channel in the usual way, incidentally displacing Marxism in at least two hitherto Marxist journals. That one belonged to the Communist Party of Great Britain and the other had CP members on the editorial board was very much a sign of the changing times. In the US influence was not left to chance, and the French post-structuralist and post-modernist leading theorists were systematically imported, with the Modern Language Association as the key staging post. Unlike the Frankfurt School's refugee presence in New York, which did little to influence US cultural life, the French presence was to rapidly permeate the

US humanities. The epistemological shift within philosophy, cultural studies and social theory, most neutrally spoken of as the literary turn, became a hugely influential current. Derrida, Baudrillard and Foucault became the new theoretical gurus. Both post-modernism and post-structuralism were professionalized and depoliticized in this new context and then re-exported to Europe and re-absorbed into the *avant garde* academic and cultural scene, where, though under considerable challenge, they are highly influential today.

Above all it is social and environmental activists who find themselves uncomfortable with this nominalist/relativist wave. What may be absorbing to academic theorists has negative purchase in conflicts in the court room or the political arena. Truth claims still matter when sexual violence or levels of radiation pollution are the stakes. I am painfully conscious that as academic feminists, we have gained access, even advance, within the university, but have theoretically and therefore politically often lost connection with the agonies of women in the world.

Political defeat was less evident to the left in other European countries and the USA so that, although the French inspired theoretical moves which challenged the possibility of any meta-narrative-weakened Marxism, in Germany, North America and Britain, it remained a significant cultural and political current into the eighties. Some such as the Canadian sociologist Dorothy Smith sought get the best of both approaches by fusing ethnomethodology – which could be read as a precursor to post-structuralism – with Marxism in a typically feminist 'both/and' move (Smith, 1988).

However, the *coup de grâce* for Marxism was unquestionably the collapse of the Soviet system in 1989. This made little intuitive sense to new leftists, as the Soviet system was seen as having rather little to do with socialism and in consequence its collapse should have helped, not hindered. With Marxism either dead or just resting, and the leading post-structuralist and post-modernist theorists retreating from social engagement behind a barricade of arcane and obscurantist prose, the popular cultural space was left open, to be filled with a resurgence of biological determinism. The economic determinism of Marx with its optimistic if qualified space for human intervention has been replaced by a widespread genetic determinism with the great biologist Darwin as its legitimator. The Human Genome Project has fostered a profound geneticization of culture. The new genetics claims to explain not only physiological but behavioural difference including any and everything from homosexuality, IQ, schizophrenia, to criminality and even homelessness. In setting itself up to causally explain phenomena, which decontextualized, have little meaning, the new molecular biology sustained the biologizing turn of both sociobiology and the new evolutionary psychology. While sociobiology removed human agency by making genes determinant, evolutionary psychology sought to explain human nature in that struggle for existence of our Pleistocene forbears, concluding that only patriarchal and market structures were properly in accordance with our evolved natural natures. Darwin@LSE, as the email address for the LSE based 'Darwin seminars', which sought to colonize the social sciences under the banner of biology, is an icon of this shift.

## Enter the Science Wars

It was into this changed culturescape that the Science Wars broke out with the publication of *Higher Superstition* by Gross and Levitt (1994). This was an all-embracing survey of critical writing about science from sociologists, historians, Marxists, philosophers, feminists, post-colonial theorists, to environmentalists and new age theorists. These were argued to be part of a conspiracy to denigrate science. The authors had a truly Catch-22 argument; recognizing that these groups did not actually have much to do with one another, they moved to the irrefutable argument that because they failed to attack one another, it was therefore clear evidence that they were in actuality part of a dangerous political grouping – the academic left. This claim to be defending science turned on a mix of an undergraduate textbook construction of 'the' scientific method, framed in an anti-'left' rhetoric. When the debate came to Britain the denunciatory rhetoric was translated from being anti-left and anti-feminist to being exclusively anti-sociology of knowledge. Thus even though in the Higher Superstition it was feminists who bore the brunt of their attack, when the debate crossed the pond it became an exclusively androcentric debate. Whatever the British natural scientists and the sociologists of scientific knowledge disagreed about, they agreed on the inevitability of androcentricity.

Not only do Gross and Levitt take for granted the permanent hegemony of science as privileged knowledge, the science warriors have clung on to an epistemological universe in which there is no problem between the word (or perhaps that should be the symbol) and the thing. Because of the grounded nature of biological research this may be a good enough description of the necessary realism of experimental biologists but it is not necessarily shared across the sciences. Theoretical physicists are divided. There are those such as Roger Penrose who think there is a connection between theory and the physical world, and those such as Stephen Hawking who think that providing the mathematics are beautiful such a relation is irrelevant. At that moment we get, we are assured by Hawking, to 'know the mind of God'. Were a sociologist to make such a claim we would find ourselves put firmly among the new agers, or seen as crackpots but theoretical physicists have always seen themselves as the Brahmins of the knowledges and such comments are relatively routine (Wertheim, 1997). Unsurprisingly these the highest priests of theoretical physics have not had much to say about post-modernism and the death of truth; they live at another rarer level altogether.

For general social theorists too, the 'either or' debate within the sociology of science between social constructionism and realism has commanded little interest. Most, such for example as Bourdieu, have seen the debate as simply not an 'either or' question. But within science studies and particularly within the sociology of scientific knowledge, the advocacy of strong social constructionist views of natural science knowledge has unquestionably generated sharp conflict in both epistemology and politics. Strong social constructionism as close kin to post-structuralism unquestionably works to erode the truth claims of science and the scientists and many radical activists don't like it.

Let me take two very different examples: the Collins/Wolpert debate at the British Association for the Advancement of Science meeting in 1994 and the women primatologists' response to the book *Primate Visions* by the feminist historian Donna Haraway. First the debate. This was between Harry Collins, a leading sociologist of scientific knowledge, and developmental biologist Lewis Wolpert, who after Bodmer became chair of COPUS. Collins, together with fellow sociologist Trevor Pinch, had published *The Golem: What Everyone Should Know about Science* (1993), and Wolpert, *The Unnatural Nature of Science: Science Does Not Make (Common) Sense* (1992). These rival and polarized texts claim to extend the public understanding of science; the former by claiming that science is socially constructed, the latter by its insistence that scientific knowledge is unitary, with unique truth claims derived from its capacity to hold a mirror to nature visible to its illuminati.

The confrontational debate made a considerable impression on those who saw it, or as I did, reviewed it on video, as an extraordinarily vituperative and unpleasant event. To the extent that considerable sections of the academy have given up those highly adversarial exchanges, long criticized in feminist circles, as fostering the non-meeting of minds the debate was a return to a past from which academic life is not yet free. The options for those sociologists who did not share Collins' position or those biologists who did not share Wolpert's, to say nothing of those who as feminists thought both were unreconstructedly macho in thought and style, were shrivelled down to the binary choice of either Collins or Wolpert.

I have many sympathies with Collins' and Pinch's political project, which is to increase the public understanding 'about' science rather than merely to increase the public understanding 'of' science, as in the COPUS deficit model. I might use different language but we share a common sociological impulse that people are expert in their own lives and that a desirable cultural and political objective is to move to a dialogue between the several publics and the sciences.

Set plain, the Collins Pinch thesis is that 'the scientific community transmutes the clumsy antics of Golem Science into a neat and tidy myth'. The central theoretical weakness (echoing the science is social relations thesis) lies in the failure to treat the knowledges equally. Thus while they show us the scientists as actively socially constructing their 'neat and tidy myths', we are invited to believe that their own sociological accounts of science are real. They tell us their subjects construct science, while they offer one true sociological story which everyone should know. Arguably they thus reproduce for sociology the authoritarian scientific voice they criticize in natural science. Worse, their tactless – to put it no more strongly – use of the word 'myth' to describe the slow patient work of laboratory scientists, pretty much forecloses the possibility of conversation with them.

Those who want to privilege the discourse of the natural sciences such as the sociobiologist Richard Dawkins were quick to pick up the myth word and to attack relentlessly. 'It is often thought clever to say that science is no more than a modern origin myth. The Jews had their Adam and Eve etc. . . . What is evolution some smart people say, but our modern equivalent of gods and epic heroes, neither better nor worse, neither truer nor falser . . . There is a fashionable saloon philosophy called cultural relativism which holds in its extreme forms that science has no more claim to truth than tribal myth: science is just a mythology favoured by our modern Western tribe' (Dawkins, 1995, p. 31).

Collins's, and for that matter Steve Fuller's, claim, that the sociology of scientific knowledge is only methodologically relativist does not quite match up to the ontological slippage which is taking place certainly in Collins's work, which renders it vulnerable to Dawkins' attack.

Thus while the understanding that science is socially shaped finds increasingly wide cultural acceptance, it does not follow that because scientific claims are socially shaped they are precisely interchangeable with myths or even stories. What is called the good science/bad science debate remains – just as it does in sociology or for that matter plumbing and dressmaking – without it our whole structure of knowledge fails. Carefully analyzing bad science is tedious work. The introduction to Anne Fausto Sterling's *Myths of Gender* (1992) audibly sighs as she faces the unappetizing but politically necessary task of clearing away the bad science of inadequate samples, poor controls and feeble design which serve to sustain wild misogynist inferences.

Until recent hints of conversion not least towards feminism, demonstrated for example in Bruno Latour's enthusiastic reception of Haraway' work, this highly professionalized grouping of the sociologists of science has been singularly hostile to normative critics of science, dealing with them by erasure and silence. Instead their sociology, despite their claim to be interested in the political role of science, has chosen to mirror science's claim of being a gender-free, value-free culture. In consequence this radical impulse concerned with the political role of science and technology is so hedged in by a professionalized and pale male construction of the political that its capacity to build alliances with other critics, whether within or without the sciences, has been severely restricted.

Wolpert's book *The Unnatural Nature of Science* is, for anyone with a more than cursory familiarity with current philosophy of science, an astonishing essay in glassy mirror ideology. It sees no gap between the word and the thing. Science, Wolpert claims, is unnatural knowledge in that many of its truths run counter to everyday beliefs – for instance that the sun goes round the earth or that heavy bodies fall faster than lighter ones. However, he never tries to define what he means by common sense, or to consider that this too is a historically relativist concept. Indeed as a standard natural scientists' joke goes, today's common sense is merely yesterday's 'good science'. Or by common sense does he want to invoke the counterintuitive, which is surely the stance of every systematic approach to knowledge from the arts to the sciences and by no means the unique property of any single one? Fatally what Wolpert does is to confuse a scientific grasp of the issues with a scientist's grasp of the issues.

My second example is the response to the book *Primate Visions* written by the feminist historian of science Donna Haraway. This has been rapturously received in women's studies, cultural studies and science studies and has been uniformly criticized by the women primatologists she studied, feminist and non-feminist alike. The *New Scientist* review (Jolly and Jolly, 1990) written by the primatologist Alison Jolly and her daughter, a post-modernist, said it all. The mother loathed it: the daughter loved it. Haraway is too skilled a word-smith and too good a feminist to casually antagonize the scientists she respects, but unquestionably the primatologists feel that her work explains their work away. Although, as a more sophisticated and more even-handed social theorist than Collins, she constantly insists that like those she studies she too only writes narratives, nonetheless the production of any counter-narrative invites belief. And there lies the rub. The strain is not like the sharp antagonism of the original conflict within the radical science movement but it is still there. Conversation is now predictably difficult. By contrast, in a critical realist project which assumes, as Mary Midgley puts it, 'one world but a big one', we can proceed more easily. Here there is no necessary reason why the sciences should compete for explanatory dominance. At the same time, setting aside my personal theoretical stance, I am convinced that feminism needs all the epistemological stances and the important task is to find ways of making difficult conversations between them possible.

Both the vituperative Science Wars and the fundamentalist Darwinism currently on offer get in the way of quieter and more serious arguments about science theory, the place and kind of of evolutionary theory useful to biology or the social sciences. Or should we focus on the discussion about the changing production system of knowledge (Gibbons *et al.*, 1994) with its move towards 'post-academic science' (Ziman, 1996)? And if this is the case, what does it mean culturally and politically? At my most optimistic – and that of the will remains desirable – I can read these changes as opening up the possibility of many new actors entering the production system of science, which could indeed include those Others historically excluded by modern Western science – not least Nature herself. This is not to lose sight of the huge losses brought by these changes, not least the casualization and the feminization of that casual sector of the research labour force. There is nothing mechanical or guaranteed about the possibilities, but this new system is developing in a context where dreams of localized, embodied, responsible knowledges press from multiple currents in both the South (Shiva, 1989) and the North (Haraway, 1985).

Lastly there are some modest auguries of change. Public hostility to GMOs is having an effect. It's not just the posturing of the supermarkets vaunting themselves as the first or most GMO-free zones, but the financial columns report a more general reduction in investment in agrochemical biotechnology. These are new cultural politics, combining massive consumer resistance based on a refusal to defer to the claims of a reductionist science and technology, underpinned by a critical environmentalist science. Crucial within this resistance has been the destabilizing of reductionist science's authority, or more accurately, science's authoritarianism. Scientific authority is a precious resource: science's authoritarianism has a good deal to answer for. Thus at my most optimistic I think that what we are seeing, despite the posturing of the science warriors such as Gross, Levitt and Wolpert, is not an anti-science movement (though in the new age movement there is more than a touch of that) but a more diffuse desire to restore natural science to its proper place, setting out its take on the world but not claiming that this is the only possible view. It would be arrogant, as well as just plain wrong, to claim that this move to stop deferring to science's authoritarianism has come about through any one social movement or science theory research programme (even those I am most committed to). This achievement has been the mutant product of conflicting cultural currents and plural epistemologies. Such mutants signal to us that there is creative theoretical and political life beyond the Science Wars.

## References

Bodmer Report (1985) *The Public Understanding of Science*, London: The Royal Society.

Bohlan, I. (1995) 'Through Malthusian specs: a study in the philosophy of science studies, with special reference to the theory and ideology of Darwin historiography', PhD Dissertation, Goteborg University.

Collins, H. and Pinch, T. (1993) *The Golem: What Everyone Should Know about Science*, Cambridge: Cambridge University Press.

Dawkins, R. (1995) *River Out of Eden*, London: Weidenfeld and Nicolson.

Fausto Sterling, A. (1992) *Myths of Gender: Biological Theories about Women and Men*, New York: Basic Books.

Fee, E. (1981) 'Is feminism a threat to scientific objectivity?', *International Journal of Women's Studies*, 4: 378–92.

Gibbons, M., Limoges, C., Nowotny, H., Schwartzmann, S., Scott, P. and Trow, M. (1994) *The New Production System of Knowledge: the Dynamics of Science and Research in Contemporary Societies*, London: Sage.

Gross, P. and Levitt, N. (1994) *Higher Superstition: the Academic Left and its Quarrels with Science*, Baltimore, MD: Johns Hopkins Press.

Haraway, D. (1985) 'A manifesto for cyborgs: science, technology and socialist feminism in the 1980s', *Socialist Review*, 80: 65–107.

Haraway, D. (1989) *Primate Visions: Gender, Race and Nature in the World of Modern Science*, New York and London: Routledge.

Harwood, J. (1976) 'The race intelligence controversy: a sociological approach. Part I. Professional factors', *Social Studies of Science*, 6: 369–94.

Harwood, J. ( 1977) 'The race intelligence controversy: a sociological approach. Part II. External factors', *Social Studies of Science*, 7: 1–30.

Irwin, A. and Wynne, B. (1996) *Misunderstanding Science? The Public Reconstruction of Science and Technology*, Cambridge: Cambridge University Press.

Jolly, A. and Jolly, M. (1990) 'A view from the other end of the telescope', *New Scientist*, 21: 58.

Pustilnik, A. (1995) 'Looking through "not in our genes": debunking, epistemology and practice between biological determinism and the dialectics of liberation', *BA Thesis*, Harvard University.

Rose, H. (1994) *Love, Power and Knowledge: Towards a Feminist Transformation of the Sciences*, Cambridge: Polity, p. 260.

Rose, H. (1996) 'My enemy's enemy is – only perhaps – my friend', *Social Text*, 46–7: 61–80.

Rose, H. and Rose, S. (1979) 'Radical science and its enemies', in Miliband, R. and Saville, J. (eds) *Socialist Register*, London: Merlin.

Shiva, V. (1989) *Staying Alive:Women, Ecology and Development*, London: Pluto.

Smith, D. (1988) *The Everyday World as Problematic: a Feminist Sociology*, Milton Keynes: Open University Press.

Wellcome Report (1998) *Public Perspectives on Human Cloning*, London: The Wellcome Trust.

Wertheim, M. (1997) *Pythagoras' Trousers: God, Physics and the Gender Wars*, London: Fourth Estate.

Wolpert, L. (1992) *The Unnatural Nature of Science: Why Science Does Not Make (Common) Sense*, London: Faber and Faber.

Young, R.M. (1977) 'Science is social relations', *Radical Science Journal*, 5: 65–129.

Ziman, J. (1996) ' "Postacademic science"; constructing knowledge with networks and norms', *Science Studies*, 1: 67–80.

# 3

## Film theory and bogus theory[1]

DEREK BOUSÉ

> It is a capital mistake to theorize before one has data. Insensibly, one begins to twist facts to suit theories instead of theories to suit facts.
>
> **Sherlock Holmes**

Would that more of those in film studies had taken Holmes's advice. Yet as anyone knows who followed the literature in this field during the last decades of the twentieth century, much of the theorizing put forth to explain the workings of *cinema*, in particular its putative ability to 'position' viewers as both ideological subjects and sexual beings, seemed to rest more on speculation and intuition than on real data or evidence. It now seems, moreover, that film theorists' taste for speculative theory, much of which was expressed in imprecise or exceedingly metaphoric language, undermined much of their apparent political agenda, and their chances of initiating an effective social critique.

By the late 1970s it was already becoming apparent that towering theories were being constructed on foundations of sand. Observers began to sound calls of alarm, the loudest of which, as well as the most cogent and comprehensive campaign of counter-statement, was that of Noël Carroll. His 1988 book *Mystifying Movies* summed up a decade of frustration with the way film theorists had mystified our understanding of cinema by way of 'extravagant ambiguity and vacuous abstraction', as well as by 'using the wrong [theoretical] tools for the task at hand'.[2] Chief among these, especially in the theoretical positions being staked out at the journal *Screen*, were Althusserian Marxism and Lacanian psychoanalysis. Although Althusser had been the darling of 'the generation of students and academics who encountered Marxism after 1968',[3] he proved the less enduring of the two. In 1978 E.P. Thompson fired his broadside *The Poverty of Theory*, after which Althusserianism began to weaken, if not to crumble.

The Lacanian edifice, however, proved more resistant to assault, and even, it seems, to erosion. By the mid-1980s, Althusser seemed all but forgotten, while Lacan remained current, and has continued to do so.[4] This has been in part because of the persistence in film theory of linguistic and psychoanalytic models, and their absorption of ideological arguments once bearing the Althusserian stamp. As feminist perspectives focusing on notions of *sexual difference* moved to the centre of film theory it was argued, for example, that 'for cinema, as for Lacanian psychoanalysis, sexual difference [not ideology] is the central, determining force',[5] and one thought to permeate the entire cinematic *apparatus* (defined loosely as the nexus of film form, technology, institutions, and spectatorship). Sexual difference theories owed in part to the concept of linguistic difference (binary oppositions) central to Saussurean linguistics and Levi-Strauss's structural anthropology, and in part to Freudian notions of sexuality and sexual identity, which had their own built-in oppositions of ego/object, masculine/feminine, active/passive, etc. All were seen as essential to understanding movies, now virtually defined by their complicity in gender construction. '[T]hat the cinema is obsessed with the polarities of masculine and feminine', it was further argued, 'is a basic assumption of feminist film theory'.[6] It seems worth considering that such 'obsessions' were not those of cinema so much as of critics and theorists, but the 'basic assumption' nevertheless became that of film theory in general.

As feminism was drawn into alliance with Lacanian psychoanalytic theory, Althusserian notions of the way in which cinema positions subjects ideologically were assimilated into Lacanian arguments about how it constructs *gendered spectators*. Ideological critique focusing on the role of motion pictures in sustaining economic and political power was meanwhile taken up (somewhat more competently) by theorists employing some variation on 'cultural studies' (in the wake of the influential work of Stuart Hall and others at the Birmingham Centre for Contemporary Cultural Studies[7]). Much of this, however, with its grounding in Marxist economic theory, seems now to have been banished to the outermost of film studies circles.

In addition to its alliance with psychoanalysis, feminist film theory also became allied in the 1980s and 1990s with a number of other perspectives and '-isms', including *post-modernism*. Both feminism and post-modernism were seen as 'oppositional discourses' challenging many of the dominant culture's basic assumptions, especially about representation.[8] Post-modernism even came to be regarded in the 1990s as 'part of a triumvirate, along with poststructuralism and multiculturalism, each representing what its advocates believe are the highest forms available today of thinking in art, theory, and politics'.[9] Yet such easy and automatic congruity between widely varying theoretical perspectives too often tended to be perceived or assumed where there was actually little evidence of real compatibility. Post-modernism, for example, in whatever manifestations, can surely not be considered a progressive social movement comparable with feminism.[10] It is difficult to imagine it, to use another example, enlisted in the struggle for racial equality and civil rights.

Yet I do not intend to review each and every film studies paradigm, or to revisit their arguments. Rather, I prefer to address here, at a more general level, some problems (not *problematics*!) in film theory, particularly in its post-*Screen* period of ascendancy, that rendered much of it politically ineffectual, and an intellectually masturbatory activity: (1) its failures *as theory*; (2) its isolation from other areas of media study that might have offered better answers to some of its questions (had they been clearly formed), in particular that of the presumed ideological 'effects' of motion pictures; and (3) its parallels to the recent 'Sokal Affair', which demonstrated that retreat behind a veil of dense theoretical jargon is self-defeating in any attempt at progressive social critique.

## 'What we need is a theory'

For over thirty years, film studies has been largely theory driven and text based. That is, speculative theories have been put forth, then given the appearance of being 'proved' when someone showed how they might be applied to a given film text or genre. Some of the theoretical speculation was not only careless, however, but made in defiant disregard for findings from research elsewhere that were derived from more systematic observation. 'How have we gotten into this state of affairs', Dudley Andrew asked, rhetorically:

> where direct approaches to the field are unfeasible, where theory aims at explanation or 'picturing' rather than at 'prediction' and 'verification' as it does in the sciences and social sciences?[11]

Indeed, some theorists asked us to renounce commitment to evidence, proof, verification and checks on validity, and to settle instead for a 'form of consensus' embodied in theoretical statements that were often incomprehensible, but that produced a 'comprehension effect'. In an aura of philosophical speculation, knowledge was replaced by 'a sense of knowledge' (elsewhere called a 'knowledge effect'), as well as by 'assumptions . . . mutual understanding . . . [and] shared perspectives, not provable predictions'.[12] In a word, we were asked to *believe*, to join a faith of which the tenets were meaningful precisely because they could not be proven. 'Verification is irrelevant', one writer noted, 'for a method based on speculative metaphors, analogies, and psychoanalytic hypotheses'.[13]

As the hybrid discipline of 'cinema studies' began to take shape, its practitioners were understandably fraught with status-anxiety.[14] Seeking theoretical and methodological legitimacy, they turned first to structural linguistics, and then to a politicized psychoanalysis (so to the latter did feminism also turn for rigour[15]), both of which seemed to promise scientific *terra firma*, but without all the methodological mire in which empirical media studies seemed to get bogged down, and which also made such studies, in some minds, complicit with powerful institutions, and therefore with the dominant ideology.[16] Yet despite the appearance of rigour, the approaches favoured in cinema studies could deal with viewers only as constructs (code word: 'spectators'), and with viewing experiences almost exclusively in abstract terms rather than through research on real human viewers.[17] This ultimately had the effect of making film theory *less* scientific by justifying its refusal of scientific method. Where there might thus have been a series of testable theories or hypotheses, film theory became instead a kind of philosophical *total system* that proffered answers even before the questions had been properly formed.[18] Indeed, much of it did not provide means for framing, asking or answering questions, and admitted of no procedures for verifying or falsifying its propositions. Rather than a process of inquiry,[19] film theory seemed at times little more than a network of unproved assertions, with a good deal more verbiage than substance. Much that was simply conjecture was taken as gospel, and, in place of evidence, was used as the basis for more theorizing; film theorists often cited the equally speculative work of other theorists in place of data or findings from actual research. As a result, much film theory neither summarized systematic observations nor seemed to reflect a good faith effort on the part of theorists to reduce, distill and clarify. Much of their work even appeared deliberately obscurantist, often seeming to heap on layers of theoretical and linguistic obfuscation where they should have been attempting to strip them away.

It was telling that theorists of film, as well as of art, literature and other areas of culture, often spoke of setting out to 'problematize' some object or area of study, rather than of attempting to clarify or (heaven forfend!) *simplify*. In an intellectual climate in which theory was seen as explanation, rather than as a means of seeking explanations, it therefore became a conclusion rather than a point of departure. Theorizing – 'doing theory', as was often said – was an end in itself, as well as an inherently elitist pursuit in its willing remove from real experience. In truth, however, most claims to be 'doing theory' really referred to acts of generating new interpretations or 'readings' of texts or genres – 'twisting facts to suit theories', as Holmes might say.[20] Consistent with this, it seemed that theory was seen as a necessary prerequisite to any form of understanding, and that claims to knowledge not supported by theory (or not within the dominant theoretical frameworks) were insupportable, if not anti-intellectual. Film theorists therefore called not for more research or data or evidence, but for more theory. Consider these variations on the 'what-we-need-is-a-theory' argument (or, in Heideggerian paraphrase, 'only a theory can save us'):

> We must theorize the very perception of images . . . We need a tentative theory of perception to undergird any useful theory of film perception.[21]

> Understanding how viewers interact with films requires a theory of subjectivity.[22]

> The only way in which cinema can circle back into an adequate, productive relationship with 'politics' is thus through the transformation of itself into a 'theoretical' practice.[23]

Even Carroll seems convinced that more theory is needed – although, happily, not more totalizing *grand theory*: 'We are in need of piecemeal theorizing', he writes, 'in need of theor*ies* about film rather than Film Theory'.[24] If by this he means *testable* theories, open to some sort of verifying or falsifying procedures, I am sympathetic to the argument, yet still unconvinced that we actually *need* more theorizing just now, especially if we have not collected data – that is, made systematic observations on which to build theories in the first place.

## Mythic effects

Contemporary film theorists have attributed a great many 'effects' to motion pictures, but never satisfactorily demonstrated them, adequately defined them or even used the term consistently. Nichols, for example, in addition to the 'comprehension effect' mentioned earlier, uses 'effect' six times on one page in at least two different ways: 'ideological effects . . . particular ideological effects . . . textually specific effects . . . ideological effects . . . effect of a text . . . effects cast in terms of a "textual system" . . .'. It is unclear whether 'ideological effects' and 'textual effects' are the same or different, or what either of them really is. Two pages later there is even less consistency: 'A gulf opens between . . . effect and the production of effects . . . agency cannot be a subject, since the subject is itself an "effect" . . . Effects just happen to us . . . modernist texts that produce "knowledge effects" about ideology and the cinematic apparatus . . .'.[25]

With regard to 'ideological effects', if we can take that to mean something roughly equivalent to what media researchers elsewhere refer to as the 'socialization function of the media',[26] many of the arguments put forth by film theorists have been, or can be, invalidated by research undertaken in a more systematic fashion.[27] The reverse, however, has not been true. Film theories derived from post-structuralist and post-modernist literary, semiotic and psychoanalytic models have hardly demonstrated the superiority of their assertions over the findings of cognitive research, audience analysis, content analysis and other more systematic approaches.[28]

Where there might have been evidence from audience research, for example, there were instead presumptive assertions about spectators as trans-cultural, trans-historical[29] and apparently helpless beings, easily duped by 'illusionistic' film images containing ideological messages aimed straight at the unconscious. Bertolt Brecht provided much of the early inspiration for such thinking, arguing that dramatic narrative induces viewers to identify or to empathize so strongly that they come to believe the fiction, mistaking it, and its ideological premises, for reality.[30] Viewers have 'the illusion of being present at a fleeting, accidental "real event"', he writes, in which the impression of naturalness is so great that 'one can no longer interpose one's judgments, imagination, and reactions'.

In the end, he concludes, one 'must simply conform'.[31] This pessimistic, deterministic conception of the helpless, completely vulnerable and gullible spectator, sitting in rapt attention believing what is on stage or screen is real, and thus allowing ideology straight into the unconscious, was taken up enthusiastically by film theorists. Indeed, the premise that ideology works mainly at the unconscious level not only motivated the Althusserian–Lacanian union but also has been seen as justifying the refusal of actual audience analysis using survey data, questionnaires, focus group studies, etc. After all, how can they really *know* what they are thinking? That is for film theorists to decide. Yet the Brechtian thesis now seems simplistic and naive. Mere exposure to even the most subtle of ideological messages in no way determines that they will be believed, accepted, complied with or acted upon by anyone, let alone by everyone.

Carroll is especially emphatic in his argument against the tendency among film theorists to invest movies with too much ideological and political power. In his book he rejects the notion that movies perform 'a major role in positioning capitalist subjects' (p. 88), that they can 'paralyze the spectator's capacity to make judgments, notably judgments of a politically critical nature' (p. 91), that cinematic illusionism 'makes us susceptible to ideological falsehood' (p. 92), that it can 'neutralize our critical capacities in such a way that we become suckers for ideology' (p. 93), that movies put spectators 'in a kind of trance which paralyzes their critical faculties in respect to believing social falsehoods' (pp. 103–4) and that film 'stuns our powers of criticism – with illusions of reality – consequently inducing us to endorse propaganda' (p. 104).

Yet in the overall absence of intellectual commerce between the world of film scholarship, of which Carroll is a part, and that of social-science-oriented media studies, even he appears at times to embrace ideas that have been struck down by research. He writes of the 'phenomenally widespread effectiveness' of movies (p. 212), that 'a spectator may acquire an ideological belief in the course of viewing a film narrative' (p. 158) and that movies 'obviously exert a great deal of power over large masses of people' (p. 238n). Notions of 'widespread effectiveness' and of 'power over large masses' echo what has been called the 'legacy of fear' inherent in several models of media effects that have either been disproved or discarded over the decades in favour of more moderate conceptions of limited and indirect influence.[32] Moreover, while it is possible that a viewer might 'acquire an ideological belief in the course of viewing a [single] film', such conversion experiences are exceedingly rare, and would surely owe far more to individual predisposition than to some power hidden in the message itself. Carroll knows this, however, and these lapses of expression do nothing to blunt the power of his critique.

The problem was that film scholars seemed unaware of the massive body of media effects research that had been accumulating since the Payne Fund Studies in the 1920s.[33] Although the two camps were in agreement on more recent notions of the 'social construction of reality', the arguments of contemporary film theorists regarding the ideological effects of cinema nevertheless suggested that they remained committed to their own version of the 'Hypodermic Needle Model', with its presumptions of widespread *uniform influence* and *direct effects*.[34] If this were so (and it now appears it was), then in some important ways films theorists seemed to be well behind empirically based media research, which had demolished much of the case for the massive, all-powerful effects so often asserted in film theory, in favour of more cautious statements about how media messages interact with other social and cultural influences, and may do so differently with each individual. What has been shown clearly is that *some* media messages can affect *some* people, in *some* ways, under *some* circumstances, *some* of the time. While virtually no one argues today that film images or other media messages have no effects, or that their influence on audiences and culture are merely negligible, in the end their effects appear neither broadly systematic nor reliably predictable, and thus not to support many of the assertions put forth by film theorists basing their statements on broad notions of ideological hegemony, let alone on speculation.

A more productive, and ultimately more politically useful, model than those offered by film theorists for analyzing how dominant ideological values are systematically disseminated and reinforced by media images can be found in the literature on 'cultivation theory' – that is, whether policy is a goal, rather than just philosophical criticism or invective. Here, rather than vague and unwieldy notions of textual and ideological effects on spectators who are themselves effects of textual positioning, has been systematic research relating the viewing experiences of *real* viewers to their political and ideological values and attitudes.[35] Researchers in this area have testified before Congressional committees, and their findings have had demonstrable effects on policy. Film theorists, by contrast, have offered only abstract, unverifiable political critique that has ultimately amounted to little more than philosophical naysaying within academic circles. Even Nichols admits the 'inability of this form of academic critique to establish a foothold elsewhere in society', and that 'neither the concepts nor the articulation of the concepts presents a very useful political model'.[36] The word *irrelevance* comes to mind.

## The emperor's tailors

Arguably, late twentieth-century film theory's greatest folly lay in its practitioners' frequent disregard, if not contempt, for clear expression. The problem was not a new one, of course. In his 1946 essay 'Politics and the English language', George Orwell wrote of such language:

> The writer either has a meaning and cannot express it, or he inadvertently says something else, or he is almost indifferent as to whether his words mean anything or not.[37]

Film theorists in the late twentieth century often seemed to be in the third category. Amid post-modernist assumptions that the 'real' world 'is understood through language, but because language changes its meaning in use . . . "reality" also changes and is never absolutely defined or agreed upon',[38] the opacity of much of the language in film-theoretical writing suggested that language itself, not the communication of meaning, had become the object. Structural linguistics had taught that since language pre-exists us and endures after us, it is, in a way, even more 'real' than the reality it describes.

With language seen as 'surface' rather than as mirror, lamp or window, some film-theoretical writing even seemed to take the form of a language game or performance, written, and perhaps read, for its own supposed *jouissance* (using French words was also part of the game) rather than for the content of its ideas or arguments. Thinkers such as Nietzsche, Heidegger, Derrida and Foucault are often said to have found ordinary, expository language inadequate to the grandness of their ideas, and so turned to other forms of expression. The result, some argue, is that their writing must often be read as a kind of verbal work of art.[39] This may be all right for Nietzsche, but it is difficult to see such metaphysical or aesthetic grandeur in the writings of most film theorists (let alone among their graduate student acolytes, who, of course, were quick to mimic the style). Were they, then, 'doing' theory – or poetry? Were they attempting to explain the workings of motion pictures, or to exploit them as fodder for self-indulgent 'belletristic musing'?[40] 'The basic objection', Nichols writes:

> is that too much of the writing is 'difficult' and that it uses this difficulty to tyrannize the reader. Frequently, such writing strains, or even violates, grammatical conventions. Often its meaning remains elusive even after much reading.[41]

Nevertheless, he mounts a spirited defence of deliberately obfuscating language, resting largely, it seems, on a pair of fallacies. First, the fallacy of *two wrongs*: 'Difficult language has no monopoly on tyranny', Nichols fights back. Why, there is also a 'tyranny of lucidity'. So there. Catherine Belsey is then allowed to call the kettle black: the effect of difficult language, he quotes her, 'is to alert the reader to the opacity of language, and to avoid the "tyranny of lucidity", the impression that what is being said must be true . . .'.[42] Is this another way of saying that obscurity equals profundity? Language is not opaque, of course, but if it were, would not a good faith effort to alert us to the problem in the clearest available terms give us the best chance to confront it? Without being let in on the charade, we are left looking for literal meaning in film theorists' words, when all along, apparently, some of them had avoided putting any there – for *our* own good. Turgid prose, Nichols suggests, may be 'a necessary condition for challenging familiar views, especially about language'. Yet what good is any alert or challenge if it is not understood as such by its receivers? Nevertheless, a 'semiopaque form of discourse is part of the radical critique'.[43] Yet is a critique that cannot be understood, or, worse, that is not be meant to be understood, an effective critique? Is it a critique at all? It seemed that among film theorists the goal of effective social critique had given way to self-indulgence and solipsism.

The argument, however, that difficult ideas can only be expressed in difficult language illustrates the second type of fallacy, often called the *imitative fallacy*, or *fallacy of imitative form*. Accordingly, a film *about* boredom must actually *be* boring, or an essay about imprecision must be imprecise, or perhaps even a condemnation of sloppy reasoning must be sloppily reasoned. This, presumably, would produce a 'comprehension effect'. In this case, however, it seems simply an admission that a writer feels no obligation to make an effort to communicate clearly with his or her readers, and may even be doing them a service by refusing to communicate (perhaps the best course, then, would be to refuse to write). Nichols grants that 'poststructuralist writing remains vulnerable' to such criticisms, but concludes nevertheless that those who do criticize its style as 'elitist and obscurantist or imprecise' are only being 'intolerant', and, anyway, are probably 'already entrenched within the academy', where post-structuralism 'remains the underdog'.[44]

Underdog? Post-structuralism? Hardly. By the end of the twentieth century, the jargon and ideas of post-structuralism (under the false assumptions that these were somehow inherently related to the ideas of post-modernism, multiculturalism, feminism and cultural studies) had enjoyed years of dominance in film and literature studies, and were consolidating their power in other university humanities programmes by way of 'culture wars' aimed, evidently, at *ideological cleansing*. It was often difficult to know who the enemy was, and many were afraid to express scepticism, let alone to speak out against the excesses of the new paradigms, lest they be branded politically incorrect neoconservatives in league with Dinesh D'Souza, Roger Kimball, George Will and even Rush Limbaugh.

This is what seems to have happened to Alan Sokal, a New York University physics professor who set out to expose 'the arrogance of theory' by seeing whether the journal *Social Text* would 'publish an article liberally salted with nonsense if (a) it sounded good and (b) it flattered the editors' ideological preconceptions'.[45] The journal did publish it, after which Sokal exposed the hoax in a separate publication in which his description of its strategies sounded uncannily like those of the dominant trends in film theory:

> . . . appeals to authority in lieu of logic; speculative theories passed off as established science; strained and even absurd analogies; rhetoric that sounds good but whose meaning is ambiguous; and confusion between the technical and everyday sense of English words.[46]

The article was written to make no sense, but to sound good nevertheless to those accustomed to post-modernist writing. It was not surprising, then, that some found significance in the 'play of signifiers' that made up its linguistic 'surface textures'. It was also not surprising, however, that a recurrent image in much of the discussion and criticism afterward was that of the emperor's new clothes, for it seemed that few, if any, had been willing to admit that the article was naked nonsense. More alarming was the cognitive dissonance that emerged when some insisted, even after the hoax had been exposed, that the article had actually contained profound theoretical significance in spite of its calculated unclarity. If the case showed anything, then, it was, once again, how easily obscurity is taken for profundity, or, as Sokal explained, how easily incomprehensibility becomes a virtue, and metaphors and puns a sub-stitute for evidence and logic.[47] This, he warns, poses a serious threat to left politics by undermining its prospects for progressive social critique.

Insofar as film theory in the late twentieth century was presented as a form of ideological analysis, its political agenda and prospects for effective social critique were no less undermined by its rhetorical strategies. Having asserted that motion pictures concealed from us the real nature of reality by illusions that were ideologically motivated, film theorists then proceeded to replicate this very set of circumstances in their use of dense language. This obscured reality no less than the medium they set out to expose, and for even more explicit ideological purposes. Arguably, the real political danger was not from motion pictures, but from film theory's degradation of political discourse.

## Notes

1 This essay is dedicated to Stewart Justman, whose commitment to clear thinking was its inspiration.

2 Carroll (1988, pp. 2, 8, 32).

3 Clarke (1980, p. 7). Perhaps the key essay in the volume that includes Clarke's is the one by Kevin McDonnell and Kevin Robins, a blistering critique of the absorption of Althusserian Marxism into film theory, in particular at *Screen*. The authors write that by 1975 they had found 'Althusserian concepts extremely abstract and impossible to apply in practice', and also 'found it extremely hard to continue reading *Screen*' (1980, p. 157).

4 See, for example, Bill Nichols's introduction to volume II of *Movies and Methods*: Althusser is already forgotten, while the value of Lacan continues to be extolled. Lacan's durability resulted also from the fact that he was actively embraced in literary studies in way that Althusser was not. He became even more deeply institutionalized after being touted by the likes of Frederic Jameson and Geoffrey Hartman, and celebrated in a special issue of *Yale French Studies* (Felman, 1982). Bill Nichols even argued that 'Jacques Lacan is a necessary prerequisite for a specifically feminist film theory' (1985, p. 12). This is not to say that Lacan's presence in film theory, in particular feminist film theory, went unchallenged. The late 1970s and early 1980s saw some, at least, questioning whether the 'ideologically positioned spectator' derived from Althusser and Lacan left any room for political action or hope for change (see Gledhill, 1978). Strangely, however,

Lacan fell from prominence among French film theorists, who have persisted along linguistic and semiotic lines (see Bordwell, 1996).

5 Mayne (1994, p. 56). Also on sexual difference, see Walker (1994) and the book-length study by Rodowick (1991). The seminal text in the body of secondary (i.e. post- or neo-Freudian) thinking about sexual difference, Lacan and cinema is Mulvey's oft-reprinted essay 'Visual pleasure and narrative cinema' (1975).

6 Mayne (1994, p. 61). On the cinematic 'apparatus' as a masculine, indeed, *phallic* projection, and therefore as marker of sexual difference, see Penley (1989), especially her use of the machine metaphor in the chapter entitled 'Feminism, film theory, and the bachelor machines' (pp. 57–80). de Lauretis (1984) has described the 'apparatus' of cinema more as a social technology, but one whose modes of address apparently determine modes of spectatorship, thereby defining different sexual and social positions for spectators (a variation on the 'subject positioning' argument).

7 See Hall *et al.* (1980). See also Fiske (1987) and Turner (1990).

8 This argument is made by Kaplan (1988). Owens (1983) also argues that feminism (a critique of patriarchy) and post-modernism (a critique of dominant forms of representation) intersect at the point where both 'upset the reassuring stability' (p. 58) of the dominant culture and 'expose the system of power that authorizes certain representations' (p. 59). See also Nicholson (1990), a collection of varying perspectives on feminism and post-modernism.

9 Carroll (1997, p. 93).

10 Carroll cautions, 'Theorists who claim to find a deep conceptual link between postmodernism and progressive political movements like multiculturalism, feminism and anticapitalism, and intellectual tendencies like post-structuralism are allowing their preferences and enthusiasms to obscure their analysis' (1997, p. 93).

11 Andrew (1984, p. 4).

12 Nichols (1985, p. 5). See also Sokal's critique of supposed 'alternative ways of knowing' (Sokal, 1997, p. 126).

13 Nichols (1985, p. 16).

14 For a discussion of the status anxiety of cinema studies, see Carroll (1988, pp. 3–5) and Nichols (1985, p. 2). For a brief history of the development of the field, see Andrew (1984, pp. 3–18) and Bordwell (1996).

15 '[I]s there a feminist theory of cinema', Judith Mayne asked, 'that might borrow, as it were, from other discourses, but that would nonetheless constitute a theory in its own right? Such questions about the very status of feminism as a theory of the cinema are just beginning to be raised' (1994, p. 57).

16 Steve Prince has also noted the propensity of those in film studies 'to view concerns about evidence as the hallmarks of an ideologically suspect empiricism' (1996, p. 76). See, in this regard, Bordwell's distinction between 'empiricism' and 'empirical inquiry' (1996, p. 34, n. 63).

17 The use of the terms 'spectators' and 'viewers' has long separated cinema studies from more empirically oriented media/television studies and audience analysis – even though a great deal of film viewing is actually done on TV screens. For a particularly effective example of bridging film theory and empirical research on *real* viewers, see Messaris (1994). See also Prince (1996).

18 Film theorists, David Bordwell has argued, 'are too often in search of what Freud called a *Weltanschauung*, an "intellectual construction which solves all the problems of our existence uniformly on the basis of one overriding hypothesis . . . in which everything that interests us finds its fixed place" ' (1989, p. 12).

19 Andrew seems to reject the very idea of theory as a step in a 'process of inquiry', as I have described it, arguing instead that 'Too much of our vocabulary relating to research

derives from the "allegory of the quest" ', and that this results in 'heroic and aggressive terms' such as ' "pursuit" of knowledge'. His solution: to substitute terms like 'discourse' and 'adequation', such that 'theory sets us reasonably before a picture of our field'. Although one may find getting such a picture to be personally pleasurable, it is difficult to see any point or social value beyond this somewhat narcissistic goal. Andrew therefore adds, 'so that we can see it in a comprehensive and *fruitful* way'. But if the point is not to embark on a process of inquiry, and to avoid the heroic and aggressive 'pursuit of knowledge', then it is difficult to see what 'fruitful' means in this context. That is, what purpose is served by getting this 'picture of our field'? (see Andrew, 1984, p. 4).

20 Bordwell (1996) has called this 'top-down' or 'doctrine driven' inquiry.

21 Andrew (1984, p. 25).

22 Bordwell (1996, p. 14). I am cheating a bit here; Bordwell is paraphrasing a tendency he too has noted.

23 Harvey (1978, p. 38).

24 Carroll (1988, p. 232). The concluding line to the book reads: 'New modes of theorizing are necessary. We must start again' (1988, p. 234).

25 Nichols (1985, pp. 7, 9).

26 For a brief overview, see Wright (1986, pp. 185–201).

27 See, for example, Gerbner *et al.* (1982), Lowery and DeFleur (1988), Messaris (1994, pp. 48–160) and the collection of essays in Bryant and Zillman (1994).

28 For an analysis of 'claims about specific effects on audiences' put forth 'without adequate evidence', see Stromer-Galley and Schiappa (1998).

29 On the matter of whether this spectator is trans-cultural and trans-historical, Carroll has suggested that some film theorists may get around this by portraying the cinema as 'the answer to culturally specific desires of the nineteenth and twentieth centuries' (1988, p. 30).

30 See, for example, Walsh (1982). More valuable, however, is the critique offered by Smith (1996).

31 Brecht (1964, p. 219).

32 A recent set of studies by the Glasgow Media Group (Philo, 1999) suggests that the media remain powerful agents of influence, but in ways more subtle and diverse than those conceptualized in the film theories discussed here.

33 For an easily digestible historical summary of 'effects' theories and research, see Lowery and DeFleur (1988).

34 The neutralizing of audiences' critical abilities, a central assumption in contemporary film theory, had, in fact, been a specific research focus in one the very earliest empirical media studies, conducted in relation to the famous 1938 'War of the Worlds' radio broadcast. The results showed even then that the gullibility of audiences varied significantly according to education, religion and other personal and social factors (see Cantril, 1940).

35 See Gerbner *et al.* (1982, 1994), Gross and Morgan (1985) and Signorielli and Morgan (1990).

36 Nichols (1985, pp. 23, 24).

37 Orwell (1982, p. 250).

38 Philo (1999, p. ix).

39 See Megill (1987).

40 The term is used by both Carroll (1988) and Bordwell (1996).

41 Nichols (1985, p. 20).

42 Quoted by Nichols (1985, p. 21).

43 Nichols (1985, p. 21).

44 Nichols (1985, p. 23).

45 Sokal (1996b, p. 63). The original article appeared in *Social Text, 46/47* (Sokal, 1996a). A website has been established as a clearing house of information, arguments, and reactions relating to the 'Sokal affair': www.astro.queenssu.ca/~bworth/Reason/Sokal/.

46 Sokal (1996c, p. 93).

47 Sokal (1996b, p. 63).

## References

Andrew, J. D. (1984) *Concepts in Film Theory*, Oxford: Oxford University Press.

Bordwell, D. (1989) 'A case for cognitivism', *Iris*, 9(Spring): 11–41.

Bordwell, D. (1996) 'Contemporary film studies and the vicissitudes of grand theory', in Bordwell, D. and Carroll, N. (eds) *Post-Theory*, Madison, WI: University of Wisconsin Press, pp. 3–36.

Brecht, B. (1964) *Brecht on Theatre* (translated and edited by John Willett), London: Methuen.

Bryant, J. and Zillman, D. (eds) (1994) *Media Effects: Advances in Theory and Research*, Hillsdale, NJ: Lawrence Erlbaum Associates.

Cantril, H. (1940) *The Invasion from Mars: a Study in the Psychology of Panic*, Princeton, NJ: Princeton University Press.

Carroll, N. (1988) *Mystifying Movies: Fads and Fallacies in Contemporary Film Theory*, New York: Columbia University Press.

Carroll, N. (1997) 'The concept of postmodernism from a philosophical perspective', in Bertens, H. and Fokkema, D. (eds) *International Postmodernism: Theory and Practice*, Amsterdam and Philadelphia, PA: John Benjamins Publishing Company, pp. 89–102.

Clarke, S. (1980) 'Althusserian Marxism', in *One-Dimensional Marxism: Althusser and the Politics of Culture*, London and New York: Allison & Busby, pp. 7–102.

de Lauretis, T. (1984) *Alice Doesn't: Feminism, Semiotics, Cinema*, Bloomington, IN: University of Indiana Press.

Felman, S. (ed.) (1982) *Literature and Psychoanalysis*, Baltimore, MD, and London: Johns Hopkins University Press.

Fiske, J. (1987) *Television Culture*, London: Methuen.

Gerbner, G., Gross, L., Morgan, M. and Signorielli, N. (1982) ' "Charting the mainstream". Television's contributions to political orientations', *Journal of Communication*, 32(2): 100–27.

Gerbner, G., Gross, L., Morgan, M. and Signorielli, N. (1994) 'Growing up with television: the cultivation perspective', in Bryant, J. and Zillman, D. (eds) *Media Effects: Advances in Theory and Research*, Hillsdale, NJ: Lawrence Erlbaum Associates, pp. 17–42.

Gledhill, C. (1978) 'Recent developments in feminist criticism', *Film Quarterly Review of Film Studies*, 3(4): 457–93.

Gross, L. and Morgan, M. (1985) 'Television and enculturation', in Dominick, J. R. and Fletcher, J. E. (eds) *Broadcasting Research Methods*, Boston, MA: Allyn and Bacon, pp. 221–34.

Hall, S., Hobson, D., Lowe, A. and Willis, P. (eds) (1980) *Culture, Media, Language: Working Papers in Cultural Studies, 1972–79*, London: Hutchinson.

Harvey, S. (1978) *May '68 and Film Culture*, London: BFI.

Kaplan, E. A. (1988) 'Feminism/Oedipus/postmodernism: the case of MTV', in Kaplan, E. A. (ed.) *Postmodernism and its Discontents*, London: Verso.

Lowery, S. and DeFleur, M. (1988) *Milestones in Mass Communication Research*, 3rd edition, New York: Longman.

Mayne, J. (1994) 'Feminist film theory and criticism', in Carson, D., Dittmar, L. and Welsch, J. R. (eds) *Multiple Voices in Feminist Film Criticism*, Minneapolis, MN: University of Minnesota Press, pp. 48–64.

McDonnell, K. and Robins, K. (1980) 'Marxist cultural theory: the Althusserian smokescreen', in *One-Dimensional Marxism: Althusser and the Politics of Culture*, London and New York: Allison & Busby, pp. 157–231.

Megill, A. (1987) *Prophets of Extremity: Nietzsche, Heidegger, Foucault, Derrida*, Berkeley, CA: University of California Press.

Messaris, P. (1994) *Visual 'Literacy': Image, Mind, & Reality*, Boulder, CO: Westview Press.

Mulvey, L. (1975) 'Visual pleasure and narrative cinema', *Screen*, 16(3): 6–18.

Nichols, B. (ed.) (1985) *Movies and Methods II*, Berkeley, CA: University of California Press.

Nicholson, L. J. (ed.) (1990) *Feminism/Postmodernism*, New York: Routledge.

Orwell, G. (1982) 'Politics and the English language', in Howe, I. (ed.) *Orwell's Nineteen Eighty-Four: Text, Sources, Criticism*, 2nd edition, New York: Harcourt Brace Jovanovich, pp. 248–59.

Owens, C. (1983) 'The discourse of others: feminists and postmodernism', in *The Anti-Aesthetic: Essays on Postmodern Culture*, Port Townsend, WA: The Bay Press, pp. 57–82.

Penley, C. (1989) *The Future of an Illusion: Film, Feminism, and Psychoanalysis*, Minneapolis, MN: University of Minnesota Press.

Philo, G. (ed.) (1999) *Message Received: Glasgow Media Group Research 1993–1998*, London: Longman.

Prince, S. (1996) 'Psychoanalytic film theory and the problem of the missing spectator', in Bordwell, D. and Carroll, N. (eds) *Post-Theory*, Madison, WI: University of Wisconsin Press, pp. 71–86.

Rodowick, D. N. (1991) *The Difficulty of Difference: Psychoanalysis, Sexual Difference, & Film Theory*, New York and London: Routledge.

Signorielli, N. and Morgan, M. (eds) (1990) *Cultivation Analysis: New Directions in Media Effects Research*, Newbury Park, CA: Sage.

Smith, M. (1996) 'The logic and legacy of Brechtianism', in Bordwell, D. and Carroll, N. (eds) *Post-Theory*, Madison, WI: University of Wisconsin Press, pp. 130–48.

Sokal, A. D. (1996a) 'Transgressing the boundaries – toward a transformative hermeneutics of quantum gravity', *Social Text*, 46/47 (Spring/Summer): 217–52.

Sokal, A. D. (1996b) 'A physicist experiments with cultural studies', *Lingua Franca*, May/June, pp. 62–4.

Sokal, A. D. (1996c) 'Transgressing the boundaries: an afterword', *Dissent*, 43(4): 93–9.

Sokal, A. D. (1997) 'A plea for reason, evidence, and logic', *New Politics*, 6(2): 126–9.

Stromer-Galley, J. and Schiappa, E. (1998) 'The argumentative burdens of audience conjectures: audience research in popular culture criticism', *Communication Theory*, 8(1): 27–62.

Turner, G. (ed.) (1990) *British Cultural Studies: an Introduction*, Boston, MA: Unwin Hyman.

Walker, J. (1994) 'Psychoanalysis and feminist film theory: the problem of sexual difference and identity', in Carson, D., Dittmar, L. and Welsch, J. R. (eds) *Multiple Voices in Feminist Film Criticism*, Minneaopolis, MN: University of Minnesota Press, pp. 82–92.

Walsh, M. (1982) *Brechtian Aspects of Radical Cinema*, London: BFI.

Wright, C. R. (1986) *Mass Communication: a Sociological Perspective*, 3rd edition, New York: Random House.

# 4

# Free market feminism, New Labour and the cultural meaning of the TV blonde

ANGELA McROBBIE

What follows is a partial sociology of the present, one that is concerned with the emergent condition of women and young women in Britain today and hence with the making of new political subjects. This will entail consideration of three issues: (1) women in New Labour politics, (2) feminism in the academy and (3) TV blondes in the media. I use the word 'condition' to suggest the broad social and political circumstances which allow a single subject or a group of persons to exist. What designs does the present New Labour government have on women and on girls? How do they envisage and propel the passage of women today through the lifecycle, from the teenage years to full adulthood? Or, echoing Foucault, what 'regime of truth' emerges for women today? I want to propose that women, for good and bad reasons, occupy a new centrality in political culture. But this has happened through a series of critical displacements. In government, women's issues are centre stage, but not the feminist arguments that made this possible. More broadly, the working mother replaces the house-wife; the woman at work replaces the woman (or mother) on welfare; feminist pedagogy in the academy replaces feminist politics in the outside world (a bold claim, but warranted I think); the TV blonde marks what Susan Sontag has called 'the arrival of women's ambition' (Sontag, 1999); but ambition and mobility replace any sense of the social, while in the expansive field of culture the seduction of celebrity and the appeal of feminist populism replace serious-ness and the public role of the feminist intellectual. But surely this must change? Aware of these displacements and wary of the dire political consequences of untrammelled individualism and free market feminism, the feminist intellectual must struggle to avoid the temptation of melancholic withdrawal. But neither must she embrace Germaine Greer's public misanthropy which proclaims only future pain and suffering for the young women of today (Greer, 1999). It is perhaps part of our role to reverse the de-legitimation of the social, and the devaluing of the feminist.

## Women and New Labour

Since coming to office in May 1997, the de-traditionalization of the female role in society, which has been taking place over the last twenty years, has provided the government with one of its biggest challenges. Across the boundaries of class and ethnicity, adult women are becoming less dependent on the male breadwinner and girls show little signs of reversing this trend. Indeed quite rapidly we are seeing a new condition of existence which is that of relative independence or as sociologists including Beck and Giddens have described it 'individualization'. Ideally sexual relationships will become equal partnerships, in love and in money, and the era of the housewife appears to have gone for good. Indeed in late summer 1999 the news media reported that the Chancellor Gordon Brown was recommending that on marriage or cohabitation women should be advised to keep their finances separate from that of their partners. Individual bank accounts protect women against the imprudent fiscal mismanagement of male partners.

Over the last fifteen years the weakening of the tie of marriage has shifted responsibility for women with children and out of work to the state and it is this simple fact which has prompted the flurry of governmental activity. The New Deal, as we know, is the attempt to replace welfare with work. New Labour has sought to seduce women voters with the idea of becoming working mothers. It is by this means that it implements one key strand of its modernization process. The Conservatives feared doing this because it offended old ideas about women's place being at home looking after children. But New Labour have swept this aside and proposed to women a new settlement on the basis of participation in the labour market, come what may.

Various commentators have described the practical difficulties and obstacles in implementing this plan, particularly in the lack of childcare provision. They have also argued that the real purpose is to target women as part of the much bigger project of overhauling welfare, reducing entitlements to benefits and unburdening the state. Or else it has been seen as a way of restoring family values as alternative living arrangements become more difficult, well nigh impossible, to sustain. That is, don't have children unless in a relationship with a highly paid partner who will provide for the child during and after marriage. Others, closer to New Labour, have seen the introduction of Working Family Tax Credit as a decisive intervention against poverty, with a redistributionist logic through the re-routing of benefits into the pay packet. There is some novelty in witnessing a New Labour government pursuing a policy with women at its centre which can be construed, simultaneously, as new right by stealth and also old left by stealth, or indeed, in the style of a triple decker sandwich, as layering left on top of right on top of left policies which appears to be the tactic favoured by Gordon Brown.

The commitment to 'women at work' comes at a cost, as a string of feminist academics have observed. As young women are becoming, as Suzanne Franks has put it, 'the most desirable workers of all', older women and single mothers find their new conditions of existence as working women more difficult (Franks quoted in Segal, 1999). This is a self-definition now foisted upon women; indeed only twenty-five years ago 'to count as a woman' as Judith Butler might put it, meant prioritizing marriage and children. 'We' academic women now in our forties with full-time jobs are actually in a small minority. The great majority of older women have already been disadvantaged in a labour market which has continually underpaid them and failed to reward them with promotion and the benefits of full-time employment. There are no mechanisms in place to help them improve their position, moving from low-paid to well-paid work. Anne Philips has recently argued for the 'importance of substantive social mobility' (Philips, 1999). Only opportunities to move occupations mid-life will shift otherwise ineradicable inequalities; it's not enough to aim for this through improved educational qualifications in the first twenty years. But it is difficult to see how a woman who has worked part time when her children were young, let's say as a university administrator, and who finds herself forty something and divorced, could realistically embark on a change of career to become for example a solicitor. There are no grants, no WFTC to go back to college and few banks would risk a loan. Gordon Brown might tell a women like this to look for a venture capitalist, but her chances of finding one, in let us say Dundee, are slim. The intensification of labour and longer working hours are making evening classes increasingly difficult. So how can older women catch up? They can only do so if they have private means. Indeed women now in their forties, as Walby has argued, 'face an older life in poverty'; they are, as Ginn and Arber have pointed out, 'twice as likely as men to live in poverty' (Walby, 1999; Ginn and Arber, 1999). This is a result of long-term low pay, erratic working patterns and pension disadvantage. In addition it is a grim future for women in their fifties who have already worked and looked after children now having to speed up to overtake the men and to make up for time 'lost' at home.

Either the government would need to embark on a much more radical plan to provide a whole infrastructure to allow for this social transition to the world of the working mother, *pace* a reinvention of the state, or else we will see the work ethic as a moral standard promoted as a political ambition aimed at granting women notional participation as citizens without necessarily addressing economic inequality. The enthusiasm of young women to succeed might well then result in new divisions, between young female 'go getters' just about able to buy into private pension plans and plug into the new global economy, and the others (including the old, the unwell, the psychologically ill, the damaged, but also the young and lazy, the dreamers, poets, musicians and artists, and those temperamentally unsuited to fit in with the new disciplinary regime of 'work') now suffering a further loss of status through not having these attributes of success, not possessing the right kind of human capital. The problem with the 'ethno-politics' of New Labour (as Nikolas Rose has called them) is that the imperative of self-improvement can only make more of us feel even greater failures when judged against the new gold standard of success embodied in the image of Mrs Blair (Rose, 1999). As soon as 'having it all' enters the blood-stream of the culture, it also becomes a new norm, a seemingly achievable goal.

But let us stand back for a moment. The overall aim is to tackle sexual inequality through education and work and at the same time to de-politicize the issue by eliminating the word feminist from the agenda, since that word renders New Labour, it seems, potentially unelectable. Even in the most aus-picious circumstances with local affordable childcare can work be socially transformative to this degree? Or is the focus on work a means of fostering a greater degree of self-sufficiency, while at the same time further stripping those social groups who fail to perform in this way of their status and identity? Can education and work compensate for society? And yet, in opposition to Nikolas Rose, for example, I am reluctant to too hastily dismiss this elevation of work as a mere ideological strategy, a symbol of moral purpose, a way of construct-ing a new ethical horizon in society. The wastage of women's intelligence and capacities throughout at least the twentieth century, the extent to which it is only literally in the last twenty-five years that female ability has been offered some scope for expression, remains one of the founding premises of the feminist movement.

Women's success in education and in work is still circumscribed by class and racial inequalities. But maybe there are opportunities within the new work ethic to re-think or re-articulate work as a force for revitalizing the now defunct 'social'. In the society we live in and in the absence of widescale social trans-formation, it remains the primary source of self-actualization, self-realization, and it marks the decisive entrance of women into the public world. Ulrich Beck has recently argued for 'civic labour', voluntary but socially valuable work in a post-employment society (Beck, 1999). I would propose instead that we bring a greater range of activities, especially those that women have done, into the realm of paid work, creating a new category of 'social work' to allow women otherwise marginalized from the labour market to use their skills and talents independent of age, class and ethnicity. For example, it is not so unusual for women to become involved in local interest groups which connect with their own experience, let's say breast cancer awareness, or mental health issues or drug problems, and through precisely some form of unpaid involve-ment, they have discovered organizational and administrative skills which quite quickly turn into a paid job (e.g. the role of Diana Lamplugh in setting up the Suzi Lamplugh Trust). This in effect paves the way for work, politics and citizenship to converge and for individualization, even in the form of personal tragedy, to give way to association. Wages for housework, as feminists used to call it, is as unrealistic as the call for a citizen's income, an idea which echoes Beck's 'civic labour'. But job creation for part-time and diverse forms of work right across the public and social field ought to be a viable way of encouraging wage earning capacity during and long after the child-rearing years. In short, we cannot abandon the political terrain of New Labour on the basis of the moral purpose which underlies the new work ethic, or because our presence as feminists is unwelcome; there is simply too much at stake and there are also some real possibilities for women. I am calling then for a greater degree of political inventiveness on the part of feminists. There has been a noticeable quietness on the terrain of the pilot studies and 'good ideas' so beloved by the 'policy wonks' of New Labour. To fail to engage on this front is in effect to discount oneself from the terrain of policy, since increasingly this is where it happens.

## It's all on the reading list! Feminism and the academy

I have suggested that feminism has been denied a legitimate space in public political discourse. Instead we have a timid band of women MPs and the New Labour image of the 'working woman'. Reviled creatures, we feminists have to an extent survived this abjection by maintaining an existence in the academy, and in particular in the arts and social sciences. Indeed it may well be that it is in education that feminism, in another fifty years' time, is seen as having had the greatest impact. While our skills of social, political and cultural analysis are our very *raison d'être*, it is surprising that there has been so little attention paid by feminists in regard to our own pedagogy. This is all the more strange given the flooding into the universities of female students, something which might be expected to provoke discussion among feminists. And given our political and public revilement, our relative popularity inside what Spivak has called 'the teaching machine' might also have prompted some degree of self-reflexivity about our own practice (Spivak, 1993). The emotive vocabulary of love and passion for political involvement which remains encrypted in our own memories of the early days of feminism is no longer something we might expect to find among students, but there is nonetheless a real enjoyment and pleasure in their studies. Of course there are many ways in which this could be interpreted; by the time students get to college they have already selected their subjects by choice; or else, as the critics of cultural studies suggest, we academic feminists have become too populist in our courses; and then there is also the widely noted enthusiasm for education right across the spectrum on the part of young women.

But let me suggest that we take this line of thinking a little further. The radical democratic tradition has looked to education not just for social mobility and advancement but also for critical understanding and political change. This shaped the British cultural studies tradition and also the diverse and inter-disciplinary ways in which feminism entered the academy in the late 1970s. More specifically there was a recognition that certain aspects of history, sociology, cultural studies and women's studies offered points of critical connection with the students' own experience. Even at its most abstract, Judith Butler's analysis of the desires which must be relinquished in order 'to count as a woman' and, following this, the way in which women then find themselves going through the motions of being a woman, 'acting out' the housewifely role, while dreaming of doing other things, resonates now as history across the field of gender studies. Thus the discourses of feminism in the academy offer points for identification and recognition. However, with one or two exceptions, notably Spivak and Charlotte Brunsdon, the complexities which arise in the course of an encounter between feminist teacher and female students have been overlooked (Spivak, 1993; Brunsdon, 1991).

Spivak describes allowing the Asian/black female student to claim some representative status on behalf of those of whom she speaks and whose experience of otherness she brings to the classroom. But she then follows this 'strategic use of essentialism' with a question to the student, which, to paraphrase, goes along the lines of asking her about what gives her the right to speak on behalf of those other Asian/black women who are not there alongside her in the classroom? What forces have brought her, but certainly not all of them, to education? 'Others are many' says Spivak; what gives this student the authority to speak for them? This is an illustration of the politics of representation and simultaneously a demonstration of the politics of access through the pedagogic process itself. Spivak is applying her own theory and testing it out. Most of us could provide any number of similar significant encounters with our students, but the point is that none of us incorporates our pedagogy into our writing or research. I am suggesting today that teaching actually provides many opportunities to consider the efficacy and the limits of feminist analysis and these 'conversations' need to be drawn more directly into feminist theory.

Brunsdon considers some of the consequences of feminist readings of media texts now becoming part of the academic canon, and she notes the generational dimensions of responses to what are by now almost feminist classics. There is often, she argues, a process of ironic distancing by students from some of the texts which so attracted the attention of feminists. Brunsdon points to film studies and the ubiquitousness of 'women's weepies' (and I would add to this lesbian fiction like *Well of Loneliness* on the English literature syllabus). This is a mark of the success of feminism in the academy, but it also provokes new questions for us academics. There are of course power relations inscribed in the creation and the transmission of the curriculum; we speak with some authority. Just as New Labour has its designs for women, its ways of shaping and making the new political subject, so too does the feminist teacher. Our subjectivizing discourses appear at some level to 'speak the truth of women', and yet despite what we have learnt from Butler we are still surprised when the female students often want to wriggle out of the gendered categories and feminist readings we present. They will not do as they are told, they· are recalcitrant subjects of our subjectivizing discourses. They are saying back to us, 'This might be you, but it sure isn't me'. Brunsdon describes the undergraduate strategy of going through the motions, performatively, of writing the good feminist essay. Young women do not want to be the women which feminism has allocated for them to identify with. They prefer to have their gender suspended or dissolved into something less problematic. They propose back to us feminists that feminism is no longer needed, they 'know it all already' or did it as GCSE! What this tells us is that we cannot expect to reproduce ourselves in the form of a new generation of young feminists, even when our ideas and our researches are being most positively endorsed. So there is this reaction of profound unsettling ambivalence, throughout the whole feminist pedagogic process where in effect education has become the space for political education. It's all on the reading lists now, unlike when I was an undergraduate in the early 1970s in Glasgow, having to search through the left-wing book stalls for pamphlets on 'women' in order to be able to back up my own claims in the sociology seminar group that gender was a worthy subject for discussion. Surely somebody out there had written something of relevance; actually it was usually Sheila Rowbotham.

I am proposing something quite simple here, that the institutional success of our feminist academic endeavours in the academy should attract greater sociological scrutiny on our own part. Call it self-reflexivity or call it pedagogic deconstruction, but in our interactions with young people and with mature students we are establishing a certain frame of reference, a way of looking at and understanding the world. While in recent years feminist theory has drawn attention to the limits of its Euro/ethnocentrism, in teaching where our student body is now so profoundly multi-cultural, we really do have the opportunity to test out how far feminism can go in its claims to speak to all women, and in what ways it must be modified. This is also a modest call for a return to local, empirical, interactionist, or dialogic 'educational' research which provides a counter to that trend in feminist theory towards what Michele Barrett and Anne Philips have described as 'reckless abstraction' (Barrett and Philips, 1997). The institutional power of the academy and the legitimation which has been awarded to feminist studies have put in motion a body of feminist knowledge. However, what happens to this once we let go of it, and in particular how it circulates in non-academic worlds alongside other competing discourses, is something we have little control over. How it clashes with or converges with other more popular 'knowledges about women' is something upon which at present we can only speculate. But this issue leads me to the third and final issue, the existence of 'feminist populism', the TV blonde and the importance of our being vigilant of the dangers of 'free market feminism'.

## The TV blondes

Paul Gilroy said in his inaugural lecture at Goldsmiths College, London, a couple of years ago, 'we need a political analysis that is alive to the fluidity and contingency of a situation that seems to lack precedents' (Gilroy, 1997). The situation of which Gilroy speaks is also one which finds the old categories of feminism, socialist feminism, liberal feminism and radical feminism, less capable of providing purchase in analysis and deficit around the intersection of race and ethnicity with gender. This incongruence of categories with political realities is further complicated by the shifting terrain of right- and left-wing politics within the remit of New Labour and as indicated programmatically in the title of Giddens' book *Beyond Right and Left* (Giddens, 1994). What are the consequences, it might be asked, of superimposing the shifts in feminist thinking with those between right and left? Having indicated in the previous section the existence of something akin to pedagogic feminism, let me propose the existence of feminist populism as a category which alerts us to the dangers of neo-liberal feminism slipping in the back door as we enjoy the energetic images of confident young women which now dominate visual culture. What the Tories during the Thatcher years could not resolve because of their commitment to family values, the popular Murdoch-owned media now promote as a new rhetoric of freedom and independence for young women. This is founded on competitiveness and success in careers, it is also based on the 'love of money' and is symbolized in the image of the TV blonde who also epitomizes what Paul Gilroy has called 'the glamour of whiteness', crystallized in the currency of celebrity.

This image of new womanhood exists in an oblique relation to 1970s feminism; it is not an entirely separate and monstrous formation. The love of money has a direct relation to the emphasis on financial independence, and the focus on career high flyers connects with feminist campaigns against the glass ceiling. But there is also a triumphalism which spurns feminist effort as worthy, well intended but now part of history. Nor is there much in the way of gestures towards even 'liberal feminism' in its equal opportunities mode. Instead there is the emphasis on drive and ambition. These phenomena (and the endless references to young women such as Zoe Ball on stratospheric salaries) have to be set in the context of the Thatcher years which now have an unexpected afterlife in the rise of the TV blonde. In keeping with the post-Tory times, the political element is subdued and pushed below the surface, so that it is barely visible, and the momentum is carried along by the media. The last ten years have seen a decisive shift in media culture which can be characterized in terms of tabloidization, hedonism and the cult of the celebrity. It is the blonde who embodies the visuality of this new regime of cultural meanings. Diana-like, she is its heroine, its dazzling star.

Populism implies an unstable alliance or combination of diverse elements which can be pulled or articulated in quite different political directions. At the same time populism reflects a sense of radical popular movement. As a social movement, without party affiliation or leadership or indeed even membership, 1970s feminism despite its vilification entered into the bloodstream of women as a kind of Gramscian common sense. And it has since taken up residence in the field of the media. From 'Richard and Judy's domestic violence hotline' (on the GMTV programme), to Sheryl Gascoigne's willingness to publicize her experience as a battered wife to promote the anti-domestic violence charity Refuge (and the decision to release her story to the Murdoch-owned *Sun* newspaper, 23 November 1999), there are grounds to talk about the feminization of the media. (It is also interesting to note how campaigning organizations for women's rights, legally defined as charities, are now the site for what in the past would have been described as activism.) But in this process of feminization, femininity does not stand opposed to feminism, rather there is a new alignment, a hybrid of the two. By femininity I mean, in this context, an arrangement of gendered characteristics which take their meaning through difference from those associated with men and masculinity.

Crudely ascribed gender essentialism is a defining characteristic of the new feminist populism. The images of 'slim blondeness' also exact an exclusionary violence on those not so endowed, the non-blonde, non-white, non-able-bodied. A new vocabulary emerges which interprets relations between men and women metaphorically in terms of a battlefield, and in so doing reduces and crudely demeans men to nothing more than their unpleasant attributes of maleness. The popular discourse of the young women columnists celebrates this ritual repudiation of men as 'bastards'. A new genre has evolved which comprises the true life, blow-by-blow account of the female columnist being left by her partner or husband. Often this is related Clarissa Harlowe-style, as the husband exits with his bags, leaving his grieving wife to write her column about their relationship. There is unresolved political significance in these writings around the role of irony. It appears to offer the feminist populists a kind of get-out clause, it provides them with symbolic room to 'play with' pre-feminist fixations of love and romance, thinness and the body. The love object in the Bridget Jones sequel has the Austinesque title of Mark Darcy and is also, it seems, to Bridget's horror, a Tory voter (Fielding, 1999). But the suggestion that feminist populism is post-Tory, and that these new young women are natural New Labour voters, and therefore morally upright and also modern young women, conceals the means by which the free floating elements which constitute this form of populism can just as easily be articulated to create a new 'mix', a kind of free market feminism, the political home of which is, however, no longer unambiguously with the Tories.

If winning the hearts and minds of young women has become a social and political priority, I want to propose that the *Daily Mail* now seeks to modern-ize and rejuvenate the political right by articulating ideas of success and wealth and individualism with those of female empowerment and 'women's rights'. Widely recognized as the voice of middle England and historically associated with mobilizing the success of the Thatcher government, the *Daily Mail*, despite its guarded approval for New Labour, remains richly symbolic of both the dynamics of change in society and the 'forces of conservatism'. The front page of the edition of Friday, 11 December 1998, ran the headline 'Shock rise in school girl babies'. This followed the publication of a report which showed an 11 per cent rise in the number of pregnancies to teenage girls in the UK. The *Mail* leader proposed that young people should be discouraged from having sex rather than be provided with better information about how to avoid pregnancy. The leader concluded with government statistics showing that 37 per cent of babies in Britain are now born to parents who are unmarried. The leader thus establishes a chain of association between teenage mothers, sexuality and the decline in family values. This lead column is then followed up in no less than three major pieces spreading across five pages, each of which focuses on young women and pursues the theme of young women, sexuality and family life.

Across pages 14 and 15 the story combines garish headlines, 'Relentless rise of the child mothers', with pictures and profiles of three young women who were pregnant in their very early teens and are now mothers (Lambert, 1998, p. 14). Inevitably these are all unusual and thus newsworthy cases. Two of the girls were pregnant at twelve and one at thirteen. The author of the article blames the heavily sexualized culture of everyday life, the 'ephemeral dross of the Spice Girls', the 'flagrantly suggestive gear' on sale even in 'dear old M and S', parents who fail to provide moral guidance and boys who put pressure on young girls to have sex with them.

Only a few pages later the reader is greeted with a full-colour double-page spread of glamorous pictures with the headline 'Blondes who will do anything for fame' (Cole, 1998, pp. 22–3). Granted the girls in question range from nineteen to thirty in age, but the story hinges round the willingness of these young women to exploit their sexuality including 'posing naked for a men's magazine' in the hope of securing a job in television. The paper celebrates the ambition of these young women by awarding them marks out of 10. At the complete opposite end of the social spectrum from the teenage mothers (these girls all have good academic qualifications), the *Daily Mail* is applauding their willingness to cash in on their sexuality. Success in the workplace hinges round using sex and blonde hair as a girl's most valuable assets. Then, finally, on page 27 of the same issue, the *Daily Mail* takes up the case of the single mother Miss Berry, who is described as working (which in *Daily Mail* terms means respectable) and who has lost her place in the queue for council housing because it has been allocated to 'asylum seekers'. The ideological footwork here is extraordinarily deft. The white, blonde single mother is presented as a deserving case who is being treated unfairly in favour of immigrants many of whose claims for asylum are to quote 'bogus'.

In this one issue of the *Daily Mail* the reader is left in little doubt that young women are a main subject of interest. This is apparent in the repetition of concerns and the sheer concentration of attention. No black or Asian women make any appearance on this occasion, and 'race' is implicit in the guise of the illegal immigrant taking the home (rather than job) of the British citizen who, as it happens, is now also a single mother. As the meanings around what it is to be a young women in Britain today proliferate and threaten to run out of control, the *Daily Mail* is attempting to marry a modern, sexually independent and individualistic image of young women with a more traditional language of national belonging and family values. On the one hand there are the girls who have made it to the top, on the other hand, the single mother who can at least be acknowledged as an upright citizen in that she is working and not claiming benefit. In this instance the status differences between the TV girls and the single mother are temporarily suspended through the non-innocent mark of their blondeness.

The image of the TV blonde is unanchored politically; it is literally suspended uncertainly between left and right, insofar as the centre-left policies of New Labour endorse the values of drive and ambition and young women are now the key proponents of this enthusiasm to achieve. In addition, Tony Blair is an enthusiastic contributor to the *Daily Mail*, penning articles with titles such as 'Why we should stop giving lone teenage mothers council homes' (Blair, 1999, p. 17). While the Conservative Party might have been considered the natural home for free market feminism, in fact quite the opposite is the case. Reports show low levels of interest on the part of female voters across the age range. It is as though the old guard of the Conservatives are so entrenched in their thinking (women included) that they cannot recognize an opportunity when it is literally knocking on their door. They either do not like or are scared off by the idea of ambitious young women challenging their status. Alternatively it is conceivable that this free market feminism is indicative of something quite different. Perhaps it exists primarily as a fantasy of female omnipotence, the only way to 'have it all' in the kind of society we live in. In which case it works by virtue of the distance it marks between the ideal and the real. Let me conclude by proposing its essentially ambivalent status, despite the efforts of the *Daily Mail* to tie it down to a means of rejuvenating right-wing values. If this is the case then it is still imperative that we feminists continue to intervene on this fantasy terrain, not by robbing young women of their desires for freedom and independence but by speaking up on behalf of social values and collectivity.

To conclude, there is much in what I have said so far which seems to point to the redundancy of or the transcendence of our labours as feminists. But there is also a danger that we too easily occupy a melancholic position. This beckons us and we take up our places within a field of sadness and loss. But is this not also a place which is now allocated to us in these anti-intellectual times? Are we not allowing ourselves to be positioned in this way, made complicit with our seeming ineffectivity? Surely we can squeeze some hope out of the fact that at long last in the UK more people will have access to higher education, and in our classrooms we can at least impart to our students the value of what Sontag described as 'the mind as passion'. We can appeal perhaps to what Wendy Brown (1995) has called the 'feminist political imagination' to envisage better ways of living, and we might also remain alert to and in touch with those strands of feminist populism (and I am thinking here of Tracey Emin) which refuse the happy hedonism of the TV blondes and which seek quite desperately to understand what can still make us feel wretched.

*Note*: This is an amended version of the inaugural lecture delivered by Angela McRobbie at Goldsmiths College in November 1999. The author would like to emphasize that her own views on media and cultural studies differ from those expressed by Greg Philo and David Miller in the *Cultural Compliance* section of this book.

## References

Barrett, M. and Philips, A. (1997) *Destabilising Theory: Contemporary Feminist Debate*, Cambridge: Polity Press.

Blair, T. (1999) 'Why we should stop giving lone teenage mothers council homes', *Daily Mail*, 14 June, p. 17.

Beck, U. (1999) *Schones Neue Arbeits-welt*, Frankfurt: Campus Verlag.

Brown, W. (1995) *States of Injury*, Princeton, NJ: Princeton University Press.

Brunsdon, C. (1991) 'Pedagogies of the feminine: feminist teaching and women's genres', *Screen*, 4(32): 364–81.

Cole, A. (1998) 'Blondes who will do anything for fame', *Daily Mail*, 11 December, pp. 22–3.

Fielding, B. (1999) *The Age of Esteem: Bridget Jones' Diary*, London: Picador

Giddens, A. (1994) *Beyond Left and Right: The Future of Radical Politics*, Cambridge: Polity Press.

Gilroy, P. (1997) 'Between camps: race and culture in postmodernity', Inaugural Lecture, Goldsmiths College, 4 March.

Ginn, J. and Arber, S. (1999) 'Women's pension poverty: prospects and options for change', in Walby, S. (ed.) *New Agendas for Women*, Basingstoke: Macmillan, pp. 75–98.

Greer, G. (1999) *The Whole Woman*, London: Doubleday.

Lambert, A. (1998) 'Relentless rise of the child mothers', *Daily Mail*, 11 December, pp. 14–15.

Philips, A. (1999) *Which Equalities Matter?*, Cambridge: Polity Press.

Rose, N. (1999) 'Inventiveness in politics', *Economy and Society*, 28(3): 467–93.

Segal, L. (1999) *Why Feminism?*, Cambridge: Polity Press.

Sontag, S. (1999) 'Women', essay to accompany photographs in Leibovitz, A., *Women*, London: Jonathan Cape.

Spivak, G. (1993) *Outside in the Teaching Machine*, London: Routledge.

Walby, S. (ed.) (1999) *New Agendas for Women*, Basingstoke: Macmillan.

# 5

## The 'public', the 'popular' and media studies

JOHN CORNER

The term 'media studies' is only a very broad indicator of a kind of academic course. There is little by way of distinctive ideas and methods, no broad agreement as to the most pertinent intellectual traditions and, indeed, no acceptance about what should be looked at and why. If these are unpromising conditions for consolidating an inter-disciplinary field, they are quite disastrous if you fancy setting up shop as a new discipline. It might be best to see the present situation as one in which there is a loose, nervous and indeed rather acrimonious grouping of a number of ways of studying media, some prepared to appear together in public and some definitely not. I wrote about this as an issue five years ago (Corner, 1995) in face of the growing tendency for media studies to be marketed as a confident, singular entity accelerating towards full academic independence (this was at about the same time as the media themselves were developing the indignant view that the term indicated a highly unrecommended, wholly inadequate route for misguided students seeking jobs in the sector). In fact, there had been earlier discussion of a possible problem, both from within the media and cultural studies field (see Durant, 1991) and from outside it (Davis (1993) noted the fragmentation of the area and suggested the benefits of improved sociological coherence). Since then the disarray has perhaps worsened with further expansion in the number and variety of courses. However, within this fissile and problematic mix I would want to note strands of work of just the sort that get the Philo and Miller seal of sociological approval, being empirical, problem based, alert to questions of power and keen at points to inform policy and public debate. I am also more sympathetic than they are to the widespread problematizing of how the 'real' and the 'represented' might relate to each other or, on occasion, of whether they are in fact separable. But that this issue has been the subject of repetitive, obscure and self-satisfied elaboration I can readily agree.

Here, I want to focus my attention on two terms – the public and the popular – which I think lie at the centre of many of problems discussed in the main section of this book and warrant more exploration than they have hitherto received. For the various ways of placing the media as objects of study have been influenced in their formation not only by the nature of the perceived relationship between the two – at times one of virtual synonymity, often of tension and occasionally of mutual exclusion – but by the continuing problems to which each term itself gives rise.

There is now widespread recognition of the problems which the 'public' as a normative idea faces as a way of justifying forms of funding, affiliation, identity, rights and responsibility in society and of then identifying such entities as the 'public interest', the 'public good' and 'public opinion'. The nature and performance of media systems have rightly been seen to be centrally implicated in 'the fate of the public' and, in media research, Habermas' concept of the 'public sphere' has become an organizing focus for a wide range of work. Among those factors seen to be threatening 'the public' are two rather different senses of 'the private'. First of all, the increasing hold of private capital over the primary terms of the social democratic project in Europe and elsewhere, with the stronger commodification of many sectors and values (including education), and, secondly, an intensification in many societies of the focus on personal life and on forms of individuation rather than of solidarity. The economic trends of globalization have also been seen to contribute to the problem by reducing the power of nation states to frame firmly their own public protocols.

Rescuing and/or redefining 'publicness', and the specific forms of its organization and expression within media, has not been the only project within media research, however. There has also been a radical deconstruction of the very idea, with the suggestion that it might be best not even to try to put it back together. This view of the public as a notion which, irredeemably, is variously coercive, limiting, exclusive and repressive has most often been advanced in the cause of a 'popular' which either in fact or in potential is seen to offer richer resources for self-identity, the recognition of multiplicity and contradiction and for devolved forms of power released from the constraints of the public–bureaucratic tradition. The spirit of this rejection is frequently 'romantic post-modern' in character, the stance taken is that of having crossed a deep if still narrow fissure, on the far side of which the potential of new confusion is attractively contrasted to the tired and failed versions of order left behind.

This strongly negative inflection of 'public' can be contrasted with the positive inflections which 'popular' has been receiving since the 1980s, some instances of which Philo and Miller critically cite. 'Popular' has always been an awkward term in media and cultural studies, of course, since many critics and researchers have wanted to recognize the problem of the industrial and commercial character of modern popular culture whilst also addressing the value of much popular entertainment and of, more broadly, the experiences, values and aspirations of 'the people'. This has sometimes produced a high degree of ambivalence and equivocation. I would want to argue, nevertheless, that there has often been a real integrity about this kind of wrestling, which is, for instance, to be found regularly in the work of Raymond Williams. A far easier move has been to inflect the 'popular' strongly as either bad or good, allowing qualifications (if they appear at all) to be merely token. F.R. and Q.D. Leavis produced a notable version of the 'bad popular' for literary criticism, but some Marxist media research has come close to matching it, if only by holding the future potential of a 'real' popular against the comprehensive denunciation of the 'false' one currently evident (the Leavises worked polemically on two fronts, the superiority of high culture and of the organic popular culture of the past). More recently, the tendency has been towards positing the popular as 'good', with at best a secondary recognition of the ways in which this might need to be qualified. Again, Philo and Miller bring this out well in discussing issues around sexism, racism and violence. What has caused this slow but steady shift? Here, I think the more loosely eclectic ways of posing questions of pleasure, aesthetics and audience on media studies courses, in the context of attracting and engaging students strongly oriented to careers in the media sector, have had their effect. There are doubtless broader and deeper factors at work too. I agree with Philo and Miller on the significance of the virtual abandonment of the notion of 'ideology', a pivotal term in the the development of the whole area. The full story of how this defining concept virtually dropped off the agenda altogether has yet to be written, but one part of it must involve the way in which it progressively became theorized away from any connection with actual political and social analysis. Perhaps it wasn't so much dropped as simply evaporated into the thin air of 'discourse'? But the question of ideology initially pointed to one clear reason why the media mattered; it pointed to complexity of meaning but also to systematic inequality and power and the role of the media in the attempt to secure terms of consent which fitted with the interests of dominant economic groups. However, in the post-Althusserian development of the notion, strongly present in the literary and cultural theory and the film and television studies of the 1970s and early 1980s, it quite quickly became expanded and elaborated to the point where it was unable to inform substantive research. Its edge as a critical concept disappeared in a miasma of semiotic speculation and a self-satisfied philosophical pessimism that 'nothing could be done'. In this form, it was used to dismiss work in empirical sociology as politically naive, including the first publications of the Glasgow Media Group, whose attempt to turn commonsense ideas of 'balance and bias' into tools of critical leverage was met with derision by some cultural studies writers. Any mention of 'ideology' now is likely to make many media researchers feel nervous, and quite understandably too. Some will remember the assertive and wildly totalistic versions of it in circulation, others would rather simply forget the whole thing. Still others, amongst whom I would count myself, will remember the silliness but also regret the failure to continue developing the connection between meanings and power through argument and empirical analysis. The net effect upon media and cultural studies of 'ideology's' disappearance was, in many areas, to displace and disperse the very idea of power and influence. The project of reception study, in the illuminating, early work of David Morley, had been developed precisely to refine the understanding of ideological influence by attention to specific media treatments and the forms of viewer response to them. The irony is that this was then followed by a 'turn to ethnography' in which many protagonists pursued what was in effect an 'anti-power' thesis, not so much a revision as a rejection of the idea of the media as agencies of political and social influence.

These shifts loosened one form of the interconnection between 'public' and 'popular', a form which framed the lack of fit between the two as a primary issue for argument and investigation. Study of the media as 'popular' was now far freer than before to pursue studies disencumbered of attention to the economy, to the steer of the market within and upon cultural development, to national history, the State and even to the functions of journalism (how and where, if at all, questions of journalism are positioned on media studies programmes continues to be a key variable).

What about work around 'the public'? Has this work not failed fully to recognize the problematic character of many rhetorics of 'the public' past and present (unifying and exclusionist in ways both crude and subtle)? Has it not frequently failed to engage with the terms of the modern popular, in respect both of experience and imagination (including the terms of fantasy)? I think the answer in both cases must be yes. Although the idea of the 'public sphere' continues to aid debate, there is little doubt that in some research and teaching it has been only too easily incorporated into a dominant, theoreticist approach and has settled into being an abstracted substitute for a real attention to government, publicity, media functions and citizenship, an attention which engages not only with ideas but with the data of specific circumstance. In some accounts, it now figures as a largely gestural point of orientation and of easy advocacy.

A tendency to focus exclusively on journalism in discussion of the public sphere has also undoubtedly given much work a narrowed sense of the dynamics of imagination and the complex and diverse character of the 'entertaining' (it seems to me that this problem is now coming through in some debates about 'infotainment' and 'docusoap', where the approach can often foreclose rapidly around judgement rather than open up investigation).

So I am suggesting that at least part of the messiness of current 'media and cultural studies' can be seen as the consequences, first of all, of uncertainties and tensions around the two orienting ideas of 'public' and 'popular' and then of the form of the relation between the two, where versions both of explicit opposition and of mutual lack of interest are to be found more often than real dialogue in theory and in inquiry. I think this is a much more significant polarity than that between 'political economy' and 'cultural studies', an end-lessly replayed skirmish whose chief drawback as a way of understanding the problems of the field is that its categories leave out a vast body of work on the press, broadcasting and information systems which is viewable neither as the one nor the other with any useful degree of precision.

The tensions around public and popular are importantly compounded by the way in which the fracturing of the field has developed a gendered dimen-sion. Feminist scholars interested in media, particularly those working from within what Philo and Miller term the newer 'cultural feminism', have often found it more congenial to work from a sense of the 'popular', whichever direction they then wish to pursue, than to relate their work to the idea of the 'public'. They have found discussion of this idea, both within the media industry and outside, to be framed within masculine values (see, for instance, Hermes, 1997). More questionably, they have seen it to depend on principles of truth and rationality upon which it is no longer possible to build. I understand why questions of pleasure and identity (and the other constituents of what Hermes discusses as 'cultural citizenship' (1997, pp. 85–9)) are particularly important to understanding the relationship between gender and the media, but I think anything which separates these questions off from other, and more established, questions about the funding and regulation of the media and about the political and ethical criteria for debating their performance as information and enter-tainment is unfortunate. Writers as diverse in their interests as Sylvia Harvey, Ros Coward, Jenny Kitzinger, Sonia Livingstone, Janet Wasko and Birgitta Hoijer have shown how, rather than a move to other terms of inquiry, there can be a productive feminist engagement with the media as public systems informed by public values.

Peter Dahlgren (1995), commenting on earlier remarks of mine about the difference between the 'public knowledge' and the 'popular culture' project in media research, suggested that if we reversed the terms and thought more about 'public culture' and 'popular knowledge' it might help get beyond the impasse in both conceptualization and research. His point is a useful one, but the fact remains that 'public' is inescapably a normative notion, concerning a mode of social cohesion. 'Popular', by contrast, remains in most usages a term descriptively anchored in a scale of market-based success, whatever the normative inflections placed on this (ranging from '10 million people can't be wrong' to disdain).

Media research needs to keep both public and popular as a clear and prob-lematic double focus in order to develop its intellectual agenda and to develop further the social cogency which Philo and Miller, along with many others, call for. They are right in thinking that issue-based research is a good way of doing this. The more that this crosses the genres, engages with both fic-tional and factual material (as recent Glasgow work has done) and considers 'entertainment' to be as significant as 'news' at many points in the relation between media and social life, the better.

However, it is very doubtful indeed whether most of the projects at present working under the 'media studies' label, variously connecting with the broader pastures of 'communication' and 'culture' and sometimes best regarded as a new branch of the arts rather than the social sciences, can be encouraged (or shamed) towards the research goals of an empirical sociology. The label 'media studies', unlike 'cultural studies', initially identified a pedagogic grouping rather than a research perspective. Quite apart from questions of core identity, both these designations continue to face difficulty in establishing themselves as coherent projects on the respective 'other side' of the research/teaching divide. But, as I noted at the beginning, there is a now routine overlooking of the real diversity of aims and approaches to be found in college and university programmes. Many usages of the term 'media studies' and even 'cultural studies', tend to aid misperception here, posing problems not only for advocacy but also for censure. Further pursuit of the issues raised by Philo and Miller – essentially about what is being given attention and what is being ignored, about what ideas get celebrated while others are scorned – will need to take account of this dispersed identity in order to get the best hearing and a proper response.

## References

Corner, J. (1995) 'Media studies and the knowledge problem', *Screen*, 36(2): 145–55 (reprinted in Corner, J. (1998) *Studying Media: Problems of Theory and Method*, Edinburgh: Edinburgh University Press).

Dahlgren, P. (1995) *Television and the Public Sphere*, London: Sage.

Davis, H. (1993) 'Media research: whose agenda?', in Eldridge, J. (ed.) *Getting the Message*, London: Routledge.

Durant, A. (1991) 'Noises offscreen: could a crisis of confidence be good for media studies?', *Screen*, 32(4): 403–28.

Hermes, J. (1997) 'Gender and media studies', in Corner, J., Schlesinger, P. and Silverstone, R. (eds) *International Media Research*, London: Routledge, pp. 65–95.

# 6

## The emperor's new theoretical clothes, or geography without origami

CHRIS HAMNETT

### Introduction

The 1990s have seen dramatic changes in the structure and geography of global economic, social and political organization. The power of global corporations has increased dramatically, the collapse of communism in the former Soviet Union and Eastern Europe has fundamentally changed economic and living conditions, the South East Asian financial crisis has created major problems in the region and conflicts and famines in Africa and elsewhere have led to hundreds of thousands of deaths. Nearer to home, the combination of rising employment in financial and business services and high levels of unemployment in many deprived inner city areas and peripheral estates has resulted in growing inequalities in education, health, living standards and the like.

Given these changes, it might be expected that human geography would seek to deal with the geography of these and other events. In many respects it does. A significant amount of research and writing in the discipline grapples with such issues (Thrift and Leyshon, 1995; Walker, 1999; Martin, 1998). In recent years, however, human geography has undergone a radical cultural or post-modern turn (see Cosgrove and Jackson, 1987; McDowell, 1994; Matless, 1995; Mitchell, 1995 for reviews). The cultural turn has many different manifestations but, as Barnett (1998, p. 380) points out:

> Perhaps one common thread . . . is a commitment to epistemologies, often loosely labelled 'post-structural', that emphasise the contingency of knowledge claims and recognise the close relationship among language, power and knowledge. Both epistemologically and in the construction of new research objects, the cultural turn is probably best characterised by a heightened reflexivity toward the role of language, meaning, and representation in the constitution of 'reality' and knowledge of 'reality'.

For those unfamiliar with developments in human geography since the 1970s, this may come as something of a surprise. They can be forgiven for possibly assuming that it is still concerned with the topics of their school days: the old 'capes and bays' listing of places and their characteristics and old style regional geographies, which started with geology and moved through physical landforms, climate, soils, vegetation and climate before turning to economy, settlement and society. Those whose school days were a little later would perhaps associate it with the study of various types of idealized models: of settlement, agricultural land use, industrial location or urban structure. Such readers may be suprised to discover that human geography has been subject to many of the same fierce intellectual debates and revolutions which have characterized some of the other disciplines in the humanities and social sciences since the 1960s. I class it in both groups because although human geography abandoned its humanities orientation in favour of an attempt to become a rigorous social science in the late 1960s and early 1970s, the last ten years have seen an equally strong rejection of the notions of science, objectivity and abstract generalizations in favour of a strong cultural, literary and interpretative turn. Human geography, or significant parts of it, has taken on the post-modern baggage of discourse theory, textuality, representation, difference, otherness, contestation subjectivity and the like (Barnes and Duncan, 1992; Barnett, 1993; Sayer, 1993; Barnett and Low, 1996). Before discussing some of these developments it is useful to provide a brief history of the evolution of the discipline since 1970.

## From regional description to post-modernism: a brief intellectual history

Human geography has undergone several major intellectual changes since the 1970s. The first such revolution was the 'quantitative' theoretical revolution in the late 1960s which dramatically re-cast human geography away from its focus on synthetic regional description and attempted to make it a 'scientific' subject with an emphasis on mathematical modelling and quantification (Chorley and Haggett, 1967). The key statement of this approach was David Harvey's (1969) classic *Explanation in Geography* which attempted to put geography on a firm positivist footing with a stress on development of formal theory, scientific explanation and empirical testing. Human geography attempted to recast its image from that of descriptive, qualitative synthesis of specific and unique places to that of a 'spatial science' with a stress on quantitative spatial analysis and spatial patterns (Johnston, 1987).

The quantitative revolution was not to last. Within a few years of its establishment it was challenged by a radical alternative led, once again, by David Harvey (1973) in his book *Social Justice and the City* which argued that quantitative geography was sterile and reinforced the status quo. As he put it:

> mapping even more evidence of man's inhumanity to man is counter revolutionary in the sense that it allows the bleeding heart liberal in us to pretend that we are contributing to a solution which in fact we are not. This kind of empiricism is irrelevant. (p. 144)

Harvey put forward a Marxist alternative which argued that the object of geography should not be the formulation of abstract 'scientific' theories, laws

**159**

and models which achieved nothing but revolutionary social change. In retrospect, Harvey's *volte-face* can be seen to reflect liberal social disenchantment with the existing social order in the aftermath of the Vietnam war, Watts and the widespread student unrest of 1968, and his intellectual shift was parallelled by Bill Bunge who renounced 'theoretical geography' (Bunge, 1966), left academe and set up a 'geographical expedition' in the inner city of Detroit.

The influence of Marxism remained strong in certain areas of human geography until the late 1980s, although it was increasingly challenged in the 1970s and 1980s by a variety of humanist, behavioural and phenomenological orientated approaches (Ley, 1977; Eyles, 1981; Duncan and Ley, 1982) who argued that human behaviour could only be interpreted in terms of the subjective meanings and values held by human beings. In retrospect, these essentially subjective approaches, which focused on meaning, interpretation and representation, marked the beginning of the cultural or literary turn in human geography which, reflecting developments in other subjects, firmly turned its back on notions of science and objectivity in favour of a far more interpretative approach based, in part, on the anthropological work of Geertz (1973, 1983) and French theoretical notions of the significance of discourse, readings, texts, interpretation and positional knowledge (see for example Barnes and Duncan, 1992). These developments have not replaced or supplanted other types of human geographical work, but notions of discourse, reading and texts are far more important among the younger generation of academics entering the discipline. This school draws heavily on post-modernism and its epistemological bases (Harvey, 1989; Sayer, 1993). As Rosenau (1992) put it in her overview of post-modernism and the social sciences:

> Postmodern social scientists support a refocusing of what has been taken for granted, what has been neglected, regions of resistance, the forgotten, the irrational, the insignificant, the repressed, the borderline, the classical, the sacred, the traditional, the eccentric, the sublimated, the subjugated, the rejected, the nonessential, the marginal, the peripheral, the excluded, the tenuous, the silenced, the accidental, the dispersed, the disqualified, the deferred, the disjointed – all that which 'the modern age has never cared to understand in any particular detail, with any sort of specificity'. (p. 8)

I want to argue here that while many of these developments have undoubtedly been beneficial and have led to a theoretical reinvigoration of the subject, in some respects the developments have been detrimental and have led to new forms of geographical writing (I hesitate to use the term research) which simply treat theory and concepts as a sort of intellectual game which has become increasingly detached from real world problems and concerns. In this respect, much contemporary cultural geography has become indistinguishable from the intellectual society described in Herman Hesse's novel *The Glass Bead Game* where what counts is the skill with which the players can deploy and link concepts, terms and ideas to build ever more complex and elaborate structures and interpretations, rather than any contribution they make to explaining or understanding the structures and processes of the world in which they live. Indeed, like the participants in the glass bead game, some post-modern cultural geographers are isolating themselves in more complex linguistic, conceptual and terminological webs. I provide some examples of this type of work below.

This trend is not, of course, unique to contemporary geography. It is characteristic of much post-modern intellectual writing in general. Ironically, both share a concern with examining ideas of difference, otherness, subordination, polyvocality and the like, while at the same time working within a linguistic and conceptual framework which profoundly differentiates them as authors from those they nominally seek to empower and give voice to. In this respect, it can be argued that the contemporary equivalent of the glass bead game is fundamentally intellectually dishonest. Under the guise of liberation, empowerment and giving voice to those hitherto excluded, it simply reinforces the privileges of the intellectual elite to play an elaborate language game written by and for a tiny minority of participants.

On the other hand, it could be argued following Foucault's work on the relationships between knowledge, discourse, representation and power, that the complex discourses of post-modernism reflect not the privileges of the intellectual elite but, rather, its growing isolation and alienation from the centres of power in society. Given the decreasing power and influence of the social sciences in economic, technological and political affairs during the 1980s and 1990s under the anti-intellectual New Right regimes of Thatcher and Reagan, it can be argued that many academics simply gave up on any notion of progressive social change and simply retreated into a world of social critique and theoretical elaboration. Some of the debates surrounding this issue have been discussed by Bassett (1996) who suggests that, following Foucault and Bauman, 'the collapse of the modernist project means that (universal intellectuals) now belong to a bygone age' (p. 513). He adds that with the triumph of the nation state:

> Cultural hegemony was no longer so important to political domination, and the state and culture separated into different spheres. However, the intellectuals did not inherit the authority to legislate in the cultural sphere. Instead, they were rapidly displaced by market mechanisms and consumer culture as sources of values and judgement. Choice was effectively privatised and left to the determination of market forces and the vagaries of fashion and instant obsolescence. (p. 514)

I cannot comment on the situation in the United States but it has become very clear in Britain over the last ten years that academic economists rarely write or comment in the mass media on the economic issues of the day. This role has been usurped by the financial economists and analysts working for the major banks and finance houses. It is to them, and not the academics, that the media now turn for statements and analysis on employment, inflation, growth and the like. There are, of course, some prominent exceptions such as Paul Krugman and Lester Thurow in the US and John Hills, John Muellbauer and John Eatwell in Britain who engage in debate on economic policy issues but they are few and far between. Academe appears to have yielded the critical policy field to the think tanks and popular intellectuals and much academic discourse has become a convoluted linguistic game for its marginalized participants. For a full critique see Martin (2000), Markusen (1999) and Storper (2000).

## Relativism and the linguistic turn

McDowell (1994) notes that one of the most pronounced features of contemporary cultural geography, and of the social sciences and humanities more widely, has been the way in which dominant notions of truth have been disrupted. She argues that:

> There is a growing recognition that knowledge is multiple and positional, that there are many ways of seeing and reading the landscape. One of the foci of contemporary cultural geography, therefore, is the investigation of multiple discourses about place and identity. (p. 163)

This view, that knowledge is multiple and positional, that different groups perceive, interpret and represent things depending on their economic and social position, their culture, gender and their place in power relations, has become the accepted starting point in cultural geography. This, in turn, has led to a growing focus on examination of the nature and construction of representations, images and identities, among both dominant and subordinate groups. Following Edward Said's (1978) pioneering work on the construction of the 'Orient', human geographers have produced valuable work on, for example, cultural hegemony and the race-definition process (Anderson, 1988) and the representation and interpretation of landscape (Cosgrove and Daniels, 1988). Underpinning this approach is the rejection of all 'mirror' theories of correspondence between the external world and our perceptions, knowledge and representations of that world. Gregory and Walford (1989) state that: 'our texts are not mirrors which we hold up to the world, reflecting its shapes and structures immediately and without distortion. They are instead, creatures of our own making, though their making is not entirely of our own choosing' (p. 2).

One of the clearest and most systematic statements of this type of philosophy is that provided by Barnes and Duncan (1992). They state in their introduction to *Writing Worlds* that: 'once we sever the supposed one-to-one link between language and brute reality, the notion that writing mirrors the world is untenable . . . there is no pre-interpreted reality that writing reflects'.

They then go on to ask what our writing reflects if it does not reflect some bedrock reality? Their answer is that:

> it must involve yet prior interpretations. That is, our texts draw upon other texts, that are themselves based on yet different texts . . . In the vocabulary of literary theory there is only intertextuality . . . 'the process whereby meaning is produced from text to text rather than, as it were, between text and world' . . . The consequence is that writing is constitutive, not simply reflective . . . we cannot appeal to any epistemological bedrocks in privileging one text over another. For what is true is made inside texts, not outside them. (pp. 2–3)

Barnes and Duncan go on to examine to role of texts, discourses and metaphors in the representation of landscape. In the process, they nail their post-modern textual flag to the mast in a clear and explicit form:

> It is not simply our accounts of the world that are intertextual; the world itself is intertextual . . . We construct both the world and our actions towards it from texts that speak of who we are or wish to be. (pp. 7–8)

There is, it seems to me, a profound and fundamental slippage here between the valid point that reality is differentially interpreted and represented by human observers, and the false one that reality does not exist outside the text. There is, in other words, a slip from epistemological relativism to ontological relativism: from accepting that there is an external real world to which we have differential and partial access to saying that the world is not merely known, but actively constituted in our heads and in our texts. In the process, the idea of scientific 'truth' claims has all but gone out of the window.

The problems with this type of radical idealism have been analyzed and documented by Geras (1995) and Norris (1995). Just as science is regarded as just one among a range of incommensurable language games and cannot claim any privileged status, so too truth is 'just a product of localized beliefs whose origin should be sought in their cultural context or in the socio-biographical history . . . of the scientists who held them' (Norris, 1995, p. 109). The problem, of course, with this belief is that we have no basis for arguing that the Holocaust took place or that six million Jews died as a result. All we have are various interpretations and representations, the meaning, significance and validity of of which have to be deconstructed. The implications of this are profound. As Geras (1995) points out: 'If truth is wholly relativized or internalized to a language game, final vocabulary, framework of instrumental success, culturally specific set of beliefs or practice of justification, there is no injustice' (p. 125).

This is not to claim, as Geras states, that there is one correct representation or one correct description of things or historical events. There will always be a plurality of voices, accounts and representations. It is to claim, however, that some accounts, some voices and some representations are not merely better, but more accurate in their correspondence to the pattern of things or events. In this respect, it is crucial to challenge Rorty's conventionalism and to argue for the existence of an external reality which exists independently of interpretation. There is no doubt that our knowledge of this reality is imperfect and partial, and it is crucial to analyze the bases and character of that knowledge, but to maintain that the external world is partly a product of our texts as Barnes and Duncan maintain is untenable idealism.

The problem with some of this work has been that the link between representation and reality has gradually become weaker. As McDowell (1994) points out: 'Images and meanings have become detached from the real world'. They have now become objects of study in their own right. Consequently, there is a plethora of work on the nature of the 'gaze', on the production, representation and deconstruction of images, the fragmented nature of identity and the like. At its best (Anderson, 1988), this work is perceptive and valuable. At its worst, it has led simply to the secondary analysis of different 'readings', representations and interpretations and little in the way of original research. This is not suprising, since the stress on the centrality of the text, 'readings', intertextuality, discourse and the socially constructed nature of knowledge means that original empirical research on the changing nature of things is now seen as a relatively valueless exercise compared with the analysis of representations and the way in which such representations are produced and contested. As Barnett (1998) notes:

> Models of progress premised upon the refinement of theoretical understandings in relation to empirical work are being replaced by a new dynamic. 'Theory' is a seemingly endless, expanding, and self-referential field . . . This peculiarity accounts, in part, for the sense in which progress in fields of human geography most touched by 'culture has come to be characterised by the successive discovery of new, ever more sexy theorists'. (p. 387)

Barnett goes on to argue that the 'cultural turn' is characterized by the emergence of theory as 'fashion' and the rise of 'celebrity theorists', which raises major questions regarding the intellectual and political norms of judgement which regulate academic work. In the process, human geography has seen the successive importation of Lacan, Derrida, de Certeau, Deleuze and Guattari and a host of others, though what they have to contribute to geography, beyond mere intellectual and linguistic play, is unclear. A classic example is the work of Marcus Doel (1993, 1996). Doel (1993) attempted to deconstruct geography as follows (the extract is chosen almost at random):

> All that remains of human geography is a mess and a method: LIQUID THOUGHT and DISSECTION FOREVER respectively. Or again: nothing remains of modern human geography except for the FLOW OF DIFFERENCE and the VOID (words eternally suspended under erasure). (p. 378)

And, in 1996, Doel writes that:

> There is no space without folding, and therefore no geography without origami. For every act of spacing involves an imbrication of folds. As with origami, the individuation of a molar aggregrate – such as a thing, person, place, concept or animal – takes on consistency, turgescence, and rigidity by way of a regulated practice of folding. (p. 436)

> Likewise the inside is not something other than the outside, but is precisely the inside *of* the outside. Thus, because the inside is the folded double *of* the outside, we can either seek to prise away the doubles and peel back the folds – in the hope of reaching the 'stifling hollowness' of the plane of consistency – or else we can try to experiment and play with all of these doubles, folds, intervals, and joints. (p. 436)

Similarly, Massumi (1996) in a paper entitled 'Becoming-Deleuzian' writes that:

> Singularities are the precise points at which all of the variations in (of) the field are copresent, from a certain angle of approach, *in potential*. That copresence in potential is '*in*tension' as opposed to extension. The potential is not a logical possibility, closer to a 'virtuality'. (p. 397)

Blum and Nast (1996) in a paper on Lefebvre and Lacan, 'The heterosexualization of alterity', write that:

> Originally no more than the effect of a two-dimensional image (indeed the image of an image, as we discuss below . . . ), which is then processed through the defiles of the signifier (language), the spatial, relational (signifying) body does not exist for Lacan. The 'third dimension' theorised by Lacan, the dimension that founds and mediates alterity, is the phallus – the signifier without a signified – which produces and sustains all meaning in the world without itself being implicated in the meaning-making. (p. 560)

Although in their conclusions the authors seek to link their work to the position of indigenous peoples outside capitalist systems who seek to recover differences denied to them, the links seem tenuous in the extreme. The paper seems to be an exercise in theoretical play for its own sake. These are not isolated examples. The papers consist of page after page of similar text, particularly those of Doel and Massumi. They are a form of intellectual display for a limited public.

This type of writing, to me, is not research or scholarship but mere play with words: a second-hand version of William Boroughs' cut-up writing verging on obscurantism. It is the theoretical equivalent of the emperor's new clothes. The theoretical tailors point to the quality of the theoretical cloth, its elegance, its sheen, the fineness of its weave and so on, but most commentators appear unwilling to point to its rather hazy nature (but see Sokal and Bricmont, 1998). Consequently, several journals are now equipped with the emperor's new theories. One of the few observers to draw attention to this development is

Neil Smith (1996) in an editorial in *Society and Space*, entitled 'In praise of sleep'. Smith wrote that:

> sleep has thus far been radically excluded from exploration of a counter-hegemonic politics of the everyday . . . Excessively narrowed by the totalising megadiscourses of economism and historicism, social and political theory has remained innocent of the practical political instanciations embedded in sleep. If Foucault is correct that political opposition oozes from the the interstices of unexceptional daily activity, then surely sleep is a vital, unexplored site of oppositional possibility. (p. 505)

Smith was, of course, being deeply ironic although I was astonished by the number of my colleagues who either thought it was serious or, more commonly, thought it was an elaborate spoof but were not quite sure. Like Sokal, Smith used all the right terms: counter-hegemonic politics, oppositional practice, critical gaze, cultural transgression, totalizing megadiscourse, narrative, trope, liminality, alterity and the like, to create a web of superficially convincing theoretical glitter to trap the unwary (Pile, 1997). As I argued at the time (Hamnett, 1997), Smith's piece can be read in several similar ways. First, that this kind of language and analysis is sending him to sleep. Second, that sleep is a reasonable strategy in the face of the uncritical nature of much of what passes for alternative cultural politics, and third that users of this kind of language and analysis are themselves sleepwalkers. What is clear is that he is using sleep as a metaphor for his concerns about the direction of contemporary human geography (Smith, 1997).

## Writing versus analysis

Another development associated with the importance of the text is the significance attached to both 'writing' and 'reading', neither of which are any longer seen as straightforward or unproblematic (Barnes and Duncan, 1992). The so-called crisis of representation has led to the emergence of the author as stylist and writer as opposed to researcher and analyst. This, in turn, is associated with a more self-conscious search for subjective writing 'strategies'. Many examples could be given, but the one I have chosen is from a paper concerned with perceptions and meanings of space for Aboriginals and non-Aboriginals which focuses on the relationship between the Australian 'Outback' and the out back of the Australian suburban house (Muecke, 1996). He states in the abstract that:

> This paper is written in such a way that the style reproduces the epistemological problems. Memories, sounds, and feelings are part of the analysis of subjective relations to Australian spaces, accordingly these are reproduced 'ficto-critically'. The aesthetic is both nomadological and immaterial. Apprehensions of Australian space are constructed as a movement through them.

The four wheel drive settles softly into the curves, pushes the dirt around, while all the time you stare out of the window like at a cinema screen, watching parallel lines converge at the same time as the vehicle is erasing tracks and putting down new ones. These parallel lines never meet, but sometimes the road disappears . . . Already we had started to talk about an aesethics of disappearance, reading Jean Baudrillard's *America* (1988) and de Certeau. I got out my papers, the intellectual showing off even as we were almost lost. I liked the idea of being the first person in the universe to utter words like 'epistemology' in places like a turpentine scrub at dusk, two hundred kilometres from anwhere. (p. 415)

The paper contains some good examples of descriptive writing, but the question it raises is to what extent work like this, and that quoted above, can legitimately be categorized as geographical and, if so, to what extent it contributes anything of real significance to either understanding or improving the world in which we live. In this respect, I would make a sharp distinction between creative writing and scholarship. Tom Woolf's *Bonfire of the Vanities*, Jonathan Raban's *Hunting Mr Heartbreak* and Annie Proulx's *Accordion Crimes*, to take three recent examples, offer powerful and penetrating insights into contemporary America. But they are all professional writers. They do not pretend to be academics. Why should academics pretend to be writers? This is not to say, of course, that writing is not important. The best academics such as Said and Geertz are often prodigiously talented writers but, rather ironically, the work of good writers such as Woolf and Raban, or Upton Sinclair in *The Jungle*, can often provide more social insight than the work of academics caught up in linguistic word games.

## Conclusions

It will be abundantly clear from the foregoing that I am not a fan of the postmodern turn in human geography. While the new cultural geography has produced some very worthwhile research and scholarship which sheds light on the social construction of the world, a substantial amount of work appears to me to be simply linguistic game playing of minimal relevance to wider economic, social, environmental and political concerns. To this extent, the postmodern turn simply provides a theoretical playpit for academics to amuse themselves harmlessly while politicians and big business get on with their affairs unencumbered by too many awkward or critical questions. Cultural geography offers, at its best, powerful insights into the nature, role and significance of culture in the organization and reproduction of human societies and their landscapes. At its worst, it is a form of second rate journalism or experimental fiction. If I want to read good writers I turn to Upton or Ian Sinclair, and if I want to read experimental fiction I turn to Burroughs, not to academics writing in language designed to mystify and obscure. I want to see geographical scholarship and research as an intellectual project designed to illuminate, to explain (and possibly even help to change) the world we live in not as an intellectual word game for the privileged but disenfranchised few. I want geography without origami.

## References

Anderson, K. (1988) 'Cultural hegemony and the race-definition process in Chinatown, Vancouver: 1880–1980', *Society and Space*, 6: 127–50.

Barnes, T. and Duncan, J. S. (1992) *Writing Worlds: Discourse, Text and Metaphor in the Representation of Landscape*, London: Routledge.

Barnett, C. (1993) 'Peddling postmodernism: a response to Strohmayer and Hannah's "Domesticating postmodernism"', *Antipode*, 25(4): 345–58.

Barnett, C. (1998) 'The cultural turn: fashion or progress in human geography', *Antipode*, 30(4): 379–94.

Barnett, C. and Low, M. (1996) 'Speculating on theory: towards a political economy of academic publishing', *Area*, 28: 13–24.

Bassett, K. (1996) 'Postmodernism and the crisis of the intellectual: reflections on reflexivity, universities and the scientific field', *Society and Space*, 14(5): 507–27.

Blum, V. and Nast, H. (1996) 'Where's the difference: the heterosexualization of alterity in Henri Lefebvre and Jacques Lacan', *Society and Space*, 14(5): 559–80.

Bunge, W. (1966) *Theoretical Geography,* University of Lund.

Chorley, R. and Haggett, P. (1967) *Models in Geography*, London: Edward Arnold.

Cosgrove, D. and Daniels, S. (1988) *The Iconography of Landscape: Essays on the Symbolic Representation, Design and Use of Past Environments*, Cambridge: Cambridge University Press.

Cosgrove, D. and Jackson, P. (1987) 'New directions in cultural geography', *Area*, 19: 95–101.

Doel, M. (1993) 'Proverbs for paranoids: writing geography on hollowed ground', *Transactions of the Institute of British Geographers*, 18: 377–94.

Doel, M. (1994) 'Deconstruction on the move: from libidinal economy to liminal materialism', *Environment and Planning A*, 26: 1041–59.

Doel, M. (1996) 'A hundred thousand lines of flight: a machinic introduction to the nomad thought and scrumpled geography of Gilles Deleuze and Felix Guattari', *Society and Space*, 14(4): 421–40.

Duncan, J. and Ley, D. (1982) 'Structural Marxism and human geography: a critical assessment', *Annals of the Association of American Geographers*, 72: 30–59.

Eyles, D. (1981) 'Why geography cannot be Marxist: towards an understanding of lived experience', *Environment and Planning A*, 13: 1371–88.

Geertz, C. (1973) *The Interpretation of Cultures*, New York: Basic Books.

Geertz, C. (1983) *Local Knowledge: Further Essays in Interpretative Anthropology*, New York: Basic Books.

Geras, N. (1995) 'Language, truth and justice', *New Left Review*, 209: 110–35.

Gregory, D. and Walford, R. (1989) 'The crisis of modernity? Human geography and critical social theory', in Thrift, N. and Peet, R. (eds) *New Models in Human Geography*, London: Unwin Hyman.

Hamnett, C. (1997) 'The sleep of reason', *Society and Space*, 15(2): 127–252.

Harvey, D. (1969) *Explanation in Human Geography*, London: Arnold.

Harvey, D. (1973) *Social Justice and the City*, London: Arnold.

Harvey, D. (1989) *The Condition of Postmodernity*, Oxford: Basil Blackwell.

Johnston, R. (1987) *Geography and Geographers: Anglo-American Human Geography Since 1945*, London: Edward Arnold.

Ley, D. (1977) 'Social geography and the taken-for-granted world', *Transactions of the Institute of British Geographers*, 2(4): 498–512.

McDowell, L. (1994) 'The transformation of cultural geography', in Gregory, D., Martin, R. and Smith, G. (eds) *Human Geography: Society, Space and Social Science*, London: Macmillan.

Markusen, A. (1999) 'Fuzzy concepts, scanty evidence, policy distance: the case for rigour and policy relevance in critical regional studies', *Regional Studies*, 33(9): 869–84.

Massumi, B. (1996) 'Becoming-Deleuzian', *Environment and Planning D: Society and Space*, 14(4): 395–406.

Matless, D. (1995) 'Culture run riot: work in social and cultural geography', *Progress in Human Geography*, 19: 395–403.

Martin, P. (1998) 'On the frontier of globalisation: development and discourse along the Rio Grande', *Geoforum*, 29(3): 217–36.

Martin, R. (2000) 'Geography and public policy', *Progress in Human Geography*, forthcoming.

Mitchell, D. (1995) 'There's no such thing as culture: towards a reconceptualisation of the idea of culture in geography', *Transactions of the Institute of British Geographers*, 20(1): 102–16.

Muecke, S. (1996) 'Outback', *Society and Space*, 14(5): 407–20.

Norris, C. (1995) 'Truth, science and the growth of knowledge', *New Left Review*, 210: 105–23.

Pile, S. (1997) 'Space and the politics of sleep', *Society and Space*, 15(2): 128–33.

Rosenau, P. M. (1992) *Post-Modernism and the Social Sciences*, Princeton, NJ: Princeton University Press.

Said, E. (1978) *Orientalism*, New York: Pantheon Books.

Sayer, A. (1993) 'Postmodern thought in geography: a realist view', *Antipode*, 25 (4): 320–44.

Smith, N. (1996) 'Rethinking sleep', *Society and Space*, 14: 505–6.

Smith, N. (1997) 'Beyond sleep', *Society and Space*, 15(2): 127–252.

Sokal, A. and Bricmont, A. (1998) *Intellectual Impostures*, London: Profile Books.

Storper, M. (2000) 'The poverty of radical theory today: from the false promises of Marxism to the mirage of the cultural turn', *International Journal of Urban and Regional Research*, forthcoming.

Thrift, N. and Leyshon, A. (1995) 'Geographies of financial exclusion: financial abandonment in Britain and the United States', *Transactions of the Institute of British Geographers*, 20: 312–41.

Walker, R. (1999) 'Putting capital in its place: globalization and the prospects for labour', *Geoforum*, 30(3): 263–84.

# 7

# Political economy

ANDREW GAMBLE

There is a complacency visible in claims that 'history' has ended and that there is no longer any serious alternative to the institutions of free market capitalism. Capitalism it is argued is not only the best economic system on offer, but the only one that works. As Marx once suggested of an earlier version of this creed – there once was history, but there is no longer any. If this view of the world is taken seriously there is nothing left to discuss. The collapse of the Soviet Union and its satellite states in eastern Europe between 1989 and 1991 is regarded as confirmation that the socialist experiment of the twentieth century failed irrevocably, and that even moderate forms of state intervention should be avoided in the future. Capitalism works best when it is left alone; it is the horizon, the inescapable reality within which all attempts to reform or change society have in future to be conducted.

This fatalism infuses most discussion of the economy today. It can be found for instance in the omnipresent discourse on globalization. In the versions propagated by management gurus and political consultants globalization has become a mantra, used to suggest that the age of politics is over. So powerful are the forces of international finance and the logic of international competition that all forms of regulation and national economic management have become outmoded and counter-productive. All that governments can do is to open their economies and refashion their welfare policies and labour market policies to make them compatible with the imperatives of the new global order. If they seek to do anything else they risk impoverishing their society, by erecting obstacles to the logic of globalization.

What is common to such conceptions of globalization is that the economy is treated not as something which is constructed and reproduced through choices, struggles, beliefs and action, but as a natural phenomenon, a part of nature, which should not be interfered with, and which human agency can do very little about. Rather than being a contrivance of human agency it is instead something more akin to the climate, the product of forces beyond human ability to alter or to comprehend, but which provides the parameters within which social interaction proceeds.

In social science in recent years there has been a marked turn away from political economy and from an interest in the relationships of power and interest which structure societies. Instead the focus has turned to questions of identity, culture and consumption. The complex ways in which the material basis of a capitalist economy and the social relationships which define it are daily reproduced receive little attention; such matters are regarded as belonging to another tedious meta-narrative which rests on theoretical foundations which are no longer regarded as credible.

Yet an understanding of this material basis remains critical, not just for any kind of radical politics, but also in order to grasp the structures which shape our lives and determine our choices. Such a perspective has to be historical, because the capitalist economy as a dominant structure throughout the world did not just arise yesterday; it has been growing and developing for more than three hundred years. Contemporary perspectives encourage the view that history is bunk and only what happened in the last five years is of any significance for the present. The past becomes a vast reservoir of images and disconnected facts, which can be raided for instrumental purposes, but which sheds no light on the problems facing us.

It is true that history does not teach lessons, and historicist versions of the past which impose a pattern on historical events and derive predictions of inevitable progress towards a definite goal no longer attract any conviction. But the abandonment of history as an essential element in our knowledge of society, its development and its potential, would impoverish our politics. The content of the political imagination has always derived in large part from a historical awareness of past experiences, possibilities and alternatives. It is this awareness which is now threatened.

A second aspect of the closing of the critical mind is the refusal any longer to think in terms of power and relationships of power. Yet the inequalities of power both within national economies such as Britain, and still more starkly between countries in the global economy, are an overwhelming fact of our times. Whatever other differences there may be between modernity and post-modernity, the existence of profound structural inequalities of wealth and power show a stubborn persistence. With one exception, Japan, the same ten countries which were the leading economies in 1900 are the same ten at the end of the century. The idea that capitalism would set in motion competitive processes which would over time even out development and produce a balanced distribution of wealth and resources around the globe has certainly not yet occurred and shows no signs of doing so. The inequality between regions of the global economy has been growing, and except in a few instances shows no signs of diminishing.

Within national economies such as Britain, the aggressive pursuit of neo-liberal policies by the Conservative Government between 1979 and 1997 saw a marked reversal of the trend which had existed in the post-war decades towards a gradual reduction in economic inequality. Britain became once again one of the most unequal societies in Europe. The policies of the Labour Government elected in 1997 have begun to reverse that trend, but the scale of the change has been so great that so far very little change in the other direction is apparent. A more radical policy is deemed too unpopular, because it would involve increasing taxes. It will take a long time for the effects of the 1980s to be reversed in Britain, and they may never be. But even if they were, and Britain were returned to the situation of the 1970s, this would hardly be a return to some egalitarian paradise. There would still be a huge discrepancy in the life situations of those who owned productive assets and those who were excluded from ownership.

Words such as inequality and redistribution, however, are no longer deemed fashionable or appropriate. But although words can be discarded easily enough, reality is a tougher proposition. The capitalist economy has not fundamentally changed. Its driving logic, the competitive accumulation of capital, is the same, and so too are many of the consequences, including the continual reproduction of a society in which wealth and power are distributed in a highly inegalitarian manner, resulting in the very different life chances which members of different social classes and localities experience, and which inquiries like the recent Black Report on health continue to expose. The existence of differences between social groups which are systematically, not randomly, produced by the way in which the society is organized is clear evidence of the continuing relevance and centrality of class to the way in which the economy operates.

The reluctance to talk about inequality and to propose radical remedies for tackling it goes hand in hand with the view that industrial conflict has now largely become a thing of the past. There is no longer any need for trade unions to represent workers. They are now better off negotiating individual contracts. Trade union membership has declined sharply from the levels it achieved in the 1970s but, from the standpoint of the new conventional wisdom, it has a lot further to fall. Trade unions and trade union militancy are associated with a past age of industrial unrest.

Levels of industrial conflict are much lower than they were two decades ago, But what the views outlined above imply is that there is now no fundamental conflict of interest between labour and capital in how companies are managed. Instead there is a spontaneous identification of interests between the two. This judgement obscures much more than it illuminates. The decline in strikes and other forms of industrial conflict and the weakening of trade unions is undisputed. But ascribing these developments to the flowering of the natural tendency towards harmony and co-operation in a capitalist economy is seriously flawed. The cause of these developments is rather better understood in more traditional terms as a reflection of the current power of capital in relation to labour. There has been a large increase in the share of profits to the owners of capital, a large rise in unemployment, the withdrawal through legislation of most of the legal immunities granted to trade unions at the beginning of the century, a major change in the structure of work and occupations, which has seen the destruction of many traditional industries and communities, and a large growth in casual, part-time and low-paid jobs. The new Labour Government has begun to redress the balance through the introduction of a minimum wage and new employment rights, but again the distance which would have to be travelled to restore the former position enjoyed by organized labour remains huge; and even at the height of its power in the past organized labour only managed to achieve limited defensive protection of its interests. Strategic initiative always remained with capital.

There are obvious facts about our society, which are rooted in the nature of the capitalist economy, yet which are now more often denied than affirmed. Acknowledgement of these facts does not tell us what we should do. A range of responses is possible. But it is an essential starting point for thinking about the opportunities and alternatives open to us. Instead what we find is a mood of compliance with the dominant orthodoxies and their descriptions of reality, and a reluctance to investigate and expose what is actually going on.

Discussion of the economy is bedevilled by ideological myths which obfuscate the reality. One of the most pervasive of the myths is that capitalism is a system which serves human needs, that consumers are sovereign and that the whole economy is organized to provide whatever it is that individuals desire. What this ignores is that the great engine of the market, the greatest wealth-creating system in human history, is so not because it is organized around production for use but production for exchange. What drives capitalism is not what has value in use but what has value in exchange. The two are by no means the same. The pursuit of exchange value obliges capital to accumulate for its own sake. Profitability becomes an end in itself. This explains how, despite capitalism being the most productive economic system in human history, there can be such poverty and unmet human need for the majority of the world's population.

The consequences of the pursuit of exchange value and profits rather than use value are visible in many of the bizarre features of capitalist markets, particularly the periodic speculative bubbles in commodities such as internet futures, land and antiques. At times like these the irrationality of capitalism is on full display because of the extraordinary disparity which comes to exist between the use value and exchange value of commodities. What is being traded in the market casinos of capitalism is, however, not just commodities which have no discernible use value at all but the livelihoods and prospects of entire communities. The process is largely invisible and impersonal. There are no obvious connections between the huge profits which are earned in the financial markets and the economic consequences for the lives of vast populations. But the connections exist.

The pursuit of exchange value leads to great instability in capitalism. It is an economic system which drives forward through great financial crises which liquidate the (exchange) value of many existing assets and makes possible new spurts of growth and innovation. There have been many attempts to stabilize capitalism and regulate it, to reduce the costs of the way in which it works. After long and painful struggles a degree of protection was achieved in several countries in the second half of the twentieth century. But in the last twenty years, policies aimed at deregulating markets and intensifying competition have come to dominate economic policymaking. Such policies exalt exchange value over use value, denigrating security as dependency and arguing for controls on the operation of capital to be reduced everywhere to a minimum. They are presented as returning the economy to its 'natural' state and as being inevitable if the economy is to remain productive and competitive. But in fact these decisions are not inevitable, they are political decisions and there are always alternatives. But it suits those advocating them to pretend otherwise.

The big story about capitalism at the end of the twentieth century is that this is a social and economic system which is only now reaching maturity and developing its full powers and its global reach. As competitive accumulation drives the system onwards, so some of the logical consequences of its development set out in abstract form by Marx one hundred and fifty years ago are coming to be realized. Chief among them is the tendency for capitalism to create a surplus population, which becomes increasingly difficult to absorb into the economy. The expulsion of living labour from the production process Marx saw as the logical endpoint of capitalist production, the dominance of dead labour over living, the automation of production, the creation of a wholly socialized system of production, from which, however, the bulk of the population was excluded.

Such a world has moved much closer in the last one hundred and fifty years. The institutional forms in which capitalism is embedded shape the way in which the wealth which it creates is distributed and have major consequences for employment and social cohesion. It does seem to matter what those institutional forms are, and whether they create spaces and countervailing forces which set limits to the way in which capitalism operates. Where they do not the results are increasing polarization and social exclusion. One of the most telling statistics of the last two decades has been that the United States economy has grown rapidly while real wages have stagnated. The huge increase in wealth in the world's leading economy has mainly accrued to the few who already possess wealth. The American economy has been successful in creating jobs, but the majority are low-wage service jobs. In many European countries by contrast unemployment has stayed high but welfare benefits have been kept at relatively generous levels, while the wages for those in jobs have held up. In this way the growth of social exclusion and poverty has been contained.

One of the great questions for the future of the world economy is how the consequences of the new informational technologies for the organization of work and the distribution of income and wealth are handled. The idea is ceaselessly promulgated today, often with little opposition, that capitalism is inherently benign and works to promote the welfare of all members of society so long as regulation and government interference are kept to a minimum. But it is a dangerous illusion. Issues of power remain central. The way in which they are resolved determine which institutional form of capitalism predominates, and whether effective limits can be placed on the way in which capitalism operates. Capitalism continues to change at bewildering speed, introducing new technologies, new products, new forms of organization and interdependence, new cultures and new identities. But alongside this huge potential it creates there is also a huge potential for misery and oppression. Capitalism is the most contradictory form of economy known to human history. If its dynamism is to be harnessed for the creation of a society which is less cruel and less oppressive for all the people living on this planet it requires a huge effort to assert effective control. This cannot be done if we blind ourselves to the nature of this economy and fail to understand the consequences which flow from the way in which it is organized.

# Theory and practice

# 8

## Media research and the audit culture

PHILIP SCHLESINGER

Du benimmst Dich schäbig wie ein Tier!
Sei ein Gentleman, kein Elendshaufen!
Ja, was ist denn das mit dir?
Und er sah sie an, kaputt vor Gier:
Leben will ich! Essen! Faul sein!
Schnaufen!
Und im Wind fortreiten so wie ihr!

Bertolt Brecht, *Vom Tod im Wald*

### Working in a research programme

I'd like to start by asking who's involved in defining what media research is for. And I think that as we conclude this major programme in Media Economics and Media Culture, there's at least one obvious point of reference.[1] *How* is such a programme located within an ideologically governed state-wide system of funding? It's by now so obvious that this is so, that we hardly ever bother to point it out.

For the ESRC – in line with the broad ideology underlying current Research Council scientific policy – our output is there to contribute to the UK's economic performance and international competitiveness and, more loosely, to enhance the quality of life. We'd be wrong to regard these slogans as empty: their unmistakable message is that we should make ourselves both useful and virtuous.

If you take the Research Council's shilling, therefore, in a quite diffuse sense you're signing up to a particular conception of the role of the academic *qua* intellectual. You've become part of the heroic effort to engage in global competition in the so-called knowledge society. That's the way social science has sold itself for the past couple of decades to get the government off its back. And the underlying belief system has become so deeply entrenched that only fools would bother to question whether it's really as self-evidently rational as is supposed.

By signing up to the Media Economics and Media Culture Programme – just as with any other piece of ESRC research – we've taken on the broad duty to contribute to public well-being and have implicitly endorsed a particular

**179**

notion of the competitive nation state. We're often apt to overlook this, but I do think that such ideas embed themselves in every practice and also enter deeply into our self-conceptions. I don't regret at all having worked on successive ESRC projects.[2] And I'll do so again if successful in my next grant application. I certainly hope that my co-workers and I have made some new contributions to knowledge. But that said, I do think that for once it's worth asking what's implied in this funding regime and how an underlying conception of what research is *for* affects how we all make our bids for resources.

Closely related to the ideology of Research Council funding is the question of *who are the key addressees* – the audiences – the 'users' of such research. For whom has our research programme been intended? And to whom is it addressed? Who really wants to know and what for?

It's worth recalling that the Media Economics and Media Culture Programme was the result of a quite lengthy negotiated process. At one level, it's been the outcome of a protracted period of lobbying for some serious investment to be given to media research, following on from the Programme on Information and Communication Technologies (PICT) of the 1980s. We've had a further programme because we – the academic researchers – have said long and loud: 'Look here, our field is important and increasingly central to an understanding of contemporary society. Why don't you acknowledge this, give us the money, and let us find out more about it?'

Well, we *were* taken seriously: this programme has been the 1990s' big bone thrown to media researchers. And now it's on to the next campaign. You could say – though we usually leave such matters tactfully unspoken – that from the funder's point of view, one latent purpose of this media research programme has been to buy off an academic constituency as a reward for effective lobbying. That's not what research itself is for. But it's very often what the funding of research is about, as a part of the preconditions for knowledge production. From the producer end, it's the usual mixture of motives that makes us act: a desire to find things out increasingly driven by a need to generate resources in a highly competitive university system.

It's also worth recalling something else about the Media Economics and Media Culture Programme. Within the lobbying process that made it possible, we shouldn't forget the struggle between established academic interests in media research and the programme director's interest in generating new kinds of work and broadening the disciplinary spread involved. In itself, this clash generated a struggle over control of the programme agenda and over what was the kind of research to be undertaken. This kind of conflict is an inherent part of how intellectual fields operate. It produced a compromise. And however new some of the perspectives that came into the programme were, that research also had to meet the inescapable test of a certain kind of usefulness.

The manifest purpose of a research programme is to produce knowledge and understanding within a broad set of guidelines. These define a range of issues but don't determine the precise detail of the work to be undertaken; nor do they insist on the exact theorizations to be used. However, a programme does have a broad prescriptive impact and inevitably contains blindspots.

All our bidding to a programme is informed by our recognition that we have to meet a functional test. The addressees of the research therefore necessarily become inscribed in each proposal: these are the 'users'. Commonly, they consist of policy communities, business/industry/commerce, the media, academics, possibly students and something vague and good that pays us, called the public. It's an open question how this inscription of users actually affects the conduct and dissemination of the research process. It certainly requires us to use a given kind of rhetoric, and either we all assume that the policy community and business interests are the most important users, or we act as though we need to say so rather loudly.

Programmatic research engenders fierce competition. This relates to another key purpose of doing research: namely, securing funds. It's quite overt and has nothing to do with knowledge generation as such. It's the fight for resources between institutions. Increasingly, this has become a matter of brute survival in what may justly be termed an 'audit society', to use Michael Power's phrase.[3]

For most of us here today, the key framework remains the UK academic system. Of course, I recognize that the European Union is a research funding context of increasing importance and that people also engage in other forms of cross-nationally initiated or funded research. But without a doubt the UK system imposes itself most immediately on British researchers and their conceptions of who they are and what they ought to do. It shapes the dominant culture in which we work.

In the UK today, the academic research ethos is dominated by what Power calls 'rituals of verification'. These engender the ethos of periodic assessment – examination, scrutiny, evaluation, the just measure of pain – all of which are tributes placed upon the altar of accountability.

The drive to continually assess us means that research prowess, in one key respect, has suffered from a goal displacement and a revaluation: it's arguably less to do with the creation of knowledge and understanding than with demonstrating that you can meet criteria of high quality in order to generate income. This by now pathological system has generated a quite desperate and demeaning obsession with status. It's the most unambiguous obeisance that we pay to a utilitarian ideology cloaked in the language of accountability. Some of us may truly believe in it. Those who don't, however, have found that paying lip-service has by way of repetition turned into uneasy worship.

Arguably, the audit mentality of the past two decades has had a profoundly damaging impact on ideas of academic autonomy and cycles of academic creativity. In short, it's redefined for us what it is to be an academic and what constitutes valued intellectual practice. The Research Assessment Exercise has made more academics produce more publications more efficiently. At the same time, manifestly, in some fields, this one included, it has badly injured collegial behaviour, induced paranoia, insecurity, fear and anxiety. And that's just on a good day.

I'd like to suggest, therefore, that this sketch of our overall UK system is one immediate context in which we might begin to answer the question: 'What is media research for?'

## Media studies, media research, media policy

Next I'd like to say a few things about 'media studies' as a researchable area. It's an inter-disciplinary field or arena. We might contribute to it from a number of disciplinary backgrounds – sociology, political science, economics, law, anthropology, social psychology, literary studies, linguistics – or we might well cross over disciplines and combine them.

The lack of clear disciplinarity has been a great strength: it's opened up some fertile approaches. We sit in and between the humanities and the social sciences. But this interstitial position has also been a cause of weakness: it's dissipated our academic recognition and reduced our clout. Despite our best efforts in recent years, there's no well-defined subject community that acts easily in concert or can convincingly represent itself professionally. At the same time, because of the rising interest in media, the field is extremely popular among students. Then again, in the UK it has quite a negative identity with many policy makers and journalists. But, paradoxically, that disdain and mis-understanding have occurred just as media and culture have become named policy areas and, taken together with telecomms, IT, the internet, have become a pre-eminent focus for business, political and regulatory interest.[4]

It's inevitable that a lot of our present attention is absorbed by fast-moving change. Questions concerning intellectual property, regulation, cross-media ownership, virtual communities, Europeanization and communicative space, political marketing – all of these, and more, require analytical attention. The changing media/communications environment imposes its agenda on policy makers, media reporting and commentary, and the academy alike. These are powerful and seductive concerns: there's the draw of money, markets, power. Moreover, it's not just the attractive pull of the changing field that directs attention. It's also the machinery of state that increasingly shapes the intellec-tual field. In the UK today the Labour Government is actively striving to bring the underlying rationale of academic inquiry more closely into its orbit under the slogan of 'evidence-led' research. David Blunkett, the UK's Secretary of State for Education and Employment has made clear his view of the choice facing academic researchers in an important speech to the ESRC. His title told the story: 'Influence or irrelevance?' For the Secretary of State, the root choice was simple: make yourself handy on my terms or be condemned for insufferable detachment. Academic social science research is evidently seen as needing to become a service industry for government policymaking. It is clear, more broadly, that he intends the Research Assessment Exercise – the key mechanism for defining the scope and nature of university research culture – to be increasingly refocused on policy and practice.[5]

In the context of our programme the work has been conducted by academics, but of course they aren't the *only* media researchers. The more we broaden our definition of media research, the more we start to raise questions about whether the academy is presently best fitted to compete in the arena of policy-oriented or policy-relevant research. I would like to suggest that there are increasing obstacles in our path to the official telos of true usefulness and that this has a lot do with how the market-place of ideas works.

One reason it's so hard to gain attention in our own particular neck of the woods is that current policy-oriented media research shares a substantial agenda with media consultants, with think-tanks, with market analysts, with policy advisors and specialist civil servants. There's been an accelerating recomposition of the intellectual field, as Pierre Bourdieu would put it, and perhaps we haven't acknowledged it explicitly enough.[6] And maybe we haven't addressed some of the consequences for ourselves with sufficient clarity.

If you think about how public debate about the policy agenda is constructed, the pack is led by specialist journalists focused on the media/communications businesses. There are besides the policy and research units of big broadcasters such as the BBC and of the Independent Television Commission (ITC). There's research conducted by the British Film Institute (BFI). A lot of what's produced outside the academy proper is self-evidently media research, though it isn't all public. Indeed some media academics have worked for or with think-tanks such as Demos and the Institute for Public Policy Research (IPPR), or have migrated to consultancies after university training or after working on this research programme. That's quite a collection of people signed up to a problem-solving agenda and they offer a different kind of competition to the academy from that of the research assessment. They constitute a policy-focused intelligentsia that's quite external to university research and what they do is part of a still unacknowledged struggle for influence over what is regarded as the most relevant media research. We – the academy – simply haven't thought enough about this. But there's really no doubt where the influence really lies. And for the most part it's not with us.

This view is easily tested if I ask where you turn to for the everyday agenda. It's to the broadsheet newspapers' media pages, their increasing number of media business pages, the specialist trade journals, some of the weeklies. Taken together, routinely these sources offer a progress check on present developments and they tell us insider stories that academic media researchers simply can't match.

There's been an exponential growth of media and communications journalism. It's completely displaced and overwhelmed the spaces that were open to academic contributions in the 1970s and early 1980s in *The Listener*, *New Society*, the *New Statesman* and less often the broadsheets' feature pages. At one time it was possible for academic writers to contribute something distinctive to the *Media Guardian* or the *Independent*'s media pages. Now these have been almost entirely colonized by those who have a very direct interest in media businesses and in policy outcomes, and offer a sounding-off board for a range of media analysts, media executives and the think-tankerati. For the most part – and there are a very few exceptions – media academics writing about their own research or media matters of public interest have an inconsequential public influence.

Some academic media research – especially if it relates to sex or violence, or the effects of TV or video games on children or teenagers – is of prime value for reporting purposes. It might also be taken up if it relates to a producer interest – allegations of declining quality on TV, say, or insecure career patterns in media occupations. Such research fits some quite limited editorial agendas. But it's true, is it not, that if our research is partly intended for the general public, as one significant 'user', not a lot of it sees the light of day in the most accessible forms, nor, as we can all testify, does it get reported in the kind of terms that we might wish.

Journalism and consultancy jointly share some signal advantages over academic media research that attempts to be policy relevant:

- They can respond more quickly to developments, indeed spot them and by achieving media attention, set an agenda for academic research to follow.
- They have an inherently higher capacity to respond rapidly to developments because of their dedicated monitoring of events and the publication of the latest policy documents. There are very few full-time academic media researchers able to systematically monitor the developing media scene.
- Journalists and consultants have more routine proximity to the elites that make up the policy community.

In the case of think-tanks, the advantages are similar but there are other factors too:

- The ones that currently count are close to the ruling party and are very often part of a two-way traffic with government. It's for that reason that they're better called 'advocacy tanks' (in Andrew Denham and Mark Garnett's phrase[7]).

- They have an intense drive to market their product because their very survival depends on it.
- They aren't interested in subtleties but in making simple policy points and creating sound-bites that have an impact on media reporting and therefore on government. They aim for media attention to increase their credibility and market value.
- Think-tanks also have an ability still rare in the academic community to fillet, simplify and popularize research.

If you add to these the interest groups concerned with press freedom, quality television, freedom of information, media consumers' rights, you'll find that commonly media academics either are hired guns for particular causes or speak from the platform to add a touch of gravitas. But they certainly don't set the interest agenda; they support or contradict it on the basis of convictions for which their research may be relevant or conveniently mobilized. The same applies to academic contributions to the plethora of conferences and policy fora that we now have.

My sense of our relative marginality was confirmed in a presentation by David Levy, a policy adviser at the BBC.[8] His problem is how to get the best possible advice on how to solve practical problems, and he asks why UK researchers' profile is so limited in the debate on regulatory structures and policy. He notes – very much in line with my argument – that it's the consultancies (such as KPMG and NERA) that have played a key part in addressing matters of convergence, a Euro FCC and analogue switch-off. In his talk Levy mentioned approvingly work by a small number of academic economists and lawyers on public service broadcasting, competition/gateway issues and on convergence. Some of this work, it should be noted, came out of the Media Culture and Media Economics programme.

Why, asks David Levy, are so few UK media academics involved in such work? Why, he inquires, aren't we making more of a collective impact? He argues that fact-gathering is the work of consultants and statisticians but that the big issues need to be addressed by the academics because they can offer more detachment, a broader set of perspectives and thereby have a distinctive influence on policy options: he gave as one example work on pluralism and media consolidation for the Council of Europe.

Where the argument leads is that to have a discernible impact we need to match up better to the government and industry agendas, we need to dialogue more with the movers and shakers, and to become more engaged in the policy debate. This is certainly in tune with what the New Labour government is saying. And under particular conditions, most of us here doubtless more or less agree with the need to make our research count in these terms. I'm very far from opposed to this in terms of my personal practice. Yes, that's an unquestionably important game, though it's one that few in our field can claim to have played successfully. And is it the only game in town? Maybe our increasing proximity has obscured *other* possible roles that we might occupy. If being useful is what makes us relevant, what precisely makes us *academic* media researchers as opposed to say, being bargain-basement consultants with a bit of detachment thrown in?

What can we really do best in the recomposing intellectual field of media research and analysis? Is policy relevance our sole collective forte and should it be our prime aim? If we embrace that mission more enthusiastically, more exclusively, how will it affect how we define our own research agendas?

We're publicly funded to a large extent and properly obliged to contribute to the public good. If our research is there in part to influence the conduct of public bodies and the wider community, perhaps we might pause and think about how well we're doing this. Of course, we're rightly required to disseminate what we do. But there's a risk of mere publication being equated with impact or influence. Much of our dissemination does take place in a practitioner or media professional setting. But it's hard to judge how the users really use us.

To take an obvious example from the heart of the public sector, academic media research is rather marginal to the policy formation of the BBC and the ITC, though the academy has provided many of the cohorts who conduct studies inside these organizations, and indeed, who run them. The Broadcasting Standards Commission (BSC) does make a point of commissioning work from academics to address its concerns and to the best of my knowledge some of the research conducted here at Stirling and elsewhere has informed the Commission's deliberations and pronouncements, although that's very hard to quantify.[9] But none of these bodies has seen a need to appoint media researchers directly to their boards for the obvious reason that policy-related expertise can easily be found elsewhere, and academics can be co-opted as required on a consultancy basis.

Much the same applies to the latest Committees of Inquiry into the BBC. In 1986, Alan Peacock made use of academic research alongside consultancy, with economics firmly in command – unsurprisingly as the issue was BBC finance. Academic media expertise was represented on the committee itself by Alastair Hetherington, formed more by his long experience of journalism and broadcasting, it must be said, than by academic research, though he certainly encouraged its use. Move on thirteen years to the Davies Review Panel. The committee itself had no obvious need of a media economist, given its chairman's known expertise, and if you look at those submitting evidence, the academy was patently absent.

These are just some of the key bodies in public life where our collective marginality as a source of influence over questions of policy is glaringly apparent.[10]

## Some implications

In the crowded media research market-place, academics need to pose some questions about how much we sign up to the ruling utilitarian doctrine and how we might secure spaces for ourselves that emphasize our autonomy. In suggesting this, I'd like to recall the following comment by Zygmunt Bauman:

> Having reached the nadir of their political relevance, modern intellectuals enjoy freedom of thought and expression that they couldn't dream of at the time that words mattered politically. This is an autonomy of no practical consequence outside the self-enclosed world of intellectual discourse; and yet this is an autonomy all the same, a most precious and cherished consolation for the eviction from the house of power ... it offers the practitioners of such a form of life the gratifying feeling of being in full and exclusive control of the life-process and its products: truth, judgement, taste.[11]

Of course, this offers a distinctive conception of the intellectual and it contradicts the user-friendly role that we have been prescribed by the impact of the audit society and the dominant functionalism. Indeed, Bauman would regard that role as based on an utter delusion. That's not my view. There is a need for useful engagement with those who hold political and economic power. I don't think we're talking about mutually exclusive alternatives here, but rather the ability to choose to play a number of different possible roles. Intellectual autonomy now seems hardly to be a feasible choice and the poignancy of Bauman's statement lies in its acute sensitivity to something that we now seem to have almost lost. His credo captures a sense of what we *ought* at times to be doing and how we still *ought* to conceive of ourselves. We recognize this when we lament the present-day compulsion to be useful; but evidently we also believe that pressure to be irresistible. That's a matter which goes well beyond media research to the shaping of the British academic culture as such.

Bauman's pure intellectual vocation has no space in the rather crowded market-place for media research and the struggle for influence over policy that I've depicted. This contact sport has intensified in violence with changes in media markets, the invention of regulatory systems, and the consequent growth of demand for policy options and advice. I believe that we're increasingly being edged out. And if we're not to be so, we shall have bend more completely with the prevailing wind. At that point, something unique to the academic vocation will be irretrievably lost. Our academic standing may yet become merely nominal.

As of now, however, there are *still* things that we as academic researchers might do that permit us to exercise some continued independence:

- We can engage more in theory and concept production, in the provision of explanations and models, although, in the intense market for ideas that I've pointed to, if judged useful such work is apt to be snapped up and popularized rapidly through journalism, consultancies and think-tanks. That doesn't mean we shouldn't do more of it. And even if it's judged practically useless in immediate terms, it may well advance our collective thinking, which is good for us and our intellectual development. And we don't know when new thinking might after some years come into wider play.

- We can adhere to more rigorous methodologies and we can engage in the use of methodological self-consciousness in order to improve the quality of our work – though these are by no means our monopoly either.

- We can engage in critique that bears no necessary relation to immediate policy concerns, but which we regard as crucial to the development of knowledge and understanding and the advancement of the field. That, I think, substantially characterized the pre-audit culture ethos of two decades ago.

- In similar vein, we can discuss normative or ethical issues without regard to their immediate utility, although we might aspire to affect the climate of debate.

- Our time-cycles do allow us to go in for more medium-term and longer-term analysis than our competitors. We can identify trends; explain motivations and strategies; uncover structural determinants; assemble more varied and more reliable sources of evidence for the analyses we're undertaking; write histories and ethnographies. It's worth recognizing how some academic discourse may over time become part of common sense. For instance, past debates about how news is a construct have fed into the self-understanding of many journalists and sections of the public. Moreover, the theories and findings of media research inform the thinking of successive generations of our students, many of whom – contrary to the prevalent myths – go usefully into media practice, government and consultancy.

Underlying all that I've said is my mounting concern that we re-think our role and purpose and that we re-affirm the value of the autonomy of at least some academic research.[12] Of course, we all recognize that autonomy has its own conditions of existence, and we seem increasingly to believe that these have largely disappeared, engendering the view that alternatives are unthinkable. To be sure, we all live in a mixed moral and practical economy. As individual researchers we do make different choices about what to research at given times according to different incentives and constraints. Collectively, as members of the academy, we're increasingly driven by cycles that we cannot control and values that we may not espouse. That said, it's time for some of us at least to coalesce in creating more spaces for autonomous thought in our field and to be fully conscious of both the costs and benefits of that course of action.

## An afterword

When I'd delivered the above talk, I was criticized in three ways that merit a brief reply here and a more extensive engagement elsewhere. My critics, to spare their blushes, I shall call the Journalist, the Cultural Bureaucrat and the Policy-Relevant Researcher.

The Journalist (who once dabbled in media research) said I wanted academic research to be irrelevant and that I was a 'whinger'. Not so: we do need to undertake research intended to shape the public conversation, as will be abundantly clear from what I've said. But that isn't to be done in only one way. As for 'whingeing': well, I don't erroneously mis-identify an analysis with making a complaint, as some seem prone to do.

The Cultural Bureaucrat (once a hard toiler in the salt-mines of media research) thought that I was decrying the very clever people who worked in think-tanks and consultancies and couldn't understand why academics should demand autonomy. Why shouldn't cultural bureaucracies also have their independence? Once again, let me make it clear: let the think-tankerati do their business, with or without academics' help. Co-operation with think-tanks is a possible role for the academy to play, but not the *only* one. As for justifying the need for autonomy? The cultural bureaucrats must fight their own battles and no-one was asking them for any help. But more to the point, it's distressing to have to make the case for academic freedom as a precondition of creating disinterested knowledge and understanding. It's long been inscribed in the very purpose of the university as an institution. Perhaps we'll have to argue all that again from first principles. Certainly, that reaction was a more telling straw in the wind than being cavalierly dismissed as a whinger.

The Policy-Relevant Researcher was aggrieved at the thought of the careful analytical work of years being denied its chance to make an impact on the high heid-yins of the world of broadcasting. There was also an apparent belief that promoting the policy implications of this work through co-operation with a think-tank was somehow thought beneath the salt. Not at all, on either count: if broadcasting policymakers want to listen and debate academic analysis, well and good, though experience suggests that we need to go clear-sightedly into an arena where successive policy regimes recruit their academic allies to suit expedient needs, and then drop them from the party invitations. And let me say it again: let a thousand think-tanks bloom! No, there's no disgrace in collaborating with them. I've done it myself and it was quite an education. But that's not the point at all. It's surely this: we too, as members of the academy, need first and foremost to set an independent research agenda and we need to try to our utmost to secure the foundations that make this possible.

## Notes

1 The present paper was first delivered as a plenary lecture at the concluding conference of the ESRC's 'Media Economics and Media Culture' Programme, held at Stirling Management Centre, Stirling University, 27–28 January 2000. I was asked to consider the

question 'What is media research for?' The conference was on 'The Future of the Media and Media Research'. The programme was directed by Professor Simon Frith.

2 I participated in the Media Culture and Media Economics Programme as Principal Investigator on a study of 'Political Communication and Democracy'.

3 Power, M. (1997) *The Audit Society: Rituals of Verification*, Oxford: Oxford University Press.

4 The newly-elected Labour Government of 1997 created a Department of Culture, Media and Sport, whose very naming was unquestionably significant in the recognition it conferred on a field of creative and business activity.

5 Blunkett, D. (2000) 'Influence or irrelevance: can social science improve government?', Secretary of State's ESRC Lecture Speech, 2 February 2000, Economic and Social Research Council/Department for Education and Employment. For comments, see Cohen, N. (2000) 'Selling New Labour to the highest bidder', *Observer*, 13 February 2000, p. 31; Walker, D. (2000) 'Looking for evidence, *Guardian*, 24 January 2000, p. 15; and 'You find the evidence, we'll pick the policy', *Guardian Higher*, 15 February 2000, p. 3H.

6 See Bourdieu, P. (1990) *In Other Words: Essays Towards a Reflexive Sociology*, Cambridge: Polity Press.

7 Denham, A. and Garnett, M. (1998) *British Think-Tanks and the Climate of Opinion*, London: UCL Press.

8 A talk delivered to the Media, Communication and Cultural Studies annual conference at Sheffield Hallam University on 7 January 2000. My thanks to Dr Levy for making available the notes of his talk and for discussing his views.

9 The Stirling studies were Schlesinger, P., Dobash, R. E., Dobash, R. P. and Weaver, C. K. (1992) *Women Viewing Violence*, London: BFI, and Schlesinger, P., Haynes, R., Boyle, R., McNair, B., Dobash, R. E. and Dobash, R. P. (1998) *Men Viewing Violence*, London: Broadcasting Standards Commission.

10 There is some call for academics elsewhere: most importantly in S4C (the Welsh Channel 4) which is chaired by Elan Closs Stephens; also in the new Film Council, where John Hill sits on the Board, in the British Film Institute, where Brian Winston is a Governor, and in Scottish Screen, where I sit on the Board. No doubt in this kind of setting, we can each influence debate about screen policy, particularly when it comes to a cultural and educational agenda. If media research comes into these board rooms, it's rather indirect in its impact; it's embodied in people and what they can contribute on an *ad hoc* basis. And that's certainly worth having.

11 Bauman, Z. (1992) *Intimations of Postmodernity*, London and New York: Routledge, p. 16.

12 Actually, I think this is part of a larger shift that's making others also consider where they might stand. It's no accident, for instance, that thoughtful journalists, too, are beginning to consider how *their* own roles are being changed by information provision over the internet, a topic that media researchers have also been debating of late. The announcement of the Time Warner/AOL merger in January 2000 provoked another round of such speculation.

# 9

# Corporate culture and the academic left

BARBARA EPSTEIN

The university left, in the US, has changed dramatically over the last several decades. In the 1950s many left wing faculty were driven out of the universities, while others kept their jobs by virtue of keeping their opinions to themselves. In the 1960s the student movement opened up discussion of politics in the universities, and a few, mostly young, faculty, supported these movements, but the vast majority of faculty remained uninvolved in political protest. Since the early 1970s, when those who had been students in the 1960s began to take university jobs, the numbers of faculty who would use such terms as left, or progressive, or feminist to describe their views has grown steadily. In the late 1990s, in a large part of the humanities and to a lesser degree in the social sciences such views are taken for granted, especially in elite universities, particularly in those in which a large proportion of the faculty have been hired since the 1960s. In much of this arena progressive views have become more or less a professional expectation. Progressive and feminist views, and the vocabulary that has come to accompany them, constitute part of the training of graduate students in this arena. Such views tend to be expected as part of a young applicant's vita. Throughout much of the humanities, faculty can be discredited by accusations that they are conservative, or not enthusiastic supporters of feminism.

One might infer that the university left is strong and healthy, that left intellectual life is thriving in the US. Unfortunately this is not the case. Despite the large numbers of faculty who adhere to the cluster of views that are described as left or progressive in the late 1990s (feminism, anti-racism, anti-homophobia, an occasional mention of class and capitalism as problems), the left in the university lacks direction. Though probably every leftist in the university would support the defence of affirmative action, there is little sense of common commitment to anything new, or to any vision of the future. Though the university left shares a great deal in terms of intellectual and political perspective (virtually everyone has been influenced to one degree or another both by Marxism and by the 'identity politics' of recent decades) it is riven by bitter internal conflicts. Unfortunately this does not mean that the university left is full of open, free-wheeling debate. Occasional, highly publicized intellectual battles are surrounded by an atmosphere of caution bordering on timidity. It is personally risky to engage in these debates because debates easily slide into wounding personal attacks. Within the academic left aggression is rewarded. Those who inspire fear gain status and power.

The association between aggressive behaviour and success promotes bullying on the part of people who under other circumstances might not have become bullies, and it promotes timidity on the part of everyone else. When one or more people begin hurling accusations (of racism, sexism, homophobia, conservatism, essentialism), others fall silent, even if they privately disapprove. The silence results partly from a reluctance to dismiss criticisms whose content may be legitimate even if presented in an objectionable manner. Progressives want to avoid saying things that are sexist, racist, homophobic, or in other ways violate progressive values. We all carry attitudes that need to be questioned, and it can be unclear when legitimate criticisms shade over into a denunciatory style that discourages dialogue and increases the personal power of the accusers. Even when it is clear that bullying is taking place, most academic leftists remain silent. Anyone who objects to attacks on someone else is likely to open him or herself to attack as well, and no one wants to be called a racist (or a sexist, a homophobe, a conservative) even if one is sure the charge is illegitimate.

Raising questions about such attacks also raises implicit questions about the academic left as a whole that most academic leftists would prefer to avoid. The academic left distinguishes itself from the rest of academia largely in terms of its fervent rejection of racism, sexism, homophobia. Having moved away from socialism, lacking any other coherent project, and rejecting universal values as outmoded, the academic left has no political, intellectual or moral standards in terms of which charges of racism, sexism and so forth might be judged. It is of course true that the stance of an earlier left, as the proponent of universal values, often masked quests for power on the part of particular groups and individuals. But the same is true of the left's current stance as the critic of sexism, racism and homophobia: this too can be a vehicle for particular agendas and ambitions. In an increasingly competitive academic environment in which pressures to succeed have been vastly amplified, political postures have become utterly intertwined with the strategies of individuals and groups to rise within the hierarchy. Everyone in the academic left is aware of this, but precisely because the academic left itself seems to be an increasingly fragile project, anyone who points it out is likely to be accused of rocking the boat, providing the enemies of the academic left with ammunition. Rocking the boat is not good for anyone's career and most people instinctively avoid it. But this leaves the problem unaddressed. Unaddressed problems rarely go away, and often get worse.

While the academic and more broadly the intellectual left is caught up in internal tensions, left ideas appear to have a shrinking impact outside the universities and the cultural and intellectual arena that surrounds it. Leftists, progressives, feminists in the university enjoy a historically unprecedented access to publishing: articles and books written from an avowedly progressive perspective roll off the presses. But in the broader public arena the left is barely heard in public debates. The conflict over the question of Clinton's impeachment revolved around a battle between the right and the mainstream (or, one might say, between the far right and the right); the left critique of Clinton, for having dismantled the welfare state and in other ways having adopted much of the programme of the right, was not even part of the discussion. In the 1960s and early 1970s the left was a major participant in the debate about the war in Vietnam. In regard to more recent US interventions (the Gulf War, the more recent bombing of Iraq and Afghanistan, currently the bombing of Kosovo) the left has no significant voice.

Many of us who were participants in the movements of the 1960s, and younger people who have participated in movements since that time, took faculty jobs not only because we liked intellectual work but also because academia seemed to be a good place to continue working for social change, though in a different way. For many of us, I think, the university was both a refuge and a bitter disappointment. It has given many of us economic security (though this is more true for those who got faculty jobs in the 1970s and 1980s than it is for newer faculty: tenure has become harder and harder to obtain). It has given us a good deal of intellectual freedom (though this varies by university and by department). But for many of us life in the university left has been soured by bitter internal conflicts, by pressures to take particular positions and by implied threats of ostracism or denunciation if one challenges these views. Many of us also have a sense that we are not making as much difference as we would like. Over the last decade politics in the US has steadily shifted toward the right. Movements of the right have also grown steadily and now have the kind of vitality that movements of the left, in this country, have not enjoyed since the early 1970s. Though it is possible to keep this away from the centre of one's consciousness most of the time (many of us rarely talk to anyone who is not also on the left), the collective awareness that our side is not winning has a discouraging effect.

Trying to understand how the university left could be so large and yet so weak requires looking at what has happened outside the university as well as within it: the left as a whole has lost ground, and it is not especially surprising that when that happens the university left should suffer as well. What is surprising, and bears some examination, is the fact that things have gone so badly within the university left despite the fact that the universities are now the main arena for the left in the US, the place where the left is strongest, at least in terms of number and visibility. What amounts to a massive shift, on the part of progressives, into the university, in the decades since the 1960s, is historically new: this is the first time that university professorships have become a kind of routine job choice for leftists. The current state of the university left seems to me to have do to partly with changes that have taken place in the US as a whole over the last several decades (including the political and cultural shift to the right), partly with changes that have taken place in the university as the left has become increasingly identified with it and partly with the fact that once the left, a movement for social change, comes to be primarily identified with university faculty, it becomes unavoidably lop-sided.

I would like quickly to address two views that are often expressed about why the left lacks vitality and why life is often so unpleasant within the university left. First, some people argue that the reason the energy of the left has sagged is that we have all gotten older. This begs the question: why aren't there more young people on the left? Furthermore, it ignores the fact that there are a lot of young people on the left, in the universities as well as elsewhere. In cultural studies and related areas of the university, virtually all graduate students and probably most undergraduates regard themselves as progressive or on the left. Secondly, many people argue that the ugliness of conflict inside the left is the result of identity politics. The argument goes that once women, people of colour, gays and lesbians began insisting that their voices be heard, and began challenging sexist, racist and homophobic assumptions, discussion necessarily became strident and unpleasant. Finding oneself regularly being verbally beaten up for one thing or another is, it is argued, is simply the price of progress. Some would go further and equate radicalism with verbal aggressiveness. According to this view radicals are marginalized or powerless people who want more power, verbal bullying is a way of getting more power, and is therefore radical.

The view that identity politics is the cause of the current problem of the university left confuses the difference between interest-group politics and radicalism. Historically, social movements have mostly been based on particular constituencies, groups acting on their own perceived interests. The term 'identity politics' connotes a particular approach to politics in which exclusion from the mainstream becomes the basis for political claims, marginality can become a sought-after status and the manipulation of guilt becomes a major part of political discourse.[1] This style has been particularly associated with some movements of the last few decades; other movements, of other historical moments, have had different styles (not always more pleasant, but different). Identity politics is at times a necessary element in creating a movement: gays and lesbians, for instance, had to summon a certain stridency in order to effectively challenge homophobia, on the left and elsewhere. But stridency can become an end in itself, a measure of commitment; it can become a means of gaining power, for individuals or for groups. Identity politics is not the same thing as radicalism, which refers to the breadth of a movement's vision, its commitment to a thoroughgoing transformation of society.

Over the last several decades identity groups have often pursued a divisive, denunciatory style of politics; the equation of this style with identity politics is not surprising. But in fact this denunciatory style has come to be employed by the academic left as much as it is by what we ordinarily think of as identity groups, women, people of colour, homosexuals and others. Recently some on the left have turned to using the term 'conservative' to discredit others on the left. In the spring of 1998 a 'Conference on Left Conservatism' was held at UC Santa Cruz. The point of reference of the conference seemed to be the article that Alan Sokal had published roughly a year earlier in the journal *Social Text*, which embarrassed the academic left by parodying the style of writing, and reasoning, that many within it have adopted.[2] The leaflet advertising the conference attacked Katha Pollitt, Barbara Ehrenreich and Alan Sokal by name, and paraphrased an article of mine, in which I criticize post-structuralism, without attribution. Both the leaflet and the conference revolved around the attempt to attach the epithet 'conservative' to opponents in a debate within the left. This denunciatory style is tempting because it is effective: it unites those who are making the accusations, and usually silences or at least isolates the accused. But it makes the academic left a very unpleasant place, and leads some to distance themselves from it.

The above discussion raises questions of terminology: what is the left? What is the academic, or university, left? I use the term 'left' to refer to anyone who supports a fundamental transformation of society in an egalitarian direction. Terms for this position have changed over time: through the 1970s the term 'radical' was most common, more recently the terms 'left' and 'progressive' have come to the fore. At least in the university the term 'feminist' usually refers to a position in favour of a systematic social transformation. I understand the left in the university as including everyone who describes him or herself as left (or progressive, or radical). The university left is divided between those whose point of reference is Marxism and socialism, and whose politics ultimately revolves around class and opposition to capitalism, and those whose point of reference is post-structuralism or literary theory, and for whom radicalism ultimately means cultural critique. The two positions overlap in some respects (virtually everyone would agree that both class and cultural critique should have a role in left politics), and many people fall in between. Nevertheless there are camps which are often in opposition to one another. Since the post-structuralist or cultural left tends to call itself the academic left, I will use that term for it in this piece. Since there are leftists in the university who are not part of the academic left so defined, I will use the term 'university left' for that broader left in the universities.

The most obvious reason for the discouraging state of the university left is that its connection to movements on which it was based has attenuated as those movements themselves have faded. Feminism in the academy, for instance, came out of what was a mass women's movement, in the early 1970s; it was especially linked to the radical wing of that movement. Over the 1980s and the 1990s feminist consciousness has become widely diffused in the US, but there is no longer a mass women's movement; instead there are bureaucratic feminist organizations whose staff work for particular reforms. Other movements have followed similar trends. Even within the realm of environmentalism, which is probably the largest of the movements remaining from the 1960s and 1970s, there is a large gap between the wide diffusion of consciousness and the much smaller world of activism, and within that world of activism the large, bureaucratic organizations are the dominant force. In the 1960s and early 1970s the movements of the time had a dynamism and vision that gave purpose and shape to left intellectual work. In the early 1980s the radical gay and lesbian movements, the eco-feminist movement, the movements against the arms race and against US intervention in Central America also gave energy and focus to the university left, though to a much more limited extent, because these movements were smaller than those of the 1960s and 1970s and because fewer academics were connected to them. In the 1990s progressive movements became smaller and weaker and, though some academics work with particular movements, the university left as a whole is no longer connected to social movements or to any particular set of progressive goals.

The connection between the university left and social movements outside the university has weakened not only because the movements of the 1960s faded but also because the universities have changed in ways that have made maintaining such a relationship very difficult. In the 1970s and 1980s I thought that it was possible to have one foot in the university and one in the left outside the university; this seemed to me to be a good way of sustaining intellectual creativity, and also maintaining a sense of oneself based on something more substantial than university hierarchies. Accelerating pressures within the university (as well as the disappearance of those movements) have made such a stance virtually impossible. Speed-up takes place on all levels: heightened competition for jobs, more publications demanded for tenure or promotion, a growing sense that if one stops running one will fall behind. Many left faculty give money to progressive groups outside the university, some manage to donate time and some do academic work that is of direct relevance to particular social movements. But such connections are established on an individual basis, or at best by groups of faculty with particular interests or expertise. Collectively the university left has no particular relationship to social movements and no particular political project.

The university left has been deeply, if indirectly, shaped by the changes that have taken place in the universities as a whole over the last couple of decades, in particular the dramatic influx of corporate money and power. In 1980, under the Reagan Administration, the Bayh–Dole Act for the first time made it possible for a public university to declare a patent on a product of university research; before this, such a product had been within the public domain. This gave public research universities, for the first time, something of substantial value on the market. Deals between corporations and professors, departments, universities began to be struck. By the mid-1980s research in bio-technology was bringing in huge amounts of corporate funds; since then the same trend has taken place in computer science, law, medicine, engineering and elsewhere. Over the 1980s and 1990s, as the amount of public money going to the universities has gradually decreased, the amount of corporate funds going to elite research universities has increased dramatically. Most of it goes to departments and fields that are closest to the market: along with bio-technology, electronics, engineering. Most of the money goes to the major research institutions, and many universities receive no corporate funds. But this does not mean that the influence of the corporations is limited to the major institutions. Increasing numbers of universities are trying to figure out how to attract corporate funds, or how to attract more corporate funds than they already do. Sometimes this is in response to a decline in public support, or in anticipation of such a decline. Turning toward corporate support can reinforce that shift: after all, if a university is being supported by corporations, legislators may decide that public funds should go elsewhere.

The problem is that the shift away from public and toward corporate funding entails a shift in values, away from a conception of the autonomy of the university (sustained only barely during the Cold War years, but nevertheless maintained to some degree) toward a view that university teaching and research should be judged by its contribution to the market. A related problem is that as corporate funding becomes more important some arenas within the university thrive while others languish, and these decisions are not made on grounds either of what is necessary for the development of human knowledge and culture or of what might be beneficial for society as a whole. The conventional division of universities into natural sciences, social sciences and humanities does not entirely match up with the new division between disciplines that are useful to the market and those that are not: there are natural sciences that corporations have relatively little use for (mathematics, for instance) and social sciences that they do find useful (economics). On the whole, however, funding for the natural sciences has risen and that for the social sciences, especially the 'softer' social sciences, and to an even greater degree the humanities, has fallen. Faculty in the market-related departments are often able to earn very large incomes, through consulting, sometimes setting up their own businesses, and as a result of university salaries designed to discourage such faculty from taking jobs in private industry.

Within the humanities the main strategy for addressing the shift of power and resources toward the natural sciences has amounted to trying to stay afloat by playing a different version of the game that is being played there. That strategy has been, in essence, if the natural sciences have stars, we can have stars too. As in US society generally, stratification has increased in the universities in recent decades. On all levels, the gap between the rich and the poor has widened. The differences between the funding of the natural sciences on the one hand and the social sciences and the humanities, between the salaries of faculty in the best-paid fields and those in the worst-paid fields, between the best-paid faculty and the worst-paid faculty, have all increased. Since the late 1970s differences among faculty pay scales have grown rapidly, with the salaries of highly ranked full professors increasing dramatically, while the salaries of other faculty, especially untenured faculty, have increased much more slowly. There has been a widening difference between average faculty salaries in lower-prestige fields, especially the humanities, and salaries in high-prestige areas, including some professional schools (law, medicine, business) and some natural sciences. The rule seems to be, the closer a field is to the marketplace, the more rapid the growth in average salaries. This has implications for women faculty, who on the whole are concentrated in the lower-paid disciplines.

Economic stratification seems to be taking place in the humanities as quickly as elsewhere, perhaps even more quickly. In the University of California, for instance, there has been a rapid increase in the use of what are called above-scale salaries, involving cases in which a faculty member at a particular step receives pay higher than that normally attached to that step. Between 1982 and 1989–90, the number of UC professors receiving above-scale salaries increased by 48 per cent. In the humanities, the comparable increase was 106 per cent. In some cases above-scale salaries are used for fine-tuning, in the way that one may give a student a B+ rather than simply a B or an A. But above-scale salaries are also used to reward or retain stars who might otherwise leave for another university. Between 1990 and 1991, there were increases of 48 per cent to 84 per cent in the numbers of faculty receiving more than $100,000 among the life sciences, physical sciences and social sciences. In the humanities, the increase was 165 per cent.[3]

The star system in the humanities is quite different from that in the natural sciences and professional schools. Stars in the humanities earn pittances compared with stars in the natural sciences and professional schools. Faculty in the humanities rarely get research grants; this has implications for graduate students, who must work as poorly paid teaching assistants, as well as for their faculty. In the market-related fields the influence of the corporations is direct: in some places it is almost as if arenas of the university have been absorbed into the corporate world. The term 'star system' describes the hierarchy that has evolved in the humanities better than it describes the parallel phenomenon in the natural sciences and professional schools. In the humanities personality and ability to project it, performance style, sometimes even personal appearance are factors in the creation of stars. Hollywood seems to be the most immediate model, though the influence of the corporate world lurks in the background: in the humanities as elsewhere in the university what is taking place is a commodification of knowledge, the development of a culture in which what matters is what sells.[4]

The academic left is utterly intertwined with the humanities star system. There are prominent faculty in the humanities who are stars in the sense that their public lectures draw large crowds, they can command high lecture fees if they want, their names are widely known. But the humanities star system is not just the sum of prominent humanities scholars, but a distinctive set of formal and informal networks which has been constructed by, and in turn has constructed, the academic left. In its broadest sense the humanities star system includes not only stars but the circles of supporters and admirers that surround the stars. In this sense the star system and the academic left are synonymous: academic leftists are those who locate themselves within these circles. The fact that belonging to these circles is so important gives the academic left the aura of a club or a sect, for which the question of who belongs and who does not takes on great importance. When the term 'left' is used to mean those within these circles (and 'conservative' to mean those outside them) clear political discussion becomes impossible.

The star system exemplifies two of the most striking qualities of turn-of-the-millennium capitalism: the growing gap between rich and poor and the galloping commodification of all aspects of life. The star system exemplifies both of these trends. It as as if the academic left has situated itself on the cutting edge of current capitalist trends, as they enter the academy and transform it. Academic leftists did not set out to do this, either individually or collectively. But over the last decade or so, the star system is where the action has been, and smart and ambitious academics have gravitated toward it. In an arena in which the only options appear to be playing the game or being left out, there are few who would choose the latter. And since this has been the only game in town, to some degree everyone has to participate in it. The problem is that giving oneself over to this game means putting aside core progressive values. It also goes against faculty solidarity and solidarity between faculty and students. It is a stance that promotes individual ambition and undermines solidarity of any sort.

Over the past decade or so, with the upper tiers of the US economy awash in money, many Americans, especially those in the upper middle class, have been swept up in the quest for upward mobility, for wealth, status and power. Given that this appears to be the only game in town, it is not surprising that academics, including left academics, have been caught up in this quest. The upward scramble in academia has its own character: especially in the under-funded humanities and the softer social sciences, status and power are more sought after than wealth, though the three do tend to go together. The academic left has taken up the values of success, of upward mobility within the existing system, with as much enthusiasm as any other sector of academia, and more than most. For most academics the quest for upward mobility is a classic case of false consciousness. Faculty work harder, churning out more publications at an ever-accelerating pace, frantically attempting to keep abreast of the proliferating, but often mediocre, literature in one's field, trying to maintain one's intellectual focus despite computer breakdowns, the growing barrage of trivial email messages and pervasive cybernetic distraction. The pressure is even worse for graduate students, most of whom must teach to survive economically, who struggle to earn their degrees in the little time left over and many of whom will in any event not find jobs in academia. According to the logic of the market, the universities benefit from all this frantic activity. Universities in search of funding need to point to numbers of undergraduates passed through the system, volume and visibility of faculty research, and hopefully a few faculty stars. But for the faculty and even more for the students, this means a frantic pace of work and the gradual disappearance of any life apart from work. It means a life increasingly restricted to the university, and increasingly instrumental, and alienated, relations within that realm.

What can progressive faculty do to resist the encroachment of corporate values, especially in the university, but also more broadly? One answer lies in our teaching and writing. Over the past decade or two literary theory, and cultural commentary driven by literary theory, has gone a long way towards driving out concern with social issues. We need to teach, and write, about the increasing disparity between rich and poor, the growing power of the corporations and its domestic and global ramifications, and about the ways in which the current trajectory towards a corporate-dominated future might be reversed by collective action. We also need to revive interest in history, which has been weakened, within the academic left, as a result of post-structuralism's dismissal of meaningful links between past, present and future. Without an understanding of the past and its connections to the present it is virtually impossible to imagine a future other than as a projection of current trends. The battle over how to understand the past has always been a major component of the debate between right and left. It is a mistake to abandon this battle and to inculcate students with the view that history no longer matters. In arguing that we need to emphasize social problems and historical analysis in our teaching and writing, I do not mean to suggest that we should abandon theory and embrace empiricism. Tracing the links between past, present, and future possibilities, is a theoretical task. But we need a theory that helps us to do this, and post-structuralism is not that theory.

Another answer to the question of what progressive faculty can do to resist the encroachment of corporate power in the universities is that we can resist the accelerated stratification that the corporate model entails. This means creating faculty unions where they do not yet exist, and supporting the efforts of graduate student teaching assistants to gain union recognition. It means fighting against the introduction of merit systems for faculty promotion, which widen pay differentials among faculty, destroy faculty solidarity and make it impossible for faculty to predict future earnings with any confidence. It also means fighting the star culture, the mindset according to which one's worth is measured by one's fame (and, of course, one's earnings). Fighting the star culture is particularly difficult because there seem to be no alternatives. Especially in the research-oriented universities that set the tone for university culture as a whole, the star system has become so engrained that it is difficult to imagine any other measure of worth. But this is why we need a left within the university: to challenge corporate-driven market values and to present an alternative, based on a humanist/socialist perspective.

The current academic left has little relation to movements for social change outside the university. This is partly due to escalating demands for publication in regard to tenure and promotion, leaving little time for activity outside the university, and partly due to the culture that has everyone scrambling to publish the next article or book, after which, one imagines, one can relax a little and have time for other things. Given these pressures a surprising number of faculty manage to sustain some connection to progressive activism outside the university, but these individual links have little impact on university culture. More individual efforts of this sort would be a good thing: progressive movements need the contributions of trained researchers and intellectuals, and teaching and writing are enriched by involvement in movement activity. Keeping one's ties to movements outside the university can also help keep one sane in an increasingly alienating academic environment. But even the sum of numbers of faculty engaged in such work is not likely to transform the culture of the university. Faculty, or faculty–student organization, with this aim, is more likely to achieve this end. If such a movement were to emerge, it would then no doubt begin to ally itself with progressive movements outside the university. Such alliances would have a much larger impact than the sum of the efforts of individual faculty who manage to devote some of their time to progressive activism outside the university.

## Notes

1 Wendy Brown explores the relationship between wounded or subordinate status, and political claims, in her 1995 essay 'Wounded attachments' in Brown, W. (1995) *States of Injury: Power and Freedom in Late Modernity*, Princeton, NJ: Princeton University Press.

2 Sokal, A. (1996) 'Transgressing the boundaries: toward a transformative hermaneutics of quantum gravity', *Social Text*, 46–47 (Spring/Summer): 217–52.

3 These figures are based on California Postsecondary Education Commission (1982, 1984, 1986–7, 1989–90) 'Faculty salaries in California higher education, 1991–2', 'Headcount of professors at above-scale salaries', *Annual Academic Personnel Statistical Report*, Office of the Senior Vice President, University of California, and on California Postsecondary Education Commission (1991–2) 'Faculty salaries in California public higher education'.

4 The accelerating influence of the corporations on the universities is explored in Slaughter, S. and Leslie, L. L. (1997) *Academic Capitalism: Politics, Policies, and the Entrepreneurial University*, Baltimore, MD: Johns Hopkins University Press. Nobel, D. F. (1998) 'Digital diploma mills: the automation of higher education', *First Monday: an Electronic Journal*, January, is an important account of the linked impact of corporate control and technology on the universities. Several books address the relationship between growing corporate control and academic culture: Readings, B. (1996) *The University in Ruins*, Cambridge, MA: Harvard University Press; Nelson, C. (1997) *Manifesto of a Tenured Radical*, New York: New York University Press; Nelson, C. and Watt, S. (1999) *Academic Keywords: a Devil's Dictionary for Higher Education*, New York: Routledge Press.

# 10

# Privatization: claims, outcomes and explanations

JEAN SHAOUL

One of the defining characteristics of public policy in the last decades of the twentieth century, not just in Britain but the world over, has been the privatization of state-owned enterprises (SOEs) (Veljanovski, 1987; Letwin, 1988; Suleiman and Waterbury, 1990; Harik and Sullivan, 1992). Privatization has taken several forms: the public offering of shares to the stock market, sale to the highest bidder, management buy-outs, outsourcing of some public services and, more recently, the Private Finance Initiative (PFI) and Public–Private Partnerships (PPPs), known elsewhere as design, build, finance and operate (DBFO). But in contrast to nationalization, it was neither the result of a widespread movement among the public at large nor popular. Governments of all political shades introduced it at the behest of big business, not the public. Privatization was central to the project of 'rolling back the state', a task which was introduced and justified as an economic necessity in 1979 (HM Treasury, 1979) and not repudiated by the incoming Labour government.

Some of the benefits that would flow to the public from privatization included raising revenue and reducing the public sector borrowing requirement; access to finance from the capital markets which government could not provide; and the promotion of wider share ownership as part of a more participative capitalism. But the government's claims and justification for privatization were largely based on abstract economic models about the benefits of private ownership and competition. Greater efficiency would flow from the ability of the new owners, with their superior management skills, to intervene and control performance that would benefit everyone (Moore 1983, 1985; Redwood, 1988). The assumptions were very clear. The public sector was inefficient. It impeded the creation of wealth. As the private sector was more efficient, the transfer of ownership would lead to increased efficiency and increased wealth. The appeal to the national 'economy' carried with it the clear implication that all would benefit. Indeed the White Papers setting out the arrangements for privatization said so quite explicitly (Department of Industry, 1982; Department of Transport, 1984; Department of the Environment, 1986; Department of Energy, 1988; Department of Transport, 1992). Yet twenty years on, it is indisputable that life for the broad mass of the population is harder.

This chapter is divided into several sections. An initial section briefly reviews the evidence as it relates to the comparative efficiency of the public and private sectors. The second section examines empirically the outcomes of the privatization of the public utilities, who were the winners and losers, and explains the significance of the efficiency rhetoric, the change in ownership and why the promises were always chimerical. The third section considers the privatization of the public services through the mechanisms of the PFI and PPPs. The final section relates these policy changes, and the lack of an effective critique and opposition to them, to the objective changes taking place in the world economy.

## The lack of evidence of private sector efficiency

The public choice or property rights model associated with Alchian, Demsetz and Hayek, and the supposed superior performance of the private sector, had been subject to little careful scrutiny as others have noted (Crain and Zardkoohi, 1978; Boardman and Vining, 1989; Heald and Steel, 1986). Most of the comparisons of public and private sector performance centred on ill-defined costs in isolation from either outputs (i.e. on economy rather than efficiency) or the social and institutional context (Pryke, 1982; Spann, 1977). The forms of analysis and research methodology rarely permitted the cause of any differences to be established (Millward, 1982; Ernst, 1994).

The government provided little empirical evidence to support the claims for efficiency gains or even to establish whether or not the enterprises were inefficient. Still less was said about where or how the gains were to be obtained. Yet the privatization White Papers acknowledged that the efficiency of the SOEs had improved markedly. In the case of the railways, labour productivity was higher than the European average while at the same time the level of subsidy was lower (Department of Transport, 1992). But the absence of evidence supporting the superior performance of the private sector calls into question the claimed benefits of privatization.

## The outcomes of privatizing the public utilities in Britain

Let us start from the standpoint of the capitalist mode of production rather than the abstract national economy and then inject some empirical evidence derived from the annual report and accounts of some of the privatized infrastructure industries into these empty conceptual boxes, to see how this all works out in practice (see Froud *et al.*, 1996; Shaoul 1998). Under private enterprise, the surplus created by the efforts of the workforce must cover the distribution to the government (tax) and the providers of loan and equity capital who require a return proportionate to the capital employed (interest and dividends).

It must cover the replacement and enhancement of the productive capacity (investment) and meet the requirements of the capital market for future growth. So if a state enterprise is to be successfully privatized, not only must it be cash generative but the form of its capitalization or balance sheet must be such that the surplus matches (most of) the distributional requirements for tax, interest, dividends and investment, in the short term at least.

The utilities and infrastructure enterprises could be privatized because, contrary to the myths, they had always been able to generate an operating surplus. Indeed they had provided the material basis for the late nineteenth-century 'municipal socialism' and more recently for reducing prices, increasing investment or subsidizing other government projects. Even coal and rail usually made an operating profit. It was the claims of finance capital they could not meet. The public services, such as health and education, could not so easily be sold because they simply were not cash generative. Hence the requirement for a new policy – the PFI and PPPs – an issue which will be developed later.

The really crucial task for the civil servants was to ensure that the cash surplus was sufficient to meet the distributional claims and generate a satisfactory rate of return on capital employed for the new owners. They accomplished this by some combination of the following: writing off the debts so that interest payments did not constitute a major charge on the surplus; allowing losses to be carried forward (rail) and setting the capital allowances (water) so that tax would not be too burdensome; retaining unusually large or problematic liabilities such as the decommissioning of nuclear power stations, and compensation for health and safety claims (mines) within the public sector; transferring surplus pension funds to the private sector (rail and water); and injecting cash to smooth over any initial problems (rail and water). If all else failed, subsidies could be increased (rail) or sweeteners provided to sugar the pill (Rover Group).

Finally, the universally observed phenomenon – the sale of publicly owned assets well below either their current value or their historic cost – was the inexorable consequence of ensuring that capital intensive industries could deliver the required rate of return to their new owners. The alternative, setting a more realistic value on the assets, would have meant allowing prices to consumers to rise to politically unacceptable levels, thereby torpedoing a deeply unpopular policy. While the flotations brought in welcome revenues to the government, this was far outweighed by the liabilities, about which little was said. Thus the government made a loss on the sales of the publicly owned assets built up by generations of tax payers and consumers; lost a source of annual revenues, thereby contributing to the fiscal crisis of the state; and faces untold financial liabilities in the future.

Despite the virtues of private sector management, the government sold the rolling stock, ports and buses, to name but a few, to management buy-outs.

**Table 1 Cash generation of various industries and companies**

| Activity | Purchases/ sales | Value added/sales | LSVA | Surplus/value added | Surplus/sales |
|----------|------------------|-------------------|------|---------------------|---------------|
| Water industry | 0.25 | 0.75 | 0.25 | 0.75 | 0.55 |
| British Airports Authority | 0.58 | 0.42 | 0.34 | 0.66 | 0.38 |
| British Telecom | 0.44 | 0.56 | 0.33 | 0.67 | 0.35 |
| British Gas | 0.56 | 0.44 | 0.45 | 0.55 | 0.20 |
| Buses | 0.25 | 0.75 | 0.65 to 1.00 | 0.35 to 0.00 | 0.26 to 0.00 |
| Coal (RJB) | 0.44 | 0.56 | 0.56 | 0.44 | 0.25 |
| Electricity generation | 0.75 | 0.25 | 0.36 | 0.64 | 0.16 |
| British Airways | 0.60 | 0.40 | 0.65 | 0.35 | 0.14 |
| British Rail | 0.18 | 0.72 | 0.84 | 0.16 | 0.13 |
| Electricity distribution | 0.80 | 0.20 | 0.50 | 0.50 | 0.10 |
| Hospital trusts | 0.29 | 0.71 | 0.86 | 0.14 | 0.09 |

*Source:* Annual reports and accounts 1994. All except British Rail and the hospital trusts were privately owned in 1994

Private owners, it was claimed, would have the incentive to invest and enhance facilities. But far from seeing their new ownership as a means of investing in improved services, nearly all took advantage of the capital markets to sell on at several times the original price and become multi-millionaires.

Consider next the determinants of the all-important cash surplus. All businesses are not the same. They generate different levels of surplus because their costs differ. In essence, costs are two-fold: purchases of goods and services, an external cost, and labour, an internal cost. The cost of bought-in goods and services is reflected in the purchase to sales ratio (P/S) and depends on the firm's position in the value chain, degree of vertical integration and monopsonistic power, etc. The different P/S ratio results in varying levels of *value added*. Their labour costs or the share of the value added going to labour (LSVA) depends upon the processes required, the technology and capital employed, bargaining power of the unions, and the 'social wage' component (which is largely institutionally determined).

As Table 1 shows, these ratios combine in different ways to produce different surpluses. Water is the most cash generative in the country because it has the advantage of low purchases (its raw materials come free) and low labour costs (being essentially a distributive network requiring little labour). But another network business, electricity distribution, is not as cash generative because it has to pay for its raw materials and employ more labour to process the product.

This in turn means that the management task differs from business to business. One size does not fit all. There are essentially three strategies that management can pursue: cost recovery via the market, cost reduction and capital restructuring. If we consider cost recovery through the market first, the scope for management intervention to transform the enterprise was limited: most of the utilities operated in mature domestic markets that could not be expanded in the short term at least owing to Britain's geographic position. Neither was there any possibility of introducing new or niche products, except in telecoms. There was therefore little prospect of increasing revenues in the product market, especially as privatization of essentially monopolistic enterprises was accompanied and legitimized by price regulation.

Most of the utilities showed little overall growth in revenues. In the case of British Gas, between 1985 and 1995 revenues rose by 24 per cent, or less than the rate of inflation (about 50 per cent). In real terms, the electricity generators' revenues fell by 12 per cent between 1990 and 1994, while those of the regional electricity distributors rose by only 6 per cent in the same period. British Telecom's revenues grew by 89 per cent between 1985 and 1995, but most of this was before 1988 when the regulator demanded price cuts. Likewise, revenues in the water industry did rise substantially: 62 per cent in the five years since privatization in 1989. But this was of little direct benefit to the industry as the regulator had allowed prices to rise to cover the cost of the European Union (EU) determined investment in coastal water clean-up, drinking water quality and urban waste water treatment.

While the rising demands of the new owners can be met when revenues are rising, in a static market, management can only increase income by grabbing market share. But even this cannibalism is impossible when the industries are essentially regional monopolies. In a mature market, the transformatory power of management and increased efficiency means finding ways of reducing costs: either the cost of external purchases by squeezing suppliers' prices or the internal cost of labour. In the final analysis, it is the workforce which has to bear the cost of adjustment via jobs, wages, conditions, etc. The only question is whose workforce bears the cost. Thus the absence of a rising product market entails redistribution from labour to the owners.

In principle at least, other alternatives include a cutback in capital investment and replacement, loans, or government subsidies. But none of these offers a long-term solution. To take but one example – investment – rising public concerns about environmental issues, the crumbling infrastructure and safety, in the case of water and rail, mean that investment cannot be indefinitely delayed. Mergers and take-overs followed in an attempt to cut costs. But the key point is that management accomplished the redistribution in different ways, all of which were painful and resulted in gains for some social groups at the expense of others.

Table 2 shows how this adjustment was made. The electricity distributors, under intense pressure from both the regulators and their customers, squeezed the generators, the generators squeezed their suppliers – oil, gas and coal – and

**Table 2 Employment and dividends since privatization**

|  | Period | Fall in Employment | Dividends (£m) |
|---|---|---|---|
| British Gas | 1987–95 | −33,675 (−38%) | 4,354 |
| British Telecom | 1988–95 | −89,000 (−38%) | 6,745 |
| 10 water companies | 1990–5 | −3,083 (−8%) | 6,862 |
| Electricity generation | 1992–6 | −8,996 (−43%) | 1,262 |
| Railtrack | 1996–9 | −520 (−5%) | 434 |

*Source:* Annual reports and accounts (various years)

most of the remaining mines in Britain closed. The generators, gas and tele-coms cut back on their workforce by 43 per cent, 38 per cent and 38 per cent respectively. The amount saved on labour costs was approximately equal to the amount paid out in dividends.

However, the water industry, with a very small labour force that had been severely cut back under public sector management, had little room left to prune its labour costs. It shed 8 per cent of its workforce. As a result of the price increases since privatization, the water industry made a £13.5bn cash surplus. It then spent £6.9bn on dividends to the parent companies, £11.3bn on investment and £1.7bn on renewing the decaying infrastructure. Several points follow from this. First, the surplus was insufficient to cover the needs of the industry and the shareholders. Loans that mortgage the future increas-ingly made up the shortfall between the surplus and the overall distribution. Second, the expenditure on investment and particularly on renewals repres-ented a cutback on the original plans as set out at privatization and led to water shortages and the failure of the public water supply in West Yorkshire. As such, it was the means of adjusting to the demands of the new owners for dividends and dividend growth (Shaoul, 1997). But third, and even more importantly from the standpoint of the government's rhetoric, this means that without the onus of dividends, the surplus was more than enough to fund the costly investment programme. The much-vaunted capital market was not so much a source of finance as a drain. The railways present a similar story, albeit with more tragic results, as passengers lost their lives as maintenance and investment were cut back.

The management of the electricity generators, gas and telecoms resolved the distributional conflict between the stakeholders in favour of the owners and, to a lesser extent, the consumers (because of pressure from the regulator). This was at the expense of the workforce, and in the case of the gas and electricity industry, the suppliers. The water and rail industries show a different distributional conflict as a result of the investment requirements laid down by the EU and the dilapidated state of the railways. Management and the regu-lators resolved the conflict at the expense of the consumer, both present and future.

While this suggests how and why private sector can produce more economically than the public sector, none of this has established that the private sector is any more *efficient*. Efficiency is a problematic concept. Productive efficiency is concerned with the best ratio of output to cost, in contrast to economy, which is concerned with the lowest possible cost. The following evidence from the water industry (Shaoul, 1997) sheds some light on the difficulty in using the concept. There was a decline in the volume of water delivered and sewage collected. More than 30 per cent of water was lost owing to leakage before it reached consumers and this leakage had increased significantly since privatization. There were no major improvements in any of performance indicators. Indeed most of the companies failed at least one of their performance targets. Within a few years of privatization, the public water supply in West Yorkshire failed and was only maintained by a round-the-clock road tankering operation lasting three months. The improvements in water quality measures had been set by the EU and paid for by price rises set by the regulator. Finally the rate of infrastructure renewals was such that it would take more than a century to replace the water mains and five centuries to renew the critical sewers. But the degradation in the performance and status of the infrastructure threatens service delivery and public health while creating additional costs in the future. None of this indicates either productive or allocative efficiency. These findings can be replicated across many of the privatized industries, including the railways (Shaoul, 1999a).

Thus while the government's case rested upon efficiency, productivity, reducing the public sector deficit, access to finance from the capital markets and benefits for all, the real effect of privatization was the redistribution of wealth to the new owners. Workers lost their jobs, and pay and conditions declined. Consumers in most cases paid higher prices without any compensating improvement in service. Governments lost a vital source of revenue that was to contribute to the fiscal crisis of the state and the dismantling of welfare provisions. Privatization has thus played a key role in the rising inequality, not just in Britain but all over the world.

The essence of bourgeois politics consists in the development of a programme through which the demands and aspirations of the broad mass of the people for improvements in their social position can be manipulated and subordinated to the programme of capital. The government, by focusing on a concept as ambiguous as efficiency, made the distribution problem invisible in order to justify a deeply unpopular policy. The press, commentators and the public at large have bought the efficiency argument without any critical examination of its meaning, measurement and significance in the policy debate. They routinely describe the public sector as inefficient. And they have discredited the notion of public ownership. While privatization remains unpopular with the public, one of the key victories of successive governments has been the 'selling' of public sector inefficiency.

The source of the problem was not poor management, inefficiency, the lack of competition and all the other alibis of the New Right but a pool of value added insufficient, relative to the amount of capital invested in the enterprises, to meet all the claims that flowed from privatization. The 'success' of privatization in general depends upon the size of the value added fund and its ability to grow to meet all the claims on the surplus for tax, interest, dividends and investment. At best, 'efficiency' provides only a limited source of growth and for a relatively short period. Even industries as profitable as water are incapable of satisfying all the claims. Privatization and its consequences have increased the social, economic and political conflicts, e.g. utility disconnections, rail safety, that were to some extent at least assuaged under public ownership.

## The privatization of public services through the private finance initiative

Whereas right-wing governments were the chief proponents of privatization, social democratic party governments have championed PPPs as softer, cuddlier forms of privatization. The PFI and PPPs are the new policy fix being used to privatize education, health, roads, prisons, roads and other public services, which could not be privatized outright because they were not cash generative. PFI is being used to finance the building of much-needed new or refurbished hospitals, schools and other infrastructure projects. Under PFI, the private sector designs, builds, operates and owns a new hospital or school used for service delivery, and leases it back to the public sector for an annual fee. But since the government can borrow more cheaply than the private sector, it is much costlier to get the private sector to finance investment, even when they are willing to do it. Even after throwing in the existing assets and various forms of public subsidy into the deal, the PFI hospitals are both expensive and 30 per cent smaller than the hospitals they replace (Gaffney and Pollock, 1999). So enter the new Treasury mantra: whereas privatization was justified on the grounds of increased efficiency, the PFI and the PPPs are justified on the basis of *risk transfer*.

But the evidence shows that the risk transferred under PFI deals for new hospitals has at best been minimal and at worst been transferred back to the public sector. Even after cooking the books to show some risk transfer – and in the case of the Edinburgh hospital, the business case revealed that most of the risk transferred to the private sector was interest rate risk – the difference between a PFI deal and a publicly funded one was loose change (Shaoul, 1999b). The PFI consortia went on to raise finance for the hospitals on the stock market saying that 'there was little inherent risk' and they were protected by 'government letters of support'. The recent crisis over private finance schemes for the new National Insurance and Passport Agency computer systems (with private partners Siemens and Andersen Consulting) illustrates the second problem. The Public Accounts Committee noted that the government's refusal to fine the contractors 'would result in the risk purportedly transferred to Andersen Consulting under the PFI contract being transferred back to the public sector' (Public Accounts Committee, 1999). Not surprisingly, PFI deals are shielded from the public with claims of 'commercial confidentiality', despite the fact that hospitals are public bodies, costs are set to increase and service provision to decline (Gaffney *et al.*, 1999a, b, c, d). The proposed *Freedom of Information* legislation will not remedy this since information can be withheld on the grounds of commercial confidentiality. So once again, the press and commentators have accepted the rhetoric – risk transfer – that serves to legitimize a policy that enriches the few at the expense of the many, without critically examining its meaning and significance.

## Globalization and the end of national reformist programmes

The policies of the New Right and New Labour were and are presented as simply a policy shift that occurred during the 1970s (and could therefore be reversed by another policy change). But in fact, they reflected the response of business leaders to the objective changes that had taken place in the world economy (International Committee of the Fourth International, 1998; Beams, 1998). The downturn in the rate of return on capital employed in the 1960s and 1970s was the driving force for several inter-related processes: the globalization of production in order to lower costs, and the development and application of new technologies of production: computers and telecommunications. Changes in technology enabled ever fewer productive units to supply a world market. Together these processes have been responsible for a transformation of the structure of the capitalist economy. The resulting global mobility of capital spelt the end of the programme of Keynesian national regulation that formed the basis of the post-war welfare state, and the state-owned enterprises and services. At the same time the enormous technological innovations in the production process, based on the computer chip, have enormously intensified the crisis of the profit system. The cash surplus or surplus value – the basis of profit – represents in the final analysis the surplus labour extracted from the working class. But the essence of new technology and cost cutting is the replacement of value creating labour in the production process. Consequently, rather than alleviating the tendency of the rate of profit to fall, it has worked to exacerbate it, as Armstrong *et al.*'s (1984) analysis shows. While this was and is largely invisible in the public debates, it was this that lay at the heart of the policy shift and the New Right agenda. It is this falling rate of profit relative to the amount of capital employed (even though the absolute amount of profit may be rising) that lies behind the successive waves of mergers and cross-border mergers in the 1980s and 1990s: corporations sought to cut costs, sell off surplus assets – thereby reducing the amount of capital employed – and reduce the number of shareholders to whom dividends were payable.

Under conditions where the overall mass of surplus value was expanding, capital was able to tolerate the welfare state and even welcome the nationalization of basic industries. Such policies provided a means of containing and regulating the class struggle. They shifted the cost of investment in capital-intensive industries onto the taxpayers while enabling their former owners to re-invest the proceeds from compensation in more profitable ventures. At the same time the nationalized industries and services were run in ways that constituted a subsidy to industry. Indeed, the nationalizations in the 1940s were justified with claims of the increased efficiency that would flow from the restructuring and increased investment that only government could provide (Millward, 1999).

But under conditions where the tendency is for the mass of available surplus value to decline, deductions in the form of corporate taxation to finance social welfare became increasingly intolerable. Furthermore, the 40 per cent of so of GDP that did not provide a source of profit must now be opened up via privatization, PFI/PPP, outsourcing and all the rest. Privatization has spawned one quarter of the top 100 corporations on the London stock market. Outsourcing and PFI/PPPs have created a new business sector – facilities management – and corporations that are the stock market darlings. The Millennium Round of the World Trade Organisation seeks to open up health, education and social services as new sources of profit for the medico-pharmaceutical and facilities management corporations through its General Agreement on Trade and Services and Government Procurement Agreement (Pollock *et al.,* 1999). Yet these corporations are and will be almost wholly dependent upon the very state that government claimed it wanted to roll back.

Such an analysis suggests that the conflicts between the claimants on the pool of surplus value will increase as business strives to meet the demands for 'international competitiveness' in the global economy. Globalization has spawned a debate among the left. One tendency, the social democrats, recognizes that globalization has taken place and, saying 'There is no alternative', has embraced the policies of the New Right. The Labour Party in Britain has renounced its old reformist programme of 'social ownership' and is now dismantling the very welfare state it once helped to establish.

But the position of many others on the left (Harman, 1996; Meiksins Wood, 1997) is summed up by *Globalization in Question* (Hirst and Thompson, 1996). The authors describe their perspective as 'a mixture of scepticism about global economic processes and optimism about the possibility of control of the international economy and the viability of national political strategies'. They argue that social reforms are still possible 'with a modest change in attitudes on the part of key elites'. It is therefore 'essential to persuade reformers on the left and conservatives who care for the fabric of their societies that we are not helpless before uncontrollable global processes'. Followed to its logical conclusion, this would lead to a realignment with some of the most right wing forces.

Despite the apparent differences, there is an essential unity between the two positions. The 'radical' intellectuals long ago rejected the working class as an international and revolutionary class. They relied on the Stalinists, the nationalist movements, labour bureaucracies and minority groups to restrain imperialism internationally and pressure the ruling class for reforms at home (see, for example, Hall, 1983; Bloomfield, 1983). Having bought the programme of national reformism, Keynesian economics and its Stalinist variants as a bulwark against the international socialist reorganization of society, the radicals were left rudderless when globalization undermined their nationalist, and capitalist, perspective.

A third tendency sees the globalization of production as the most revolutionary factor in world politics today because it means the destruction of all the old social, economic and political structures through which the ruling class has maintained its rule. These very developments have created the conditions for its overthrow and the foundations for the construction of an international socialist society (International Committee of the Fourth International, 1998; Beams, 1998).

Globalization and the policy shifts that have followed in its wake have already produced the deep-seated social polarization and inequality which is so glaringly visible in Britain and everywhere else – a far cry from the best of all possible worlds that the government promised us. The issue is not whether this or that industry or service benefits from a particular policy, in this case privatization or PPPs. But rather this analysis poses the question whether all economic life is to be run in the interests of the few seeking ever higher profits instead of meeting the social and public needs, not just of this, but of future generations. To pose the question is to answer it. In other words, it implies a very definite social orientation and programme – that of revolutionary socialism – which is why the traditional organizations of the working class and intellectuals have been unable to mount any effective opposition or critique of the neo-liberal agenda.

## References

Armstrong, P., Glyn, A. and Harrison J. (1984) *Capitalism since World War II: the Making and Breakup of the Great Boom*, London: Fontana Paperbacks.

Beams, N. (1998) *The Significance and Implications of Globalisation: a Marxist Assessment*, Detroit, MI: Mehring Books.

Bloomfield, J. (1983) 'Labour's long haul', in Hall, S. and Jacques, M. (eds) *The Politics of Thatcherism*, London: Lawrence and Wishart in association with Marxism Today.

Boardman, A. E. and Vining, A. R. (1989) 'Ownership and performance in competitive environments: a comparison of the performance of private, mixed and state-owned enterprises', *Journal of Law and Economics*, 32(1): 1–33.

Crain, W. M. and Zardkoohi, A. (1978) 'A test of the property rights theory of the firm: water utilities in the United States', *Journal of Law and Economics*, 21(2): 395–408.

Department of Energy (1988) *Privatising Electricity: the Government's Proposals for the Privatisation of the Electricity Supply Industry in England and Wales*, Cmnd 322, London: HMSO.

Department of the Environment (1986) *Privatisation of the Water Authorities in England and Wales*, Cmnd 9734, London: HMSO.

Department of Industry (1982) *The Future of Telecommunications in Britain*, Cmnd 8610, London: HMSO.

Department of Transport (1984) *Buses and Deregulation*, Cmnd 9300, London: HMSO.

Department of Transport (1992) *New Opportunities for the Railways*, Cmnd 2012, London: HMSO.

Ernst, J. (1994) *Whose Utility? The Social Impact of Public Utility Privatisation and Regulation in Britain*, Buckingham and Philadelphia, PA: Open University Press.

Froud, J., Haslam, C., Johal, S., Shaoul, J. and Williams, K. (1996) 'Stakeholder Economy?', *Capital and Class*, vol. 60: 119–34.

Gaffney, D. and Pollock, A. (1999) 'Pump-priming the PFI: why are privately financed hospitals schemes being financed?', *Public Money and Management*, January–March, pp. 55–62.

Gaffney, D., Pollock, A., Price, D. and Shaoul, J. (1999a) 'NHS capital expenditure and the private finance initiative – expansion or contraction?', *British Medical Journal*, 319: 48–50.

Gaffney, D., Pollock, A., Price, D. and Shaoul, J. (1999b) 'PFI in the NHS – is there an economic case?', *British Medical Journal*, 319: 116–99.

Gaffney, D., Pollock, A., Dunnigan, M., Price, D. and Shaoul, J. (1999c) 'Planning the "New" NHS: downsizing for the 21st century', *British Medical Journal*, 319, 17 July, pp. 179–84.

Gaffney, D., Pollock, A., Price, D. and Shaoul, J. (1999d) 'The politics of PFI and the "New" NHS', *British Medical Journal*, 319, 24 July, pp. 249–53.

Hall, S. (1983) 'The great moving right show', in Hall, S. and Jacques, M. (eds) *Politics of Thatcherism*, London: Lawrence and Wishart in association with Marxism Today.

Harik, I. and Sullivan, D. J. (eds) (1992) *Privatisation and Liberalisation in the Middle East*, Bloomington, IN: Indiana University Press.

Harman, C. (1996) 'Globalisation: a critique of the new orthodoxy', *International Socialism*, Winter.

Heald, D. and Steel, D. (1986) 'Privatising public enterprises: an analysis of the government's case', in Kay, J., Mayer, C. and Thompson, D. (eds) *Privatisation and Regulation: the UK Experience*, London: Clarendon Press.

Hirst, P. Q. and Thompson, G. (1996) *Globalization in Question: the International Economy and the Possibility of Governance*, Cambridge: Polity Press.

HM Treasury (1979) *The Government's Expenditure Plans 1980–81*, Cmnd 1746, London: HMSO.

International Committee of the Fourth International (1998) *Globalization and the International Working Class – a Marxist Assessment*, Michigan: Mehring Books.

Letwin, O. (1988) *Privatising the World*, London: Cassell.

Meiksins Wood, E. (1997) 'Labor, state and class struggle', *Monthly Review*, 49(3).

Millward, R. (1982) 'The comparative performance of public and private enterprise', in Lord Roll (ed.) *The Mixed Economy*, London: Macmillan.

Millward, R. (1999) 'State enterprise in Britain in the twentieth century', in Amatori, F. (ed.) *The Rise and Fall of State Owned Enterprises in the Western World*, Cambridge: Cambridge University Press.

Moore, J. (1983) 'Why privatise?', speech given to the annual conference of City of London stockbrokers Fielding, Newson Smith at Plaisterer's Hall, London Wall, on 1 November, HM Treasury Press Release 190/83, reprinted in Kay, J., Mayer, C. and Thompson, D. (eds) (1986) *Privatisation and Regulation: the UK Experience*, London: Clarendon Press.

Moore, J. (1985) 'The success of privatisation', speech made when opening Hoare Govett Ltd's new City dealing rooms on 17 July, HM Treasury Press Release 107/85, reprinted in part in Kay, J., Mayer, C. and Thompson, D. (eds) (1986) *Privatisation and Regulation: the UK Experience*, London: Clarendon Press.

Pollock, A., Price, D. and Shaoul, J. (1999) 'The World Trade Organisation and the future of health services – opening the debate', *The Lancet*, 354, 27 November, pp. 1889–92.

Pryke, R. (1982) 'The comparative performance of public and private sector enterprise', *Fiscal Studies*, 3(2): 68–81.

Public Accounts Committee (1999) 'Twenty-third report: getting better value for money from the private finance initiative', London: House of Commons, Committee Office (HC 583).

Redwood, R. (1988) *Popular Capitalism*, London: Routledge.

Shaoul, J. (1997) 'A critical financial analysis of the post-privatisation of the water industry', *Critical Perspectives on Accounting*, 8: 479–505.

Shaoul, J. (1998) 'Critical Financial Analysis and Accounting for Stakeholders', *Critical Perspectives in Accounting*, vol. 9: 235–49.

Shaoul, J. (1999a) 'Railpolitik: a stakeholder analysis of the privatised railway industry', Public Interest Report, Manchester: Manchester University.

Shaoul, J. (1999b) 'The looking glass world of PFI', *Public Finance*, 29 January, pp. 14–16.

Spann, R. M. (1977) 'Public v private provision of government services', in Borcherding, T. E. (ed.) *Budgets and Bureaucrats – the Source of Government Growth*, North Carolina: Duke University Press.

Suleiman, E. N. and Waterbury, J. (eds) (1990) *Political Economy of Public Sector Reform and Privatisation*, Boulder, Oxford: Westview Press.

Veljanovski, C. (1987) *Selling the State*, London: Weidenfield and Nicolson.

# 11

## Media regulation in the era of market liberalism

JAMES CURRAN

### Introduction

During the Cold War, we were offered two contrasting models. One portrayed capitalist media as agencies of democracy and consumer fulfilment in free societies. The other portrayed communist media as serving the needs of the people under 'actually existing socialism'. Now that one system has triumphed, we are encouraged to believe that it represents the only universally valid model available. There is, we are told, no alternative.

This market triumphalism draws upon widely held anti-statist attitudes. On the neo-liberal right, it has long been thought that the best form of government is least government. Media regulation, in this view, should be minimized because it gives rise to bureaucracy, cultural paternalism and, above all, the denial of freedom. However, this right wing tradition also derives unintended support from some versions of left wing thought, rooted in traditional Marxism or radical libertarian politics. This radical tradition is hostile to the 'capitalist state', seeing it as an agency of big business or moral repression. It also opposes media regulation, believing that it can be used to silence critics of the social order, or be exploited by the moral majority to impose their intolerant views. Thus, for very different sorts of people, media regulation is associated with control by those they fear: whether they be bureaucrats, bosses or 'wonderloaf people'.

The triumph of market liberalism is supported rather than challenged by the new revisionism in media and cultural studies research. This focuses on the nature of people's pleasure in the media; the ways in which media content lends itself to multiple interpetation; and the selective nature of audience responses to the media. The implication of this affirmative research is that people love market-based media for valid reasons, and are well able to take care of themselves without nanny-ish regulation. To this has been added, more recently, a further theme: the uncritical heralding of globalization as a force of nature that is bypassing the nation state and sweeping away national regulation in a tidal wave of history.

Yet in the context of this anti-statist market triumphalism, it is important to point out that there was not before – and is not now – a simple choice between a free market capitalist model and a discredited, communist alternative.

There has long been a 'third way' embodied by social democracy and its numerous cousins (including, crucially, Christian democracy). This comes out of experience of both capitalism and democracy, and is a democratic response to the failings of capitalism. While its arguments and themes have been taken up around the world, they are especially well embedded in the political culture of western Europe owing to the strength, historically, of its organized working class.

This reformist tradition sees the democratic state not as a tool of state elites or big business but as a set of institutions that respond to the play of influence within democratic polities.[1] Certain barriers have been built up over the years to limit the abuse of state authority, including the formal separation of powers, constitutional guarantees of human rights, a cultural tradition of public service, independent media and, above all, an active civil society. Yet while this tradition is cautious, it still sees the democratic state in a positive light, as an important instrument for realizing the common interests of society. Its belief is that people can achieve desirable objectives through the state which they cannot accomplish as solitary consumers in the market economy, or as a marginalized vanguard seeking a new social order that may never dawn.

At a time when the centre of attention of media research has long been elsewhere, it is worth looking again at this tradition and seeing what it has to offer. Why did it reject free market fundamentalism? What has it to offer in its place?

## Dissenting analysis

The free market prospectus claims that anyone can say what they want in a market environment, thus creating the conditions for both free expression and media diversity. Competition ensures that the media are subject to popular control since media enterprises must respond to public wants if they are to stay in business. Private provision in the free market also guarantees, it is claimed, the media's independence from the state, and enables the media to act as a check on government. And since market-based media are subject to the sovereign consumer, they are not regulated by elites and cultural vigilantes who think they know what is best for us. In short media organized on free market lines serve the general public.[2]

Like all persuasive mythologies, this account contains an element of truth. But it has also an element of wishful thinking. This is exposed especially effectively by radical neo-Keynesians, partly because they are reared within a liberal market tradition and are especially alert to its weaknesses. Their central contention is that free market media systems are subject to a number of restrictive controls which tend to be overlooked because they are not consciously sought or are not immediately visible.

One key form of control is exerted through market entry costs. There has been a general tendency for media costs to rise because of the increasing scale of media operations in mass markets, and because of rising levels of technology, outlay and promotion. For example, it now costs over £15 million to establish a popular cable TV channel, over £20 million to establish a mainstream national daily paper, and many times this to establish a new satellite television service, in Britain.[3] The increasing capitalization of media industries has had two important consequences. It has introduced an invisible system of ideological control by preventing groups with limited finanical resources from competing in the market, and it has restricted consumer power by narrowing the range of choice. Only in some specialized markets are entry costs still low, and these are largely confined to provision for minorities.

The rise of market entry costs has influenced in turn the pattern of media ownership. In the early phase of capitalist development, ownership of the press was linked to a plurality of social groups. In the twenty-first century, by contrast, commercial mass media are owned overwhelmingly by big business.[4] This does not mean that these media serve, in a simple and direct way, the interests of big business since ownership power is significantly limited by staff and audience influence. However, some right wing media owners have promoted right wing perspectives within some of the media organizations under their control through their control over senior appointments and strategic organizational policy.[5] Corporate ownership of the mass media is not entirely neutralized by market-oriented pragmatism and the delegation of power to media staff, as some liberal analysts claim.[6] Like those Marxists who argue the exact opposite,[7] they overstate their case.

The media are also shaped by economic inequalities within society. Thus, communications on the internet are shaped by inequalities between countries, between private and commercial institutions, and between individuals.[8] The internet is not a neutral zone of expression, transcending relations of power, as it was first assumed to be.[9]

More generally, affluent groups have additional income to spend on minority media services, and tend to exercise consequently a disproportionate influence on left-over, niche market provision.[10] The affluent also have greater economic muscle because advertisers are willing to pay more to reach them. This influences the allocation of advertising subsidies, and indirectly the structure of the media. For example, nearly half the national daily titles in Britain are prestige papers accounting for a mere 20 per cent of the market,[11] and are sustained primarily by elite advertising. Media content can also be distorted by the advertising-induced shunning of low-income groups. Giving attention to their issues, as Otis Chandler, head of the parent company owning the *Los Angeles Times*, candidly explained, 'would not make sense financially . . . [because] the audience does not have the purchasing power and is not responsive to the kind of advertising that we carry'.[12] Partly as a consequence of this, the *Los Angeles Times* failed to give voice to the smouldering discontents of the city's black ghettoes that erupted in 1992 in one of the worst riots in American history.

Neo-Keynesians also point to specific failures in the functioning of media markets. The natural processes of competition tend to undermine competition, particularly in the press, music and film industries, which have large economies of scale. A high volume of sales greatly increases the marginal rate of profit because expenditure on the first copy can be spread over a larger run of production, leading to a lowering of unit costs. This generates a relationship of competitive inequality between the strong and the weak which tends to result in the latter failing or being marginalized. This is the principal factor behind the global trend towards contraction and monopoly in the Western press,[13] and helped to sustain for a long time the global dominance of movie and record majors. This in turn limited real choice, and weakened consumer power.

There is also a built-in dynamic favouring media concentration. Mergers and acquisitions offer advantages in terms of economies of consolidation, market control, the accumulation of financial resources and multi-media packaging. This has encouraged a general trend towards media concentration within single-media industries, across the media (where it has been allowed) in nation states, and more recently multi-media concentration in a global context.[14] Major media conglomerates are now strategically placed to colonize the development of information arising from new communications technologies.

The trend towards media concentration, it is argued, has fostered centralization and media uniformity, limited competition and audience control, and led to an unhealthy amassment of media power. However, media concentration is not always accompanied by internal centralization of control,[15] and market domination does not always result in the successful 'management' of market demand.[16] But the short-lived rise of Berlusconi, who controlled 40 per cent of the Italian TV market among other media interests, and was catapulted into the premiership of Italy without any prior political experience, illustrates the way in which democratic processes can be distorted by the private concentration of media power.[17]

One last theme of neo-Keynesian analysis also overlaps with a well worn cultural critique. The dynamics of mass production leads, it is argued, to provision for the lowest common denominator of mass taste, and results therefore in bland and undemanding content.[18] It also marginalizes political coverage in the mass media since this is generally a minority interest. This widens the gap between the information rich and poor, and leads to the increasing exclusion of much of the population from the political culture and decision-making processes of society. The economic pressure to maximize audiences also encourages media to converge around the consensual and conventional in order to avoid giving offence to a significant section of the population.[19] Economic processes also promote production for the global market at the expense of national production, in this way contracting the cultural space for collective self-expression within individual nation states, where democracy is still largely practised.[20]

However, all these arguments need to be qualified. The internal differentiation of the mass market can result in some degree of market specialization. A rich, multi-channel TV system like that in the US offers a wide range of programmes, including political debate, alternative comedy, classic Hollywood, specialized sport and provision for minorities. It is primarily the TV networks (still accounting for the majority of TV consumption in the US) which are oriented exclusively towards the mass market and have many of the characteristics associated with mass production content. While these networks are oriented towards the mainstream, the radicalization of society can result – as in early 1970s America – in a shift towards more socially committed and progressive programmes.[21] Furthermore, the globalization of the TV market is more pronounced in TV fiction than in other categories of content, and a wide range of TV programmes continues to be produced locally.[22] This, too, reflects the differentiation of the international market with local populations preferring their own news, sport, chat shows and certain forms of entertainment which can be produced relatively cheaply. But while the 'mass market' critique needs to be qualified, some of its central themes are valid or partly valid.

Another source of criticism of free market systems comes from examination of their operation in different national contexts. A recurrent theme of studies of media in diverse settings, from post-communist Russia to Mexico, is that controllers of major media conglomerates can have very close ties with leading politicians or the ruling party, with the result that privately owned media operate as cheer-leaders of government rather than as vigilant watchdogs.[23] In other words, the free market is no guarantee of editorial independence in a context where major media enterprises have an interest in how government policy, from taxation to labour law, is framed.

The radical sociology of media organizations provides an alternative critical perspective. Although it is not confined to market media, it is relevant here because it directly confronts the claim of neo-liberals that free market media are independent of the state and elites.[24] It points out that news organizations have routines and structures designed to manage an efficient flow of work in a marketable form. Much of the news that reaches us is pre-scheduled in news diaries filled from press releases and information supplied by reporters and takes the form of predictable events such as press conferences, trials and legislative sessions. This is because newsgathering is made easier and more manageable if the news is anticipated and if a regular network of sources can be tapped who are adept at meeting the needs of news organizations and who generate a large volume of reportable activity. It makes the job of the reporter easier and satisfies the employer's need to have the news covered on time and in a resource-efficient way.

However, this strategic approach to newsgathering has unforeseen consequences. Powerful groups and institutions are in a strong position to invest substantial resources in servicing, and in effect subsidizing, the media. They also tend to be judged authoritative and credible as sources by virtue of the position they hold in society. This encourages news media to organize their resources and personnel around them in established 'news beats', which predetermine the supply of news and create an inside track to the media. As a consequence, state institutions and powerful groups tend to be the dominant sources and definers of news. Organizations without headquarters and full-time staff, with low status, tend to be excluded.

This does not mean necessarily that the media take their cue from the 'powerful' in a single framework of news to which subordinate groups must accommodate in order to obtain a media hearing, as it has been influentially argued by some analysts.[25] This is too mechanistic and simplistic an account of the news process. It ignores conflict and competition between elite sources (including tensions within the state); overstates the passivity of the media; takes insufficient account of the relative effectiveness of rival sources; and overlooks the way in which wider changes in society can affect the composition and hierarchy of accredited media sources.[26] But what the radical social organizational critique does demonstrate convincingly is that the media are predisposed through organizational routines and values to marginalize the weak and disorganized.

This argument has a counterpart in studies of entertainment organizations. These emphasize the power exerted by genre conventions and formulae within institutional contexts where the autonomy of individual workers is severely constrained. For example, Todd Gitlin argues that the American television networks have set procedures for weeding out script ideas designed essentially to minimize risk.[27] These procedures take place within an oligarchical structure where 'inside tracking' between a small number of network officials, top suppliers and agents is the norm. The actual makers of TV fiction tend to work in teams, operating within the framework of established formats, narratives and plot lines which are repeated or recombined because they have been successful in the past. In the case of TV films, argues Gitlin, 'characters should be simple and simply motivated, heroes familiar, stories full of conflict, uplift apparent, and each act should end on a note of suspense sufficient to carry the viewer through the commercial break'.[28] The dominant dramatic aesthetic of American television is a conservative one in which problems are tacitly portrayed as being susceptible to individual-moral rather than structural-political solutions.

Mention should also be made of radical culturalist accounts which see the media as being shaped by the cultural domination of society. While this position often pays insufficient attention to countervailing trends in society – in particular the way in which economically subordinate groups can organize collectively to influence the culture and political organization of society – it does point to the way in which the unequal division of power can influence directly and indirectly the operation of the media.[29]

These wider sociological interpretations in effect contest the primacy given by the free market model to a narrowly economic understanding of the media, arguing that the media are shaped by their organizational needs and the wider social processes of society. Neo-Keynesian critics, on the other hand, operate on the same terrain as economic liberals and argue that orthodox economic interpretations are based on an idealized model that deviates from reality. Together these critiques add up to a formidable indictment of the free market prospectus. Their implication is that we should not settle unquestioningly for market regulation of the media, but instead actively explore alternatives.

## Welfare approach

The principal alternative to the free market is a 'welfare' approach, exemplified by public service broadcasting.[30] This approach argues that the satisfaction of individual wants through the free market fails to serve the wider interests of society, because these wider interests are not even taken into account in private transactions. In particular, the media should facilitate a wide-ranging public debate that allows different viewpoints and interests to be articulated. This is more likely to happen, it is argued (especially in mainland Europe), if it is staged by a broadcasting system that is under representative control and committed to representing different points of view. The broadcasting system should also contribute to the cultural needs of society, it is argued, through being committed to quality, innovation and variety.

Public service broadcasting organizations are required to pursue specific cultural goals such as delivering programme quality, and are organized in a way that assists them to pursue these goals. Regulations have also been introduced to ensure that public media facilitate a dialogue in society. These usually require that public broadcasting organizations adhere to fairness rules; give prominence to current affairs coverage; and reflect the diversity of society.

Public service broadcasting has evolved over time. In most mature liberal democracies, television has become independent of government control in response to broadcaster and public pressure. Relative autonomy from the governmental system has also been encouraged by institutional devices such as constitutional support for freedom of expression, funding through a licence fee paid direct to public broadcasters, the involvement of civil society in appointments to broadcasting authorities or the dispersal of power within broadcasting organizations.

There has also been a move away from public service monopolies towards mixed systems made up of competing publicly owned and regulated private organizations. At best, these hybrid systems have relinquished the paternalism of the old monopoly systems without surrendering to commercial values. They embody the advantages of the collectivist approach, with few of its disadvantages. But at worst, they have struck a relatively poor bargain, being either too paternalistic or too commercialized, or perhaps worst of all (as in Turkey)[31] embodying the two extremes.

There is thus a rich record of experimentation to learn from. Out of this experience it is possible to derive certain general lessons. Some forms of media organization have been more successful than others, or offer distinct advantages as well as disadvantages.

## Three public service alternatives

One approach that seems beguiling on paper but has problems in practice is the *franchised pluralism* model, based on devolving control over broadcasting to leading groups in society. This is exemplified by the Dutch television system[32] (with a politicized variant in Italy). In the Netherlands, air-time and technical facilities are allocated to representative organizations on the basis of the size of their membership and/or sale of their TV magazines. The lion's share of three public TV channels goes to seven community organizations (among them, socialists, catholics, protestant conservatives and a liberal, entertainment-oriented corporation) each of which is required to develop their own package of programmes. These are financed through a combination of public funding, advertising and membership dues, and are subject to certain public guidelines. In addition there is a separate organization, NOS, which provides the national news and covers certain key national events.

One problem with this model is that the 'representative' organizations controlling public TV are no longer genuinely representative owing to the rapid social change that has taken place in the Netherlands. Another problem is that the law still requires each major contributing organization to allocate 60 per cent of its time share to a high-fibre diet of information, education, culture and arts programmes.[33] This provoked a consumer revolt in 1989–90 when RTL 4, a commercial, Dutch-language satellite TV channel transmitting mainly American programmes, became within one year of its launch the most popular TV channel in the Netherlands. This was followed by the defection of Veronica, a popular public service organization, to the private sector in 1995.

While the Dutch public TV system has since been restabilized partly through the tacit relaxation of its high-fibre diet, it is difficult to avoid the conclusion that it is a flawed system. Franchised pluralism may be an approach that can be applied usefully in relation to supporting minority media (for example, local community radio stations). But as far as *mass* media are concerned, it seems to have a basic shortcoming. It unduly privileges minority concerns at the expense of majority pleasures.

The *liberal corporatist* model has proved to be altogether more successful. It is the principal public service approach in western Europe, and is perhaps best exemplified by the German broadcasting system.[34] This has the same objective as the Dutch model – the creation of a broadcasting system which reflects the plurality of society – but adopts a different strategy for achieving this. Whereas the Dutch model leases different parts of the broadcasting system to rival groups, the liberal corporatist model seeks to secure pluralism through the incorporation of leading social interests as partners in the management of broadcasting.

German public broadcasting organizations are subject to broadcasting councils which lay down broad strategy and appoint the chief executive. These councils have democratic representatives appointed on the basis of one of three principles. One is a civil society model in which council members are nominated primarily by various representative groups such as business, labour, pensioner, tenant, women's, consumer, charity and environmental organizations as well as political parties and representatives from science, culture and education. The second is the political-parliamentary model in which council members are elected by the local state assembly and government. And the third is a mixed model which combines elements of both these types. In addition, private broadcasting (dominated by Kirch and Bertelsmann) is subject to external broadcasting authorities, made up of community representatives, though these have less influence than public broadcasting councils.

This representative input is reinforced by a constitutional guarantee of pluralism which lays down that 'everybody has the right to free expression and publication of his opinion in word, writing and picture and the right to obtain information without hindrance from sources generally accessible'.[35] This has been interpreted by the Constitutional Court to mean that significant groups in society must be given the opportunity to air their views within the overall programme schedule of television and radio, and that the broadcasting system as a whole must give expression to differing perspectives (in entertainment as well as current affairs programmes). What makes this different from the more limited American First Amendment is that it underwrites not only freedom of expression but also the audience's right of access to diverse opinion. This has entrenched political and cultural pluralism at the heart of the German broadcasting system.

While the German broadcasting system is a successful one, it does not fully function in practice in the way in which it is supposed to in theory. Its main weakness is that is tends to over-represent dominant social blocs in its system of democratic representation, in particular the major political parties and their allies, at the expense of the unorganized, the weak (such as 'guestworkers') and new social movements. At worst, it has degenerated into the so-called 'proporz' system, in which senior and middle-ranking positions in some local public broadcasting organizations have been filled by party caucuses in proportion to the balance of party representation in local state legislatures. Party cartels have thus undermined the pluralistic conception of the broadcasting system, and filled jobs partly on the basis of party patronage rather than of merit. This said, the expansion of commercial broadcasting, and changes in the way in which some broadcasting council members have been appointed, have reduced party control over broadcasting during the last two decades.

German broadcasting has also succeeded in developing an independent relationship to the federal government partly as a consequence, paradoxically, of its politicization. This is perhaps best exemplified by the general public channel, ARD, which is made up of local organizations formed into a national network. ARD organizations in left wing regions tend to have radical broadcasting councils and a radical tradition of programme making, while the opposite is the case in right wing regions. Their combined output is fed into a nationally networked programme service that consequently contains radical and conservative elements. In effect, opposed political tendencies are embedded in the decentralized management structure of ARD in a way that prevents federal government control.

The third approach, exemplified by British broadcasting, is based on a *civil service* model.[36] Whereas the first two models forge links between broadcasting organizations and the principal social interests in society as a way of making broadcasting representative of the diversity of society, the civil service approach seeks to establish broadcasting as an autonomous and neutral zone that stands above partisan politics.

Those appointed to broadcasting authorities in the UK are, in British parliamentary jargon, 'national trustees' who represent the nation rather than a special interest. Technically they have overall control over public broadcasting (BBC and Channel 4), and in the private sector they do have a significant role as regulators upholding public service goals. But to some extent, they are a public facade – a symbolic form of public accountability – behind which broadcasters at the level of producer enjoy a considerable degree of decision-making power.[37]

This is the distinctive feature of the British system, and is the source of both its strength and its weakness. British TV producers are more autonomous than their counterparts in the more representative-dominated, politicized broadcasting systems of continental Europe. They are also more autonomous than producers in the ratings-dominated TV networks of the US because they are insulated from market pressures. The BBC is funded by a licence fee; Channel 4, with a remit to serve minorities, was protected by a cross-subsidy arrangement until this proved unneccessary; and commercial, terrestrial TV channels are subject to quality and diversity requirements which have strengthened the position of public service oriented producers within the commercial system. The autonomy of British TV producers is relative, and subject to corporate constraints. But it has generated a tradition of well-made programmes, not only in the export areas of costume drama and natural history but also in other categories such as soap opera, social realist fiction and alternative comedy.

But this quality is achieved at a price. British broadcasting is very strongly influenced by a metropolitan elite, and does not reflect adequately the diversity of British society, partly because representative pluralism is not a central objective of the system. British broadcasting is also becoming less good than it was because it has become more centralized. In the 1980s, top-down controls tightened within the BBC as a defensive response to government attacks. A similar process took place in the 1990s in commercial television in response to increased shareholder pressure and the weakening of the regulatory agency (ITC). The distinctive strength of British television, based on producer power, has been partly sapped as a consequence.

## Social market policies

The public service approach comes out of an anti-market, collectivist tradition. It gives rise to publicly owned media corporations or the licensing, under specific conditions, of private companies; the codification of the objectives of these organizations in law; and the creation of 'authorities' – whether these be supervisory boards, public regulators or other forms of public body – which are typically concerned with media content and corporate policy. In effect, the community specifies the kind of broadcasting it wants by defining through legislation the objectives, organization and funding of television and radio.

By contrast, the social market approach comes out of a pro-market tradition, and intervenes in the market only to make it work for the public interest. It is a more hands-off approach that seldom concerns itself with media content. This can take the form of watchdog regulation designed to maintain fair competition, and protect the consumer; repair shop measures in which the state seeks to modernize or reconstruct; protectionism in which national media are defended against foreign competition; and more ambitious schemes that amend the rules and processes of competition, for a public purpose.

Thus, all western European countries have some form of anti-monopoly legislation.[38] Without it, media concentration would be very much greater than it is. This said, its effectiveness is declining. This is partly because anti-monopoly law has been relaxed in a number of countries on the grounds that the media system is expanding, and economic concentration makes for success in the global market. A further reason is that some governments have been reluctant to enforce anti-monopoly controls for fear of alienating powerful media friends, or because their enforcement seems likely to prevent a failing enterprise from being saved. So far, attempts to strengthen monopoly legislation through a concerted European approach have come to nothing.

European institutions have initiated various repair shop measures. The information and cultural industries have been identified by the European Commission as a key growth area for jobs.[39] Yet Europe is falling behind in this sector, and has an audio-visual trade deficit with the US. The response of the European state has been to fund, on a relatively modest scale and to limited effect, programme and film making, research into new communications technology and European co-production projects.[40]

There was also a move to limit the import of TV programmes through the framing of a European Directive requiring that 51 per cent of programmes transmitted in the European Union should be originated domestically. This was made an objective rather than a requirement of the 1989 Television Without Frontiers Directive, which meant in effect that it became optional. However, a number of European countries have national protectionist policies. For example, British law forbids non-European control of commercial, terrestrial TV channels, while an ITC regulation requires all such channels to 'originate' 65 per cent of their programmes.

Perhaps the most ambitious social market policy is the press subsidy schemes developed in Nordic countries (with variants in Austria and the Netherlands) since they seek in effect to restructure the market.[41] Their justification is that there is a built-in propensity towards contraction in the press market. Rather than treat its symptoms unsuccessfully through monopoly controls, it is far better, it is argued, to tackle its root cause, the competitive inequality between the strong and weak, through selective subsidies.

In Sweden, grants have been introduced to encourage cost-cutting co-operation between rivals, particularly in the area of joint distribution. A production subsidy is also provided for non-market leaders. This is calculated impersonally in relation to circulation and volume of newsprint without reference to editorial content in order to prevent political favouritism. The scheme is also administered by an independent public board on which there is multi-party representation.

The Swedish scheme is not in fact abused by the government, and funds opposition papers as well as pro-government ones. It has kept alive a local political press, and sustained a much greater degree of press diversity in Sweden than would have existed in an unregulated market. Its further unplanned consequence has been to promote internal differentiation and debate within the party-aligned press partly because public finance has loosened dependence on party.[42] Its principal weakness, however, is that it has done little to introduce new blood into the press system, and its principal beneficiaries are publications linked to mainstream political organizations.

However, a similar scheme in Norway[43] supports a tradition of alternative media activism which emphasizes the value of internal democracy or co-operation, and is sustained by a political culture that is less consensual than that in Sweden. Press subsidies in Norway keep alive a wide diversity of publications, including a remarkable 'cultural Marxist' daily (*Klassekampen*) which functions almost as a training centre for the industry in the way it recruits young, unorthodox talent. The press system is paralleled by that in film. Independent film making in Norway is supported by production grants and given access to the market through municipally owned cinemas.[44]

## Conclusion

In addition, all western European countries have a framework of public law which balances freedom of expression against other rights, such as that to a fair trial, public reputation, privacy and collective security. In effect, a trade-off is calculated between freedom and the avoidance of harm to others. Restrictive moralists seek to expand the notion of 'harm' to include the giving of offence, but this is resisted by those who stress the value of freedom. Different European countries have drawn up slightly different legal boundaries between what is acceptable and unacceptable.[45]

These calculations are common to all societies ruled by a framework of public law, whereas the cultural welfare and social market policies that are embedded in western Europe are less widely adopted. How these fare in the future will depend partly upon how the global market is managed. Simplifying a little, the United States government has placed itself at the head of the media industrial lobby that wants the global market to be re-regulated through the extension of intellectual property rights and the international outlawing of state restrictions on the free movement of cultural goods. It was opposed by European governments, responding to a wider range of industrial and democratic pressures, in the Uruguay round of the GATT (General Agreement on Tariffs and Trade) talks in 1993. The result was a stand-off that has yet to be resolved.[46]

This highlights one crucial point: how the global market evolves is not in the gift of right wing ideologues and trans-national business corporations, but is susceptible to democratic influence exerted through multilateral agencies (not all of which have been 'captured') and through inter-government agreement.

The future of the welfare tradition also depends upon a political battle that has only just begun.[47] The emergence of new communications technology (notably, high-powered satellite, fibre optic cable and digital television) weakened the traditional justification for public service broadcasting based on the need to manage scarce airwave frequencies in the public interest. The rise of power-ful communications conglomerates generated political pressure to privatize and deregulate. They had in the 1980s and early 1990s the ear of sympathetic governments owing to a generalized shift to the right throughout most of west-ern Europe. Yet, despite the convergence of these technological, commercial and political pressures, public service broadcasting organizations in western Europe remained relatively resilient. With few exceptions, they retained both political and consumer support.[48]

They weathered this first storm because, for the most part, they were thought to be independent of government and produced programmes that were valued. The political pendulum has since swung back to the centre-left throughout most of western Europe, creating a vital breathing space in which public service broadcasting, and the wider tradition of media reform, can renew itself. Else-where, I have outlined one way in which different elements of European media policy can be synthesized to produce an optimal media system;[49] suggested ways in which both the conception and practice of public service broadcasting in Britain can be improved;[50] and documented the way in which young broad-casters are currently making improvements in British current affairs journal-ism.[51] This is merely part of a much wider effort on the part of researchers and journalists throughout Europe who are considering how best a worth-while tradition can be defended through candid criticism and reform.[52]

However, this approach is essentially defensive: it is directed towards protect-ing and strengthening what we have got already. Needed now is a more critical and creative response to the pressing issue of media concentration. In the late 1980s, it briefly looked as if new communications technology would generate greater real choice and increased ideological diversity. This was before leading media corporations responded to the threat posed by market fragmentation by expanding vertically, merging with rivals and developing partnership arrange-ments in new media markets. The merger between Time Warner and America Online in 2000 was merely the latest episode in a spectacular acceleration of media concentration during the previous decade. This involved a succession of mergers between film and television companies in the United States, and press and television companies in Europe, to which are now being recruited selected telecommunications and net companies.[53]

Tough limits on the expansion of giant media corporations should be imposed through national states and supra-national agencies (the European Union and Council of Europe, in the case of Europe). The editorial influence of employees within these corporations should be strengthened (by for example giving them the legal right to participate in senior appointments) as a way of promoting 'internal' pluralism within media empires. And a variety of state-supported schemes could be introduced to ensure that minority media voices are not overwhelmed by the corporate muscle of the new media behemoths.[54]

# Notes

1 The best introduction to the very large literature on this subject is Held, D. (1996) *Models of Democracy*, 2nd edition, Cambridge: Polity.

2 For a short and eloquent exposition of this viewpoint, see Murdoch, R. (1989) *Freedom in Broadcasting*, London: News International. For more qualified or elaborated presentations, see Veljanovski, C. (ed.) (1989) *Freedom in Broadcasting*, London: Institute of Economic Affairs, and Kelley, D. and Donway, R. (1990) 'Liberalism and free speech', in Lichtenberg, J. (ed.) *Mass Media and Democracy*, New York: Cambridge University Press.

3 These estimates relate respectively to Live TV, the *Independent* and BSkyB.

4 Herman, E. and McChesney, R. (1997) *The Global Media*, London: Cassell.

5 Frenkel, E. (1994) *The Press and Politics in Israel*, Westport, CT: Greenwood; Neil, A. (1996) *Full Disclosure*, London: Macmillan; Curran, J. and Seaton, J. (1997) *Power Without Responsibility*, 5th edition, London: Routledge.

6 Koss, S. (1984) *The Rise and Fall of the Political Press in Britain*, Volume 2, London: Hamish Hamilton; Alexander, J. (1981) 'The mass media in systemic, historical and comparative perspective', in Katz, E. and Szecsko, T. (eds) *Mass Media and Social Change*, Beverly Hills, CA: Sage; Gans, H. (1980) *Deciding What's News*, London: Constable.

7 Parenti, M. (1993) *Inventing Reality*, 2nd edition, London: St. Martin's Press.

8 Patelis, K. (2000) 'Political economy of the internet', in Curran, J. (ed.) *Media Organisations in Society*, London: Arnold.

9 Negroponte, N. (1995) *Being Digital*, London: Hodder and Stoughton.

10 Golding, P. and Murdoch, M. (1996) 'Culture, communications and political economy', in Curran, J. and Gurevitch, M. (eds) *Mass Media and Society*, 2nd edition, London: Arnold.

11 Tunstall, J. (1996) *Newspaper Power*, Oxford: Clarendon Press.

12 Cited in Baker, E. (1994) *Advertising and a Democratic Press*, Princeton, NJ: Princeton University Press, p. 68.

13 For classic presentations of this neo-Keynesian argument in two different countries, see Reddaway, W. (1963) 'The economics of newspapers', *Economics Journal*, 73, and Rosse, J. N. (1980) 'The decline of direct newspaper competition', *Journal of Communication*, 30.

14 Graham, A. and Davies, G. (1997) *Broadcasting, Society and Policy in the Multimedia Age*, Luton: University of Luton Press; Herman and McChesney (1997) *op. cit.*; Tabernero, A. *et al.* (1993) *Media Concentration in Europe*, Manchester: European Institute for the Media; Murdock, G. (1990) 'Redrawing the map of the communication industries: concentration and ownership in the era of privatization', in Ferguson, M. (ed.) *Public Communication*, London: Sage.

15 McQuail, D. (1992) *Media Performance*, London: Sage.

16 Frith, S. (1996) 'Entertainment', in Curran, J. and Gurevitch, M. (eds) *Mass Media and Society*, 2nd edition, London: Arnold.

17 Mazzoleni, G. (1995) 'Towards a videocracy? Italian political communication at a turning point', *European Journal of Communication*, 10(3).

18 Blumler, J. (1991) 'The new television marketplace: imperatives, implications, issues', in Curran, J. and Gurevitch, M. (eds) *Mass Media and Society*, 1st edition, London: Arnold.

19 Golding and Murdock (1996) *op. cit.*

20 Katz, E. (1996) 'And deliver us from segmentation', *Annals of the American Academy of Political and Social Science*, 546; Varis, T. (1985) *The International Flow of Television Programmes*, Paris: UNESCO.

21 Gitlin, T. (1994) *Inside Prime Time*, revised edition, London: Routledge.

22 Sepstrup, P. and Goonasekera, A. (eds) (1994) *TV Transnationalization: Europe and Asia*, Paris: UNESCO.

23 This is a central theme of a number of essays in Curran, J. and Park, M.-Y. (eds) (2000) *De-Westernizing Media Studies*, London: Routledge.

24 For example, Kaniss, P. (1997) *Making Local News*, Chicago, IL: University of Chicago Press; Protess, D. *et al.* (1991) *The Journalism of Outrage*, New York: Guilford Press; Tiffen, R. (1989) *News and Power*, Sydney: Allen and Unwin; Tuchman, G. (1978) *Making the News*, New York: Free Press.

25 Hall, S., Critcher, C., Jefferson, T., Clarke, J. and Roberts, B. (1978) *Policing the Crisis*, London: Macmillan.

26 Schlesinger, P. (1990) 'Rethinking the sociology of journalism: source strategies and the limits of media-centrism', in Ferguson (1990) *op. cit.*; Schlesinger, P. and Tumber, H. (1994), *Reporting Crime*, Oxford: Clarendon; Hallin, D. (1994) *We Keep America on Top of the World*, London: Routledge; Miller, D. (1993) 'Official sources and "primary definition": the case of Northern Ireland', *Media, Culture and Society*, 15(3); and Davis, A. (2000) 'Public relations campaigning and news production: the case of "new unionism" in Britain', in Curran (2000) *op. cit.*

27 Gitlin (1994) *op. cit.*

28 *Ibid.*, pp. 165–6.

29 Curran, J. (1996) 'Rethinking mass communications', in Curran, J., Morley, D. and Walkerdine, V. (eds) *Cultural Studies and Communications*, London: Arnold.

30 See, in particular, Avery, R. (ed.) (1993) *Public Service Broadcasting in a Multichannel Environment*, Harlow: Longman; Aldridge, B. and Hewitt, N. (eds) (1994) *Controlling Broadcasting*, Manchester: Manchester University Press; Weymouth, T. and Lamizet, B. (eds) (1996) *Markets and Myths*, Harlow: Longman; Coleman, J. and Rollet, B. (eds) (1997) *Television in Europe*, Exeter: Intellect; Goldberg, D. *et al.* (eds) *Regulating the Changing Media*. Oxford: Clarendon.

31 Catalbas, D. (1999) 'Broadcasting deregulation in Turkey: uniformity within diversity', in Curran (2000) *op. cit.*

32 Brants, K. and McQuail, D. (1997) 'The Netherlands', in Ostergaard, B. (ed.) *The Media in Western Europe*, 2nd edition, London: Sage; Nieuwenhuis, A. J. (1993) 'Media policy in the Netherlands: beyond the market?', *European Journal of Communication*, 7(2); McQuail, D. (1992) 'The Netherlands: safeguarding freedom and diversity under multichannel conditions', in Blumler, J. (ed.) (1992) *Television and the Public Interest*, London: Sage; Ang, I. (1991) *Desperately Seeking the Audience*, London: Routledge.

33 Brants and McQuail (1997) *op. cit.*, p. 159.

34 Sandford, J. (1997) 'Television in Germany', in Coleman and Rollet (1997) *op. cit.*; Humphreys, P. (1996) *Mass Media and Media Policy in Western Europe*, Manchester: Manchester University Press; Humphreys, P. (1994) *Media and Media Policy in Germany*, Oxford: Berg; Hoffmann-Riem, W. (1992) 'Development of broadcasting law in the Federal Republic of Germany', *European Journal of Communication*, 7(2); Porter, V. and Hasselbach, S. (1991) *Pluralism, Politics and the Market Place*, London: Routledge; Browne, D. (1989) *Comparing Broadcasting*, Ames, IA: Iowa University Press.

35 Cited in Kleinsteuber, H. and Wilke, P. (1992) 'Germany', in Ostergaard, B. (ed.) *The Media in Western Europe*, London: Sage, p. 79.

36 Curran and Seaton (1997) *op. cit.*; McNair, B. (1999) *News and Journalism in the UK*, 3rd edition, London: Routledge; Curran, J. (1995) 'Regulation and deregulation of the British media', in Gustafsson, K. E. (ed.) *Media Structure and the State*, Gothenburg: Gothenburg University Press; Barnett, S. and Curry, A. (1994) *The Battle for the BBC*, London: Arium; Seymour-Ure, C. (1996) *The British Press and Broadcasting since 1945*, 2nd edition, Oxford: Blackwell.

37 Tunstall, J. (1993) *Television Producers*, London: Routledge.

38 Commission of the European Communities (1992) *Pluralism and Media Concentration in the Internal Market*, Commission of the European Communities Green Paper, Brussels; Barendt, E. (1993) *Broadcasting Law*, Oxford: Oxford University Press.

39 European Commission (1994) *Strategy Options to Strengthen the European Programme Industry in the Context of the Audiovisual Policy of the European Union*, Brussels; European Council (1994) *Europe and the Global Information Society*, Brussels.

40 Humphreys (1996) *op. cit.*; Hirsch, M. and Petersen, V. (1998) 'European policy initiatives', in McQuail, D. and Siune, K. (eds) (1998) *Media Policy*, London: Sage; and for a powerful indictment, Commission of the European Communities (1994) *Report by the Think-Tank on the Audiovisual Policy in the European Union*, Luxembourg.

41 Murschetz, P. (1998) 'State support for the daily press in Europe: a critical appraisal', *European Journal of Communication*, 13(3); Gustafsson, K. E. (1995) 'The process of media integration – the case of Sweden and the Nordic area', paper delivered to the Conference on Media Concentration, Copenhagen on 13 June 1995; Picard, R. (1988) *The Ravens of Odin*, Ames, IA: Iowa State University.

42 Weibull, L. (1995) 'Media diversity and choice', in Gustafsson, K. E. (ed.) *Media Structure and the State*, Gothenburg: University of Gothenburg Press.

43 Skogerbo, E. (1997) 'The press subsidy system in Norway', *European Journal of Communication*, 12(1); Host, S. (1991) 'The Norwegian newspaper system; structure and development', in Ronning, H. and Lundby, K. (eds) *Media and Communication*, Oslo: Norwegian University Press.

44 Solum, O. (1994) 'Film production in Norway and the municipal cinema system', unpublished paper, University of Oslo, Oslo.

45 Barendt (1993) *op. cit.*

46 Tracey, M. (1998) *The Decline and Fall of Public Service Broadcasting*, Oxford: Oxford University Press.

47 Steinberg, D. (1999) 'Why Hollywood lost the Uruguay Round: the political economy of mass communication revisited', unpublished PhD thesis, London School of Economics and Political Science; Hirsch and Petersen (1998) *op. cit.*

48 Ostergaard, B. (ed.) (1997) *The Media in Western Europe*, 2nd edition, London: Sage; Coleman and Rollet (1997) *op. cit.*; Humphreys (1996) *op. cit.*

49 Curran, J. (2000) 'Rethinking media and democracy', in Curran, J. and Gurevitch, M. (eds) *Mass Media and Society*, 3rd edition, London: Arnold.

50 Curran, J. (2000) 'Television journalism: theory and practice. The case of *Newsnight*', in Holland, P., *Television Handbook*, 2nd edition, London: Routledge.

51 Curran, J. (1998) 'The crisis of public communication: a reappraisal', in Liebes, T. and Curran, J. (eds) *Media, Ritual and Identity*, London: Routledge.

52 For example, Hutchinson, D. (1999) *Media Policy*, Oxford: Blackwell; Woldt, R. *et al.* (1998) *Perspectives of Public Service Television in Europe*, Dusseldorf: European Institute for the Media; McQuail, D. and Siune, K. (eds) (1998) *Media Policy*, Sage: London; Raboy, M. (ed.) (1997) *Public Broadcasting for the 21st Century*, Luton: University of Luton Press; Williams, G. (1996) *Britain's Media*, 2nd edition, London: Campaign for Press and Broadcasting Freedom; Collins, R. and Murroni, C. (1996) *New Media, New Policies*, Cambridge: Polity.

53 Herman, E. and McChesney, R. (1997) *The Global Media*, London: Cassell; Tunstall, J. and Machin, D. (1999) *The Anglo-American Connection*, Oxford: Oxford University Press.

54 A wide range of alternative options are reviewed in Curran, J. and Seaton, J. (1997) *Power Without Responsibility*, 5th edition, London: Routledge, chapter 21.

# 12

## Alternatives in the media age

DANNY SCHECHTER

When the personification of an American news obsession jetted into London – by Concorde, of course – in early March 1999, a crisis was on its way to becoming a commodity. Monica Lewinsky's blitzkrieg through the bookstores and TV studios of Britain demonstrated again how celebrities born in scandal end up with less to tell than sell.

With the 'American Century', as *Time Magazine*'s Henry Luce once dubbed it, ending with a whimper instead of a bang, the integration of the news business into show business is virtually complete. Media mergers have multiplied with fewer and fewer companies controlling the flow of news and information globally. These cartel-like conglomerates spawned a web of interconnected strategic alliances driven by neo-liberal economics and controlled competition.

Despite the proliferation of channels, fewer voices were heard among the bewildering array of choices. Instead of difference, the multi-channel environment of American television began oozing sameness with only a few corporations and even fewer gatekeepers deciding what to show. The range of debate was narrowed to from A to B, as the media watchdog group FAIR put it. Scholars began publishing books about the 'post journalism era', pointing out that packaging and presentation techniques had become far more important than substantive reporting.

In the United States, international news were all but gone with Rupert Murdoch's station in New York running a feature called 'The World in a Minute' while the local CBS station boasted of 'more news in less time'. Serious documentaries gave way to shocumentaries and docu-soaps. Investigative reporting, except in a few outlets, had become an endangered species, A dumbing down of news and information was well underway. One of America's best known TV writers, Larry Gelbart, dubbed television a 'weapon of mass distraction'.

According to a 1998 survey, feature stories covering celebrities, scandal and human interest increased from 15 per cent to 43 per cent of the total coverage provided by the three nightly network TV newscasts, major newspapers, front pages and weekly newsmagazines from 1977 to 1997. The entertainment trade magazine *Variety* reported that the network news magazines such as ABC's 20–20 – the show I worked for and dissect in some detail in my book, *The*

*More You Watch, The Less You Know* – and NBC's Dateline say that 'celebrity stuff' got them better ratings than '*the more newsy stuff* [emphasis mine] they were airing'. Remember this phrase because it is indicative of how journalism itself was regarded – MNS – 'more newsy stuff'. TV news was clearly more about creating consumers than informing citizens.

And this was happening by design. When I was flying to Greece to keynote a conference on the dark days of the media, I met a young public relations woman on the plane from a high-profile agency in Washington, DC. I told her about this book and its assault on the dumbing down of news.

She laughed, bragging 'It's my job to keep it that way'. Joking or not, there was candor in that 'confession'. Indeed by then there were three times as many PR specialists as reporters and the journalism reviews were document-ing the impact of the new media order with its many diversions and news sitcoms like the OJ Simpson Trial or the White House sex scandal, multi-week stories that were given saturation coverage with a blather of commentary dominating its content. Opinionizing and moralizing soon displaced most reporting and analysis. The mainsteam became a mudstream.

Other cultural sectors began to comment on the degrading of the news media, especially Hollywood with films of a kind you would rarely see on TV, films castigating the media business. Oliver Stone's *Natural Born Killers* was an over-the-top assault on the rise of over-the-top tabloid TV. 'For me that film', he later wrote in a piece called 'The media beast', 'was just a vomiting up of what I saw in American mass culture . . . It was about all the crap that is produced to keep the masses entertained . . . like the Roman circus'. Later, James Bond went after a Murdoch-like bad guy in *Tomorrow Never Dies*. *Wag the Dog* won an Oscar nomination for its mocking send up of govern-ment manipulation and media collaboration. Warren Beatty topped them all with his rap attack *Bulworth* eviscerating corrupt politics and mindless TV news. And then along came *The Truman Show*, a post-modernist blast at our TV culture that created its own world and frames of reference. Some of this anti-TV sensibility occasionally popped up on the tube with HBO's *Larry Sanders Show* and very occasional documentaries.

Soon luminaries in the news media itself were contributing to a growing chorus of media criticism – some of it akin to self-flagellation. Walter Cronkite gave a speech blasting his old haunt, CBS, in more strident terms that I used. *60 Minutes'* Don Hewitt condemned the merger of show biz and news biz. Suddenly the newspapers were packed with op-eds on media industry mal-practice. A group of former newsmen formed a committee of concerned journ-alists to sound the alarm. Steve Brill, the former head of Court TV, launched a slick media review called *Brill's Content*. Outside the mainstream, a Media and Democracy Congress rallied critics while a Cultural Environment Move-ment sought to mobilize disaffection.

Inside the networks and media institutions, some media employees are speaking up in defence of the values of journalism and their own integrity. In Los Angeles, a newsroom revolt at KCBS forced a news director to resign after the staff signed a collective complaint. 'You are producing a cynical news product that very few of us can respect or take pride in', it read. 'You mock [the viewers] continually and make us carry out your daily deceptions'. Some individuals such as Ross Becker, formerly an anchor at LA's KCOP, left in disgust with tabloidization and the compromises it imposes on journalistic values. 'People are tired of wondering whether it's true that aliens are about to land in their back yards', he said. 'They don't want to be insulted anymore . . . We have had a technological revolution in this business; now we need a revolution of conscience and content'.

Sadly, much of the news business remained locked in a kind of media logic that rationalized all the sensationalized coverage in the name of 'giving the people what they want'. 'What really got dumbed down over the last year more than any other institution, frankly was ours', commented journalist Hodding Carter on the 'all Monica all the time' news. 'We managed somehow to go to the bottom faster and stay there longer than any of the participants. And if you don't think the American people don't know about that and don't feel it, you aren't following the polls.'

Those polls showed massive dissatisfaction with the TV media's focus. Fifty-one per cent of those surveyed in one poll said they believed the Lewinsky story had 'no importance, at all'. Sixty-nine per cent in another poll said the Lewinsky story was overcovered. Significantly, 80 per cent of TV news managers agreed – but then went on doing what they were doing – overcovering the story. The reasons have become institutional, deeply imbedded in the news world. Explained *Electronic Media*, a trade magazine close to the TV business, 'The proliferation of 24 hour news channels has a created a system in which one piece of scandal news is often stretched into 24 hours of analysis, hypothesis and all news network avarice for no-brainer programming.'

The consequences of all this produced a glaring contradiction: the very TV shows that media executives said would bring in an audience were actually driving it away. While pleasing a minority of scandal junkies, the constant drumbeat on this one issue 'contributed to a national Monica fatigue or scandal fatigue that hurt general news programs', admits Andrew Heyward, president of CBS News. After a year of this approach, two million viewers stopped watching network evening newscasts.

This erosion of viewership is part of a larger defection away from network viewing. Yet the networks are so wedded to their view of audience as infinitely malleable that, again according to the influential industry magazine, 'it's unlikely many television news organizations will step back for long to reflect on their missteps . . . no group seems to learn less from their follies than journalists'.

But even if journalists are wearing blinders, and even if the news system is unlikely to change from within, it is still under attack from competing technologies and critical voices.

The system as we have known it is already changing – analogue technology is giving way to digital. The internet is making convergence more feasible. And in the margins, media critics and activists are starting to be heard. Working with *One World Online* (oneworld.net), my company Globalvision is producing (as in oneworld.net) *The Media Channel* (www.mediachannel.org) as a worldwide web supersite to bring together and share information about what's happening to journalism worldwide. It is a non-profit public interest site featuring news, analysis and debate on international media. We are hoping that this initiative will spur social movements for media reform. (By June 2000, *The Media Channel* had 425 affiliates worldwide.) We will also have to reach out for support from political parties, NGOs, and advocacy groups.

We also need a program for change with at least five components:

1 It needs to build awareness of media power and irresponsibility throughout our communities. Educators, journalists and organizers have to start talking about this issue and popularizing it.
2 It needs to be placed squarely on the agendas of all organizations representing people who are effectively excluded from media discourse, including minorities, unions and issue-oriented organizations. Coalitions have to be forged.
3 An agenda for change is needed. We need to think harder and more creatively about workable and watchable alternatives to a market-dominated media system and how to create and sustain democratic public media. We need vision, ideas and plans.
4 Leaders need to be sensitized on these issues and groomed to lead public interest campaigns for media reform.
5 Funding has to be found to finance an effective nationwide organizational and public outreach effort.

As organizing gets underway, here is some of the work a media movement might do.

### I More monitoring

Everyone can and should monitor media performance. Groups such as FAIR have developed manuals and lists of criteria. If teachers and their students, labour unions and their members began tracking what's on TV and radio, and how the news is being reported, they will be able to better detect and challenge bias. One good model is the work of Rocky Mountain Media Watch, a group based in Denver that regularly examines local TV news content. They have published a small book called *Let The World Know: Make Your Cause News* which explains how to organize seminars, train staff and consult with non-profits. Media literacy has to become part of our school curricula and everyday life.

## 2 Media accountability

Once armed with current data and well-researched documentation, citizen groups will be in a better position to demand responsiveness and accountability by media corporations. When media executives meet with consumers, they do tend to get more responsive. Most are sure to resist pressure politics, but they will not be able to ignore it.

## 3 Legislation and regulation

Deregulation has given media companies a free hand to do as they will, all in the name of competition. (A year after the 1996 Telecoms Bill passed, government agencies admitted that the new law has not had the desired effect, leading instead to more concentration.) Tougher anti-monopoly laws and enhanced regulation in the public interest by a revamped Federal Communications Commission and Federal Trade Commission are also in order. 'And so we must begin a serious national debate', says media analyst Mark Crispin Miller, of NYU, 'on anti-trust, raising crucial questions about foreign ownership, the dangers of horizontal integration, the necessity of public access, the possibility of taxes both on advertising and on the use of the public spectrum and all of the other issues that this Congress has been speeding from madly in the other direction'. There are anti-trust laws on the books. They need to be enforced.

Public concern has to be focused as well on reversing the giveaway of the digital broadcast spectrum to broadcasters without fees or public interest obligations. 'Because of increased capacity, digital television will be a powerful medium', argued the Benton Foundation, 'powerful enough to do some important things for the American people. Like serving children better. Giving us political debate that really is debate. And using new interactive and on-demand features to provide the information people want and need every day. But there's no commitment from the commercial broadcast industry to serve these public needs.' Can we press to expand broadcasters' public interest obligations to match the increased capacity of digital TV?

## 4 Public television

There is no reason why America cannot have a publicly owned BBC or CBC-style public TV system to effectively compete with the commercial spectrum. It is time to put the public back into public television with more locally elected community boards to encourage PBS to return to its original mandate calling for alternative voices and more diverse program choices. Pressure will be needed to democratize and properly finance PBS. PBS could be funded through a tax on commercial television stations and their advertisers. There needs to be at least one channel that serves the public interest in the broadest possible way. The experience of Channel 4 in London might be a model worth examining and improving upon.

We also need to protect and strengthen public access to cable outlets and television and radio. Cable operators are now trying to drop their obligations to provide public access studios and channels because they say it violates their first amendment rights and costs too much. This is nonsense. A vital community-based media can challenge this self-serving logic. We can say to cities and to cable companies: don't mess with public access.

Outside of television, there is also a need to fight for funding for new public exhibition spaces for feature films and documentaries considered not commercial enough. Fewer and fewer theatres now show independent work, in part because the movie industry and the multi-plex theater operators have also become concentrated. As a result, fewer and fewer films, the majority studio releases, are being shown on more and more screens. Smaller independent distributors say they are being shut out.

### 5 Alternative programming and independent media

Creating channels in and of themselves will not make for changes in the system unless new programming reflecting a non-corporate view is available. Congress already recognized discrimination against America's independent film-makers when it created the Independent Television Service (ITVS). That agency and other media centres on the local level need to be adequately funded, with their programming guaranteed some form of distribution. The calls for social responsibility in business have so far not reached the media industry. Only public awareness and pressure can move the mountain of media inertia. Happily, some of the voices associated with reform in business are moving into the media arena.

The unflappable Anita Roddick of the Body Shop is leading the charge. 'Is the idea of a socially responsible media just pie in the sky?' she asks. 'I don't think so. I know it will be complex, paradoxical, and slightly unfamiliar but censorship by omission or indifference never works.' In her inimitable style, she calls socially responsible media, 'a bloody good idea'. But there are many good ideas. This is one that needs to be fought for.

Media critic Laura Flanders concludes in *Real Majority, Media Minority*, her thoughtful book on the shabby treatment of women in the media, 'The right to communicate is like any other right. And like any right, it will not be given. It must be won.'

# 13

## Political frustrations in the post-modern fog

HILARY WAINWRIGHT

In the audacious challenge of 'anti-capitalist' movements gathered in Seattle in November 1999, there are signs of a critical mass of people seeking radical progress against the gross inequalities of the new world order. For the first time since the ending of the Cold War the question is being raised on a world scale: what are the alternatives?

Progress often requires the rediscovery of lost tracks. To answer this question we need to return, critically as well as curiously, to the late 1960s, the 1970s and the early 1980s when egalitarian alternatives were being sought but when many of those pursuing them got lost in the fog.

In the last thirty years, governments seem to have come full circle. Tony Blair's speech to the 1999 Labour Conference promised progress instead of conservatism, just as in the late 1960s a Labour Prime Minister promised modernity instead of tradition. Important differences, however, indicate that the ground beneath Westminster politics has been severely shaken in the intervening years.

Harold Wilson's modernization turned out to involve nothing more innovative than a version of the peace-time corporatism constructed by the Attlee government, with the addition of some shiny new parts and a dynamic look. Many of Labour's younger voters had high hopes, after thirteen years of increasingly decrepit conservatism, that change would be more radically democratic. But the old institutions of Britain's mandarin and City dominated state maintained control. In the early 1970s their hold was nearly shaken by a combination of trade union power, politicized by increasing government intervention in collective bargaining, and encouraged by several ministers – most notably Tony Benn – who had learnt from experience that democratic modernization had to come from below.

By the late 1990s, Britain's hybrid political architecture of social democracy and a business oriented corporatism had been shattered by the radicalism of the right – perhaps the only way for the financial establishment to retain its control. But the legacy from the 1970s of radical democratic pressures was still a force to be reckoned with.

New Labour's 'modernization' continued Thatcherism's deference to the market and the private sector, and in one sense developed it further, into emulation. New Labour sought to run the country as if it was a corporation, complete with annual reports, streamlined executives and centralized control. Yet Tony Blair's government had been swept into office by an anti-Tory sentiment which was also fiercely pro-democracy.

The result of this contradictory mix is on the one hand, devolution for Scotland, Wales and London: on the other, intense efforts by the party machine to undermine the scope for any independent political dynamic at all. While the government itself is secure (largely through the lack of any national political challenge, a protective cushion kept in place by the first past the post electoral system) specific policies are constantly proving vulnerable to a public with a strong sense of democratic and social rights aroused by the indignities of Thatcherism.

One particular challenge rises out of the pressures built up from unfulfilled demands of the 1970s and 1980s – intensified by the new consciousness of environmental destruction. It may not be recognized in mainstream debates but, even before Thatcher, there were seeds of convincing alternative directions to the free market right. These seeds could, in principle, have been nurtured when Labour's corporatism collapsed, in Callaghan's miserable final years. In other words different, more democratic, egalitarian and ecologically sustainable responses to the challenges of the modern world could have been championed – as they have been by Green, radical left and left social democratic political organizations almost everywhere else in Northern Europe.

The belief underlying this essay is that much of what came to be described as 'post-modernism' (at least in the forms it was popularized) clouded and distorted the political choices that we faced in the 1970s and 1980s. Of course this is not the only explanation of the failure to develop democratic alternatives to the unregulated market. On the continent the political championing of radical alternatives has been helped enormously by a proportional electoral system, where generally the ideas of all parties gaining over 5 per cent of the vote are represented in mainstream political debate. Moreover the existence in Europe of competitors to the left of the main social democratic parties has considerably strengthened the legitimacy of radical left ideas within those parties. Hence in Germany Oscar La Fontaine gained the leadership of the SDP to balance the centrist Schroeder – even if the partnership in the end proved unviable – whereas in Britain Ken Livingstone is treated as a pariah.

It is not just governments which seem to have come full circle. On the streets, in communities, in universities, up trees and down tunnels, on fields planted with genetically modified crops, indeed wherever corporations threaten the quality of life and the environment, people have been taking direct action with a self-confidence that evokes the creative militancy of the late 1960s and 1970s. The repercussions of the defeat of this earlier resistance are apparent in the contemporary movements, however. The trade union presence, for instance, has been rare. It has been restricted to determined if beleaguered groups, such as the Liverpool dockers, which have made links with the new movements, seeking sources of power to replace their depleted industrial leverage. Or individual organizers with a trade union background have used their wit to contribute to innovative collective projects such as the Exodus Collective, a group of homeless and unemployed young people who have squatted an empty hospice and pooled their benefits to create a community centre, farm and regular parties (http://www.squall.co.uk/squall8/exchron.htm).

There is within these 'direct actions' a striking new ability to create alliances which could strengthen democratic power against the unregulated market. This is most evident in the use of the internet to build a practical internationalism which has already helped to delay and disrupt the latest moves to 'free' the market of all social, environmental or cultural constraints. The postponement of both the Multilateral Agreement on Investment and the 'Millennium Round' of the World Trade Organization – both intended to further free trade without social or environmental constraint – is the outcome of globally mobilized grass-roots movements working to exacerbate divisions among the governments on whom negotiations depended (Gunnell and Timms, 2000) These movements are not homogeneous or united but they do represent a new kind of internationalism, based on direct intervention in the workings of global capital rather than only solidarity of social movements from nation to nation.

The political and cultural messages of all these recent movements have strong echoes of the radicalism of the 1960s and 1970s, though the language and ideological framework – or lack of it – are different. Both generations of extra-parliamentary activists insist that there are alternatives to the corporate led technologies which threaten the health of the living and the environment of the yet to be born; that participatory democracy and the decentralization of both political and economic power are feasible and desirable; that wealth owned in common need not mean a command economy – common ownership can take many forms; that equality of gender, race, culture and wealth is a condition of liberty and diversity rather than a threat to it. These continuities are clear in retrospect but in real historical time there was a marked severing, during the 1980s and 1990s, of links with many of the institutions and traditions which could have nurtured and strengthened the current generation of radical activists and the possibility of a powerful, cumulative political alternative.

I would point to three developments which in combination were responsible for this sharp break. First, the political victory of the free market right; second, the consequent defeat of organized labour and with it the steady erosion of public provision, public space and public resources; third, and less noted, the turn of a significant number of intellectuals to turn towards treating culture and discourse as if they were disembodied from other levels of reality. This tendency is generally described as post-modernism, although many writers

**241**

– Foucault, most notably – who have been lumped under this label in fact have a far more complex understanding of the world. By the time this diverse intellectual trend reverberated into the political culture, however, it was its dematerializing character that came to the fore, in Britain and the US if not elsewhere.

In many ways this was an understandable reaction to a reductive, materialist, structuralist orthodoxy which denied the distinctive reality and importance of culture and subjectivity. It was a reaction, too, to the narrow and rigid politics that often accompanied this theoretical orthodoxy, both on the far left and the Labourist left. The end result of this exclusive concern with discourse, however, was a marginalizing of that intellectual work on the left which paid detailed and critical attention to changes in political and economic realities, as well as to the inter-relations of these changes and their relationship in turn with culture and consciousness.

My sceptical approach to 'the post-modern turn' stems not from a loyalty to structuralist orthodoxy or indeed from a denial of the importance, in their own right, of some of the particular studies carried out by writers who are described as post-modern. I approach post-modernism from an intellectual tradition that had never espoused the theoretical framework from which it was a turn. Perhaps 'tradition' conveys too mature and rounded an impression. In truth, I'm referring to a cluster of critical ideas that presented a cultural and humanist materialism, whether in the Frankfurt tradition or the more empirical tradition of the British New Left, as an alternative to both economistic Marxism and structuralist sociology. It is a tradition which by the 1970s had been further developed by the influence of emerging social movements, in particular feminism. These new movements found orthodox Marxism and consequently its Althusserian elaboration inadequate to the complex interplay of the cultural and the material, embodied in their own active combination of struggle and self-realization.

It was exactly this cultural/material inter-relation which was at the centre of our concerns within the women's movement. We traced the ways, for example, in which women's cultural subordination helped to underpin the ability of employers to get away with paying women significantly less than men. Our focus on sexism in the everyday use of language specifically was part of an effort to achieve greater public awareness of the way in which women's secondary position is taken for granted. We did not believe, however, that we needed to change only the word and that in itself would change the world. Our very character as a movement – combining 'consciousness raising' with campaigns over economic conditions and legislation – presupposed that liberation involved the victims of oppression becoming active, self-conscious subjects transforming relationships which they would otherwise tend, out of habit, inertia or powerlessness, to reproduce. In that sense we rejected in practice, even if it was not fully spelt out in theory, the determinism of a crude, one-dimensional materialism. Yet, on the other hand, our debates about how to achieve this personal liberation and structural change were much more than the diverse-but-equally-true statements of personal rebellion implied by post-modernism. Generally, our debates presumed an independent reality, a common reference point against which strategies can be tested in practice.

To be faced with the post-modern turn was like progressing confidently along a path that, albeit difficult, was leading somewhere only to be blocked by a giant bunch of signposts bearing multiple destinations, but no path, and, on protesting, being told that the only alternative was backwards. I hoped the shiny signposts would melt into air so that I and others could continue along our roughly beaten track. Indeed they might have disappeared had post-modernism been an isolated cultural and academic development, surrounded by the continued voices of socially rooted political alternatives. But by the late 1970s, those alternatives, whose cultural politics were grounded in a challenge to material realities of power and wealth, faced severe setbacks.

Geographically post-modernism was most influential in France, where, in the late 1960s, the early radical social movements were at their strongest, and yet where they suffered their severest defeat. Post-modernism thus tended to become a theory for ex-members of social movements which had been defeated – it was loyal to the culture of which these movements had been a part, but confirmed a disillusionment with the slow and uneven process of bringing about social change.

One of the political frustrations of post-modernism for those of us on the left whose socialism was shaped by recent social movements is that there is a considerable overlap between its apparent concerns and those of the movements of which we have been a part. We share with post-modernists, for instance, a commitment to scrutinize and deconstruct the cultural consensus; to challenge simplistic uses of universal concepts such as 'citizenship' and 'human rights' to hide differences and inequalities; to subvert modernist optimism in techno-logical 'progress' and reveal values embedded in this apparently neutral notion; to draw attention to the role of language in shaping our cultural and social life rather than simply reflecting a reality 'out there'. All these are character-istics of the feminist, lesbian, gay, green and anti-racist movements as well as a feature of the best post-modern writers. Post-modernism, however, with its denial of any extra discursive reality, takes these ideas out of their original context of purposeful collective effort to transform powerful institutions.

The politically debilitating result is that these ideas, bereft of context, boom-erang back into the political culture, often being pitched against – rather than debating with – older labour movement ideas and practices which do try, however inadequately, to challenge material power.

The result has been a series of polarities which appear increasingly mis-leading as people once more find the confidence and resources to challenge concentrations of wealth and power. So we have identity/cultural politics versus struggles over economics; social movements versus the labour/working class movement; civil society versus state action: and as their political climax, Old versus New Labour – where New Labour deletes from vision and political language alike the innovative thinking and practice emerging on the left over the previous twenty years. These polarities are not simply false at the level of descriptive 'discourse'; they can also by the very elisions and omissions they make block out lines of thinking and hence forms of action. This is best illustrated by exploring what is blocked out, with what consequences, by the false polarization of Old versus New Labour.

One crucial line of thought lost in the post-modern fog has been ideas associated with democratizing public provision and public industries. The crucial idea here is that of holding on to the social, redistributive assumptions behind the welfare state, and the wider, social notions of efficiency, profit and loss that weakly underpinned public industries, but at the same time proposing a radical democratization of the way these public resources are managed, the means by which these social assumptions are put into practice. 'New Labour' thinking has tended to counterpose the old bureaucratic welfare state with various forms of business dominated public–private partnerships (often de facto privatization). The implication is that the private sector has the only antidote to the bureaucratic failings of past forms of public provision: that the discipline of the market is the only feasible stimulus to efficiency. This false dichotomy has meant that much work and experience developing the discipline of democracy could be lost to public policymaking in the UK.

This is not necessarily through wilful denial of this genuine 'third way' – often the evangelists of New Labour are genuinely ignorant about existing thinking on democratizing the public sector.[1] There is a common phenomenon of labour politicians who used to be wedded to the 'old' command economy or traditional public sector model simply turning away from this model in favour of its opposite. They are unaware that a highly developed critique of their old beliefs already exists: a critique that issues from a democratic as distinct from a market view point (London, Edinburgh Weekend Return Group, 1980; Cockburn, 1977; Whitfield, 1992).

The innovative politics of the 1970s and early 1980s, which began to evolve this democratic and egalitarian critique of traditional 'Old' Labour public sector thinking, remained incomplete. In practice, rather more than in theory, they were critiquing both the limitations of 'actually existing socialism' – its social democratic and its Soviet forms – and the changes occurring in capitalism. Radical workers in the social sector, health, education and local government campaigned to democratize the management of public services. They proposed ways of making them responsive to diverse and rising expectations, challenging the almost military hierarchies on which many parts of the public sector were built. Politically confident trade unionists drew on their practical experiences of effectively controlling production to push towards a variety of forms of industrial democracy, rejecting old style nationalization. Socialist feminists created subversive networks in the trade unions to drag labour organizing into the age of the mass retail, finance and cleaning workers (who are predominantly female) and to face up to the growth of a part-time and often casualized female workforce. Radical, critical scientists questioned the neutrality of scientific research in areas such as the military, food and genetics in ways which anticipated the challenges which have since become the basis of powerful popular movements (Rose and Rose, 1976).

Sometimes radical scientists worked on exemplary practical alternatives with technologists and engineers on the front line of industry – like the shop stewards on the shop and office floors of Lucas Aerospace. In an uneven way these developments held out the possibility of an alternative form of modernization to the global market driven version that dominates us now (Cooley, 1987; Wainwright and Elliott, 1984).

Ken Livingstone's GLC was the concentration and most direct expression of this alternative modernization (Carvel, 1999; MacIntosh and Wainwright, 1987; Rowbotham, 1989). A theorization of this alternative, democratic modernization, at a time when the practice was under threat, would have greatly increased the chance of a challenge to the neo-liberal consensus. But this required intellectual work of an engaged kind, interested in material practice as well as symbolic representations. Although by the late 1970s this was under way (Beynon, 1973; Cockburn, 1977; Kaldor, 1981; Wilson, 1977; Rowbotham, 1989) it was not to be sustained through the 1980s and 1990s. By then the baleful influence of post-modernism had gained a hold in both the universities and the media. In the universities it diverted many well-meaning intellectuals from the difficult empirical work needed to identify new trends in transformative practice. In the media it drew public attention away from the continuing development of 'alternatives'.

The 1980s and 1990s saw an erosion of many of the public institutions and workplace and community bonds on which this innovative left had depended. The abolition of the GLC for instance was a particularly stark reminder of how far this left depended on, at the same time as transforming, the old institutions. There were many practical and often invisible ways in which the radical left attempted to adapt the old institutions to the changing times, drawing on innovations of the previous decades. A number of trades councils turned their organizations from being primarily workplace based to being a focal point for community campaigns to defend local services and facilities. Parts of the co-operative movement began once again to promote forms of common ownership rather than simply the survival of their own infrastructure. Constituency Labour Parties, inspired by their experiences of campaigning during the miners' strike, opened themselves up to debates and joint activity with campaigns outside the Party. More radically, some left activists used a strong commercial position to reach out to disaffected youth, for example Asian Dub Foundation in the music industry, with its political message and encouragement of radical self-education and organization. Others, like the women who had organized the mining communities during the strike, drew on the skills they had learnt to run a variety of democratically controlled community resouces, especially for young people and women.

Comparing these political innovations with architectural theory – a rich source of post-modern thinking – sparked off some personal reflections. In the architecture journal *Blueprints* in July 1999, Iain Borden describes the death of *avant garde* architecture, whose architects he describes as 'conceived as an elitist group, small in number, somehow apart from yet ahead of the rest of society and prescient of its singular future direction'. He goes on to describe 'today's radicality', saying:

> It comes from a different position. Those who take up the challenge are not those who set themselves apart from society, but those who are knowingly within it, working not wholly oppositionally but with irony and agitation against the dominant systems of capitalism, colonialism and their constitutive agents. They are those who, through their various practices, including architecture, say something that is not only a negative critique but also a proposition – a critical suggestion as to what might be done next. Their purpose is not to enact a total-all-or-nothing revolution but to make radical difference. (Borden, 1999)

This, I would argue, is an accurate description of the revolutionary or radical gradualism that is emerging from a range of left, labour and green organizations as they react creatively, not adaptively, to their changing environment.

A particular problem in Britain has been that none of these efforts at an alternative, egalitarian form of modernization has had any direct political expression because of blockages in the electoral system referred to earlier. The GLC was the exception that proved the rule. Recent developments in Scotland, most notably the success under a proportional electoral system of the Scottish Socialist Party – a radically renovated party well to the left of Labour – and the Green Party, provide positive evidence of the influence of the electoral system on the wider political appeal of the radical democratic left. In the absence of a democratic electoral system, other forms of public representation rise in significance.

In Britain at the time when many of these left alternatives were facing serious political threats and were in need of a wider public presence, magazines and public intellectuals became briefly very influential, often out of all proportion to their circulation. The *New Socialist*, under the editorship of James Curran in late 1970s and early 1980s, began to play an important role, providing a positive platform for the debate of these radical left ideas. So did the Socialist Society, founded by Ralph Miliband, Raymond Williams and others in younger generations of the new and social movement left.

The official theoretical organ of the Communist Party, *Marxism Today*, was influenced by this stirring of public debate on the left. Indeed Martin Jacques its editor was a member of the Socialist Society's steering committee in its early days. It was in many ways an impressive magazine many of whose writers, most notably Eric Hobsbawm, Stuart Hall, Andrew Gamble, Robin Murray and Doreen Massey, made positive and useful contributions to understanding the changing economic and political circumstances. It was never, however, fully of the 'new' or social movement left, coming as it did from a tradition which had always opposed the democratizing impetus of the original new left, from 1956 onwards. And although Martin Jacques broke the magazine away from orthodox communism, as a publication it never fully acknowledged the existence of a reforming democratic left which was independent of and pre-dated its own moment of rethinking. Without roots in this critically materialist left, and with a somewhat cavalier if not downright philistine attitude towards critical left thinking that it could not corral, *Marxism Today* became one of the main political vehicles of the post-modern turn. In this role its cannily promoted articles often served in effect to spread the dichotomies, like that between social movements and the labour movement, which, as we have seen, drained and paralyzed much public political debate on the left in Britain.

*Marxism Today* made an impact beyond its traditional circles by giving a platform to the first detailed analyses – most notably by Stuart Hall and Andrew Gamble – of the distinctive politics of the Thatcher regime. These accounts highlighted Thatcherism's combination of the free market and the centralized state; analyzing the way it took the high ground with a unique authoritarian populism.

There were problems, however, with these analyses, and hence the implications drawn from them (Williamson, 1989). The first problem was *Marxism Today*'s description of the left. As Judith Williamson puts it, 'Sometimes from MT-speak, you would think that the labour movement was the enemy and Thatcherism the ideal – sensitively tuned to people's needs while socialists in hobnailed boots stomp all over them' (Williamson, 1989). The left was described essentially in terms of the Communist and Labour left of the 1950s and 1960s – economistic, statist, often male chauvinist and generally not notably open to new ideas. Even at that time this was often a caricature. All the new thinking and practice of the 1970s and early 1980s were either ignored or 'captured', that is treated as if they were nothing to do with the left but were somehow virgin territory, as if the 'new social movements' had been discovered by MT and pitched against 'the left'.

Related to this was an absence of any sense of history or of the role of the Communist Party and its failure to open up to the new left of the late 1960s and 1970s, let alone its treatment of the original new left associated with E.P. Thompson and those who left the party over Hungary. The second problem was a more general lack of history – a portrayal of change as if it came in the night and stabbed everyone but the all-seeing MT in the back. Methodologically, the influence of post-modernism, for whom history is little more than a variety of equally valid stories, enabled *Marxism Today* to get away with this travesty. A third problem, where again the fingerprints of post-modernism can be traced, was an over-estimation of the popularity of Thatcherism. Post-modernism's rejection of the existence of distinct levels of social and economic reality contributed to an overloading of the category 'cultural' to explain Thatcher's power (Williamson, 1989).

Surveys carried out throughout the Thatcher years but only published in 1998 (Jowell *et al.*, 1997) show how free market, anti-public-service, anti-union values were not internalized to anything like the degree implied by MT. Indeed MT writers made no effort to report on or analyze evidence about how effective and how sustained the impact of Thatcher's populism actually was. Implicit in the magazine's politics was an ungrounded leap from characterizing her ideology to the conclusion that this had become the popular common sense of the day. As Williamson argues, the concept of 'hegemony' was used as if it was a purely cultural. And in the process popularity was confused with populism. Thatcher was certainly *populist*. Stuart Hall was right about this (Hall, 1988). But her *popularity* was shallow and uneven. In fact, surveys show that she was never personally popular and that her popularity dipped markedly whenever she got involved in public campaigning (Scammell, 1995).

The final problem with MT's politics was the celebration of the market as not simply a force for change, but a force for progressive change; in the words of the 'New Times' document published in 1989 in conjunction with *Marxism Today*, 'the market would encourage flexibility, diversity and dynamism'. Here again is evidence of analyzing a complex, many-levelled phenomenon almost exclusively in terms of the discourse used to describe them. Shopping was elevated to a liberating experience, a political platform in itself. No regard was paid to the issues which have now produced a highly critical politics of consumption: the super-exploitation of the labour and the environment of farmers, agricultural and industrial workers in the South, on whom the pleasures of Western shopping depend. Neither was any attention paid to the ways in which those pleasures posed both a threat to our health and a boost to the profitability and power of multi-national corporations.

What was missing was a social and economic critique of the market. Again we have come full circle. Issues of regulation and even public ownership are back on the agenda. The movements and organizations pressing for them, however (for instance the direct action movement against genetically modified foods or the railway workers and users), know that new answers are needed to new questions. Much has changed since the time of Robert Owen and the decades in which capitalism began. Some of the tools we need to find these new answers lie buried beneath screeds of post-modernist discourse. The process of re-excavation has begun, aided by various helpful spectres. Ghosts of 1970s and 1980s, feminism, radical trade unionism, even the GLC, just won't leave us alone. Now they have contemporary allies with their own egalitarian, democratic and sustainable vision.

### Acknowledgement

Many thanks to Hilary Bichovsky.

## Note

1 An exception was Geoff Mulgan who was part of such a democratizing experiment at the GLC and yet an essay in a book by Charles Handy rubbishes the whole experience in a most cavalier manner: 'Because the GLC was also badly mismanaged and politically self-indulgent it was ineffective and ultimately doomed' (1999, p. 187).

## References

Beynon, H. (1973) *Working for Ford*, London: Penguin.

Borden, I. (1999) *Blueprints*, Summer.

Carvel, J. (1999) *Red Ken*, 2nd edition, London:

Cockburn, C. (1977) *The Local State: Management of Cities and People*, London: Pluto Press.

Cooley, M. (1987) *Architect or Bee?*, London: Chatto and Windus.

Doyle, L. with Pennel, I. (1979) *The Political Economy of Health*, London: Pluto Press.

Gunnell, B. and Timms, D. (eds) (2000) *Globalisation and Its Discontents*, London: Catalyst Trust.

Hall, S. (1988) 'The great moving right show', in Hall, S. (ed.), *The Hard Road to Renewal*, London: Lawrence and Wishart.

Handy, C. (ed.) (1999) *The New Alchemists*, London: Hutchinson.

Jowell, R., Cutice, J., Park A., Brook, L., Thomson, K. and Bryson, C. (1997) *British Social Attitudes*, Aldershot: Ashgate and SCPR.

Kaldor, M. (1981) *Baroque Arsenal*, London: Allen Lane.

London, Edinburgh Weekend Return Group (1980) *In and Against the State*.

MacIntosh, M. and Wainwright, H. (1987) *A Taste of Power*, London: Verso.

Rose, H. and Rose, S. (eds) (1976) *Political Economy of Science*, London: Macmillan.

Rowbotham, S. (1989) *The Past is Before Us: Feminism in Action since the 1960s*, London: Allen Lane.

Rowbotham, S. (2000) 'Why Londoners love Ken', *Red Pepper*, January, pp. 19–21.

Scammell, M. (1995) *Designer Politics: How Elections are Won*, Basingstoke: Macmillan.

Wainwright, H. and Elliott, D. (1984) *The Lucas Story: New Trade Unionism in the Making*, London: Alison and Busby.

Whitfield, D. (1992) *The Welfare State: Privatisation, Deregulation and Commercialisation of Public Services*, London: Pluto.

Williamson, J. (1989) 'New times', *New Statesman and Society*, 7 July.

Wilson, E. (1977) *Women and Welfare*, London: Tavistock.

# Index